BEFORE AND AFTER DISASTER STRIKES

DEVELOPING AN EMERGENCY
PROCEDURES MANUAL

FOURTH EDITION

Professional Review

Lawrence W. Baiamonte, CPM®
Natalie D. Brecher, CPM®
David Mistick, CPM®
Debbie Mistick, CPM®
Richard F. Muhlebach, CPM®, SCSM, CRE, RPA

IREM Education Publishing

Ronald Gjerde
Vice President, IREM Knowledge Center

Nadia Geagea Pupa
Managing Editor, Publications

Zachary Tarvin
Editorial Assistant

BEFORE AND AFTER DISASTER STRIKES

DEVELOPING AN EMERGENCY
PROCEDURES MANUAL

FOURTH EDITION

IREM Institute of Real Estate Management

Printed in the United States of America
10 9 8 7 6 5 4 3 2 1

ISBN-10 1-57203-171-9
ISBN-13 978-1-57203-171-5

Publishing Department
Institute of Real Estate Management
430 North Michigan Avenue
Chicago, IL 60611-4090.

This publication is designed to provide accurate and authoritative information in regard to the subject
matter covered. Forms or other documents included in this book are intended as samples only.
Because of changing and varying state and local laws, competent professional advice should be sought
prior to the use of any document, form, exhibit, or the like.

This publication is sold with the understanding that the publisher is not engaged in rendering legal,
accounting, or any other professional service. If legal advice or other expert assistance is required, the
services of a competent professional should be sought.

Cover Photo © Steve Dunwell

Text and Cover Composition:
Nadia Geagea Pupa
Managing Editor, Education Publishing

Library of Congress Cataloging-in-Publication Data

Before and after disaster strikes : developing an emergency procedures manual.
    p. cm.
"Fourth edition"--Pref.
  ISBN 978-1-57203-171-5 (pbk. : alk. paper) -- ISBN 1-57203-171-9 (pbk. : alk. paper) 1.
Real estate management--United States. 2. Commercial real estate--United States--Manage-
ment. 3. Emergency management--United States. I. Institute of Real Estate Management.
  HD1394.5.U6B44 2012
  333.3068'4--dc23
                            2012034732

Preface

In the context of emergency procedures planning, there are two types of disasters: natural and manmade. At its core, an emergency procedures plan provides real estate managers, their staff, and the occupants of the buildings they manage with information and training to respond to both types of disasters. Emergencies may largely arise without notice, but real estate managers can still be prepared to respond. From everyday emergencies, such power outages, fires, or medical emergencies to large disasters such as hurricanes, earthquakes, or tornadoes, real estate managers can use this book as a frame of reference to help develop emergency procedures for both anticipated and unanticipated disasters and emergencies.

This fourth edition of *Before and After Disaster Strikes: Developing an Emergency Procedures Manual* is designed to take real estate managers one step further in their preparations for (and recovery from) disasters by providing updated information on a number of topics. These topics include emergency alert systems, document storage and retrieval, and—new to this edition—an introduction to business continuity strategies.

Section 1: The Basics of an Emergency Plan outlines the key components necessary to each and every emergency response manual—including who should comprise the emergency response team and how the manual should be devised—but also information on other key practices in managing both the physical and financial damage to a property.

With the universal concepts established, *Section 2: Emergency Planning by Property Types,* will lead you on a walk through residential, commercial, industrial, medical office, and mixed-use properties. This section highlights and contrasts critical considerations to be made for each property type when preparing for, faced with, or following a disaster.

Building upon the considerations for each property type, *Section 3: Preparing for Specific Emergencies,* details the preparations that can be made for specific emergencies which affect every type of property. From power outages and fires to hazardous materials spills, the vast majority of emergencies covered in this section could happen anywhere. Notable in this section is a newly extended chapter on medical emergencies—featuring additional content on bloodborne pathogens.

Section 4: Natural Disasters asks real estate managers to further customize their emergency response manual to the environment around their property. Specifically, which kinds of natural disaster may threaten their properties. This section has been updated to make mention of new technology and the ways it can be used to disseminate alerts and updates on a disaster.

Section 5: Crime and Terrorism explores the threat of manmade disasters from crime prevention measures to responding to bomb threats and terrorist acts. This section helps prepare real estate managers to acts of violence and emergencies that provide very little in terms of warning.

Concluding this book is a new section, *Section 6: Business Continuity Strategies,* which defines what business continuity is and how it can and should be implemented into every emergency procedures plan. This section helps you identify which of your business processes are absolutely vital, while also helping you identify which of your systems should remain online during a disruption caused by an emergency or disaster.

This fourth edition of *Before and After Disaster Strikes* also includes a series of updated forms to be included in your emergency procedures manual or in planning your emergency response procedures. These forms have been designed to be as customizable as possible in order to save real estate managers the time and effort of having to create new forms for each property. These forms have been assembled from resources of the Institute of Real Estate Management (IREM®), with some being graciously provided by the IREM industry partners.

IREM is an industry leader in providing its members and the real estate industry with timely and comprehensive information necessary for developing emergency procedures and implementing responses to emergencies. This edition of *Before and After Disaster Strikes* combines new content with updated and re-evaluated content from previous editions to create the most comprehensive publication for real estate managers on emergency procedures and emergency planning. While this book is not an emergency procedures plan in and of itself, it is a guide to help you prepare for emergency procedure plans for residential, commercial, medical office, and industrial buildings.

—*Richard Muhlebach CPM, CRE, RPA, SCSM*

Acknowlegements

The Institute of Real Estate Management (IREM®) gratefully acknowledges the contribution of the following individuals, who read the manuscript carefully, providing insights from their experience in real estate management and emergency planning: Lawrence Baiamonte, CPM; Natalie Brecher, CPM, president of Brecher Associates, Inc.; Debbie Mistick, CPM, CCM, vice-president of Circumspex, LLC; David Mistick, CPM, CBRM, president of Circumspex, LLC; and Richard Muhlebach CPM, CRE, RPA, SCSM.

IREM would also like to thank David and Debbie Mistick for their work in reviewing the text and also providing the material that became *Section 6: Business Continuity Strategies*, as well as their company, Circumspex, LLC, for providing some of the forms included with this text.

Table of Contents

Chapter 5: Public Relations   47

Chapter 6: The Emergency Procedures Manual   55

SECTION 2: Emergency Planning by Property Type   69

Chapter 7: Residential Properties   71

BEFORE AND AFTER DISASTER STRIKES

DEVELOPING AN EMERGENCY PROCEDURES MANUAL

FOURTH EDITION

CHAPTER 1:

The Scope of Emergency Planning

Every property, regardless of size or function, should have an emergency procedures plan that establishes written procedures and guidelines for the preparation and response to an emergency. The emergency procedures plan is the backbone to an emergency response manual that will be used by tenants and staff and is tailored to fit the property's unique needs, while also helping to minimize or prevent loss of life and property.

Your emergency procedures plan should spell out how staff and tenants should respond to different types of emergencies. In developing emergency procedures, the real estate manager's primary responsibilities are to protect the lives of the building's occupants, employees, and visitors, while also protecting the property owner's investment.

Before and After Disaster Strikes: Developing an Emergency Procedures Manual offers guidance in constructing and implementing a well-designed emergency procedures plan, which will enable the property staff to be prepared *before and after* a disaster occurs.

Preparing an emergency procedures plan requires thorough research and teamwork, involving in-depth knowledge of the property and its occupants, the neighborhood, and the community in which the property is located. The planning process should also be formulated in cooperation with an emergency planning and response team, which may be comprised of the property owner, police and fire department officials, disaster recovery contractors, outside service contractors, and community service agencies, as well as the property's onsite management staff and the management firm's office staff. The property owner's insurance carrier may provide written materials or identify consulting resources that can be helpful. Local, state, and federal emergency agencies may also be consulted. Individuals and organizations provide their expertise in specialized areas to help determine what is needed for the emergency procedures plan. However, not all of the members of this planning team will be involved with the implementation of the plan if a disaster should occur.

An emergency procedures plan also includes an emergency management team, who will see the plan through to completion in an emergency situation. This team will be comprised primarily of management staff personnel with participation by tenant employees, where appropriate (see *Chapter 2*). As the planning process develops, begin to formulate an emergency procedures manual (see *Chapter 6*), which will be an important reference guide for the emergency management team in the event of an emergency.

BEING AWARE OF FEDERAL REGULATIONS

Real estate managers should also be aware that there may be specific requirements for aspects of an emergency procedures plan that are dictated by various rules and regulations. In particular, the Occupational Safety and Health Administration (OSHA) requires businesses that employ more than ten workers to have a written action plan in place for an assortment of emergencies. These plans—commonly in place for evacuations or sheltering in place—cover "designated actions that employers and employees must take to ensure safety from fire and other emergencies."[1] Individuals who manage properties that house government agencies should be aware that the Government Services Administration (GSA) requires those agencies to have an Occupant Emergency Program (OEP) in place to cover evacuations as a response to fire, explosion, severe weather, and other emergencies.[2]

PREPARING THE EMERGENCY PROCEDURES PLAN

Before a plan can be developed, there must be an assessment of the property's vulnerabilities and an evaluation of capabilities. The following questions and points will help you start thinking about basic elements that should be included in an emergency procedure plan. As a group, answering the following questions will form the base of a plan, which can then be further expanded to suit your property in the face of any emergency:

- What federal, state, and local laws affect your procedure planning? Consider the fire, building, and other codes or ordinances or regulations that affect the property.

---

1. Specific requirements and details of OSHA regulations can be found in a number of sources available on the OSHA website, *http://www.osha.gov.*

2. The GSA has published an Occupant Emergency Program Guide (available at *http://www.gsa.gov*), which provides comprehensive guidelines that can be adapted for use in the private sector. Emergency plan templates are available in publications from a company called Emergency Planning Solutions (*http://www.emergencyplanningsolutions.com*).

- How will staff and building occupants be alerted of an emergency situation?
- Where should staff report in an emergency (if they are called to the site)?
- Is there a logical place where external emergency response personnel may set up a command center onsite?
- Are there specific points to assemble for evacuation, as well as sheltering points if the order to take shelter is made?
- Are there occupants or staff that will require special needs? If so, how can you prepare to address those in an emergency?
- Is there a chain of command established? Who will communicate with entities such as fire or police departments and the media?
- How can critical business data, such as records or client files be preserved through data backup or storage?

An emergency plan should address how information about an emergency will be communicated to those who need to know. It should also include strategies for beginning recovery efforts and handling the property's public relations.

Gathering as much information about the property and becoming knowledgeable about its surroundings, should be some of the first steps when creating an emergency plan. Knowing all you can about a property and its neighborhood allows for an effective response to emergencies with minimal human injury and property loss. This book is divided into the following six main sections to help you develop and implement your emergency procedures plan:

1. Basics of an Emergency Plan
2. Emergency Planning by Property Type
3. Preparing for Specific Emergencies
4. Natural Disasters
5. Crime and Terrorism
6. Business Continuity Strategies

The Basics of an Emergency Plan

Crucial to the execution of your emergency management procedures plan is the emergency management team. This team can be made up of administrative, onsite, and maintenance staff members and is the group responsible for ensuring that the emergency procedures plan is correctly executed to help save lives on the property. The emergency management team should be involved in the development of an emergency procedures plan with regard to the creation, training, testing, and correcting of evacuation and other safety procedures through practice drills or demonstrations.

While the emergency management team is a very important part of the emergency procedures plan, in the end, they are only as effective as the procedures that guide them. It is important to establish the grounds for evacuation of the property in the emergency procedures. Consider if there are scenarios in which only part of the property would need to be evacuated:

- How will the order to evacuate be communicated to occupants?
- Should the building be evacuated, what conditions would need to be met before allowing staff or occupants to re-enter the building?

Your emergency procedures should reflect careful thought and consideration for a wide range of variable conditions and emergency situations for both the people who live, work, or occupy the building *and* the building itself.

Develop a procedure as part of the property's emergency plan for dealing with damage to the asset itself following a disaster. This part of the plan should give careful consideration to how existing damage and loss can be documented, while ensuring that actions are taken to eliminate further harm to the asset. Consider what kind of contractors or other authorities may be involved in the restoration and resumption of building operations.

How will you handle an inquiry or complaint from tenants or the media? Establishing a public relations policy is a critical part of mitigating a disaster because it helps ensure that property staff will deliver a consistent message regarding what happened, what is being done, and when the property may resume operations.

Establishing these general procedures will help create your emergency procedures manual. This manual will serve as the definitive guide to emergency and disaster situations for staff, tenants, and management. While it may not be exhaustive—some forms of disasters and emergencies cannot be anticipated—it offers to minimize injury and loss by providing necessary information when an emergency arises. The emergency procedures manual should be the go-to resource following a disaster.

Emergency Planning by Property Type

No two properties are identical in terms of their emergency response needs. While similarities exist amongst properties within the same property type, each individual property must be examined on its own when developing emergency procedures to ensure that all needs for the property and its occupants have been met.

Properties fall into the categories of residential, office buildings, medical office buildings, shopping centers, or industrial properties. Though each property has distinct needs and considerations in terms of emergency planning, classifying the property type helps identify characteristics that lend themselves to a general emergency procedures plan that may be built upon with detailed, property-specific elements.

Each property type has a vastly different number of occupants. Regardless of the property type, an excellent place to start with any evacuation or emergency procedure development is to examine the demographics and needs of a building's occupants. Emergency procedures should be adapted to help those with decreased mobility or awareness—especially in a scenario where children, senior citizens, or disabled individuals are present.

As part of this occupant analysis, think about occupant readiness to respond to an emergency. Successfully evacuating a residential apartment building may be more difficult than evacuating a commercial office building. Residents in the apartment building could be less practiced at evacuating—they may have never had a full-scale evacuation drill, whereas office buildings may hold mandated drills several times a year.

How many people will be present on the property when a disaster strikes? Are there different procedures that should be created for peak hours? The answers to these types of considerations are especially important for commercial office, medical office, industrial, and retail properties. As part of examining the individual needs of a property, performing a general headcount might go a long way in determining best practices for your emergency procedures manual.

As a final consideration, be sure to document and record any and all hazardous materials that may be kept on a property. Especially in the industrial and medical office property types, hazardous materials may be used daily as part of a regular business process. It's important to create special policies and procedures for the handling, securing, and disposing of hazardous materials to help alleviate the threat of a hazardous-materials incident. Having detailed records of what materials are located on the property will help in the creation of emergency response procedures if exposure to those materials occurs.

Preparing for Specific Emergencies

Not every type of emergency or natural disaster threatens a property. Certain events might be unlikely due to the property's type, use, or geographic location. There are, however, universal and also specific emergencies that can arise at any property. These would include the following:

- Power outages
- Medical emergencies
- Fires
- Winter storms
- Hazardous-materials incidents

The fact that these incidents can occur on any property further underscores the importance of examining and evaluating the needs of each individual property when creating an emergency procedures plan. Periodic testing of emergency equipment helps to provide an opportune moment to discuss the basics of safety and the property's emergency procedures plan with tenants and residents. Build procedures into your emergency plan that provide preventive and responsive measures for these specific types of emergencies. At a basic level, this might be as simple as establishing a protocol for the testing and replacement of smoke and carbon monoxide detectors on the property or performing scheduled inspections and maintenance on a backup generator (if needed).

Another specific emergency to plan for would be major power outages, which could be caused by natural disasters or other larger forces. For instance, consider the effects that a power outage can have on elevators. Although elevators should not be used in an emergency, it is possible that tenants or visitors could become trapped in one during a power outage. If an elevator is present on the property, maintain regular safety inspections to ensure emergency contact lines, etc. are in working order (for detailed information on elevator emergencies, see *Chapter 12*).

Other specific emergencies to plan for would be medical emergencies. If real estate managers are faced with medical emergencies on their property, the only real recourse is to provide treatment to the best extent possible. Because a medical emergency can range from a sprain, burn, or broken bone to internal bleeding, cardiac arrest, or death, it's difficult for a real estate manager to be fully prepared. Some ways to create a sense of preparedness is to have a first aid kit onsite for the property, reinforced with a policy in the emergency procedures plan that dictates it be periodically evaluated and restocked. Doing so may help ensure that tenants or visitors suffering a medical emergency will receive the treatment they need. Whenever possible, consider designating staff members as emergency responders, trained in basic first aid procedures, but also CPR, the Heimlich maneuver, etc.

Depending on the geographic location of the property, it may be affected by winter storms. Severe winter storms and blizzards can pose significant dangers to buildings and human life on their own; however, it's equally important to analyze the potential damage that can arise even when ice and the effects of extreme temperatures outweigh snowfall. Your emergency procedures should include a breakdown of the types of winter weather advisories and warnings that may be apply to your area. Doing so will help increase tenant education about dangerous weather conditions, which also leads into more specialized disaster planning for specific emergencies caused by natural disasters, as described in the next section.

Natural Disasters

Natural disasters frequently strike with little to no warning, meaning that the best action a real estate manager can take in safeguarding their property is to know how to be prepared for the types of disasters that threaten their property. Given that many natural disasters, including tornadoes, hurricanes, and floods, are the direct result of severe weather, the National Weather Service (NWS) will be an invaluable asset in preparing a property against an incoming disaster.

Identify the types of natural disasters common to the area in which your property is located. Is there a history of tornadoes or hurricanes hitting the area? Are there potential floodplains or bodies of water that may swell into a flood located nearby?

Floods and hurricanes may especially be prone to contributing to secondary disasters such as landslides. As part of evaluating the properties needs, it's always important to consider the surrounding landscape.

Earthquakes also pose a significant danger to a property—particularly in areas that have little to no experience with them. Properties which frequently experience earthquakes have likely been constructed or altered in such a way that it protects itself against weak to moderate earthquakes. These properties will likely have extensive, well-practiced emergency procedures for responding to an earthquake. Evaluate the need to include earthquakes in your emergency response plan as needed.

Crime and Terrorism

Natural disasters are not always the cause of an emergency; many disasters that affect a property may also be the result (directly or indirectly) of a crime. It's imperative to survey the area surrounding your property. Is there a high crime rate or a trend of crimes? Is there evidence or history of gang activity in the area? Gathering this level of research will help determine specific actions that may need to be implemented into your emergency procedures plan.

Create an overarching procedure for notifying law enforcement and other local authorities (as needed) during a crime. Doing so helps to ensure the safety of property staff and tenants, while hopefully making an impact against future crime on the property, if only for a period of time.

Terrorism poses a more complex threat to a property. Since the September 11, 2001 attacks on the World Trade Center and the Pentagon, it has become increasingly important for real estate managers to develop, tighten, or refine their emergency procedures plan with regard to suspicious packages and bomb threats.

Ask yourself if the property could be a direct target for a terrorist attack. Consider the location of the property and the nature of the surrounding properties. Regardless of the outward threat of terror, your property should be prepared to respond to a suspicious package, bomb threat, or explosion. (More information about guarding your property against specific crimes can be found in *Section 5*.)

Business Continuity Strategies

It's easy to think of your emergency procedures plan in terms of actionable items like leading an evacuation or holding a fire drill. It's just as easy to say that a lot of thought, time, and resources are being applied to preparing for events that may never happen to a property. Emergency planning is vital to continued operation, but equally as important is a business continuity strategy.

Business continuity is an understanding of what might go wrong and having a plan in place to overcome it. Real estate managers frequently do this for their properties, so why not for their business? Because business

RECORDS STORAGE

The emergency plan and emergency procedures manual need to be available in the event of an emergency. Other property records—such as the business records needed for day-to-day operations—will be needed to resume operations after an emergency. These records should also be backed up to removable disc (such as a DVD, USB flashdrive, or external hard drive) or online storage.

Real estate managers may also wish to explore other possibilities for offsite data storage. These include use of disc media to back up computer data, retention of hard copy records, or both.

Determining which records need to be regularly preserved will help determine the amount of storage space needed to transfer these files to digital storage. When choosing an online storage option or a physical storage option, be sure to choose one that can house the amount of data being archived. It may be advisable to choose an option that provides double the data space needed—allowing for growth down the road.

continuity includes recovery and resumption of normal business operations, there is an element of planning that goes beyond preparing for fires and floods, winter storms, and power outages. Business continuity planning also includes the ability to efficiently and effectively handle an insurance claim to reduce rent loss and business interruption costs.

For many real estate managers, business continuity entails an understanding of what records—tenant records, property schematics, business records, etc.—are vital to continued operation. How will those be accessible should a disaster strike? What protections are in place to prevent loss or corruption of records from a power outage, fire, or theft?

Business continuity considerations should ask you to look at what the staffing needs are when resuming business following a disaster. Is a backup operations site necessary? What will the property's insurance coverage provide in terms of financial assistance? By choosing to think not only about what could disrupt your business, but also how to get it back on track, you do a great deal to protect a property against any disaster.

LEASE INSURANCE REQUIREMENTS

Real estate managers may wish to conduct a comprehensive review of all of the leases to identify specifics of insurance requirements. As part of this analysis, the following questions could be asked:

- Who is responsible for insuring the leased premises?

- Who is responsible for insuring the building (to the extent that it differs from the leased premises)?
- What are the insurance amounts called for in the lease?
- How much damage does there have to be before the leased premises is considered uninhabitable and who has authority to determine such condition?
- What duty does the lessee have to pay rent if the leased premises are not habitable?
- How will commercial tenants be affected from a business standpoint in the event of a large-scale natural disaster? Should tenants be required to carry business interruption insurance?
- Does the lease require tenants to include the landlord as an additional insured?
- Is a current certificate of insurance on file? What procedures are in place to monitor expirations?

Also to be considered is the amount and type of general liability insurance carried by the property owner, management company, and tenants.

PROPERTY INSURANCE REQUIREMENTS

In addition to the basic property casualty and liability insurance coverages that a property owner may carry, there may be special coverages that are required or desired. Rent loss insurance should be considered if it is not currently carried.

Flood insurance is available through the National Flood Insurance Program (see *Chapter 19*). Special earthquake coverage can also be obtained. Many lenders require owners to carry flood or earthquake insurance in areas prone to these types of events. Insurance premiums are high and large deductibles are required.

As a consequence of September 11, 2001, lenders may want some form of terrorism insurance on prominent buildings. The Terrorism Risk Insurance Act (TRIA), which became law in 2002, requires insurance carriers to offer such coverage to their customers. Discussion with a competent insurance professional is suggested, especially in regard to the need for terrorism insurance, what this coverage costs, and the types of exclusions that apply.

Consultation with an insurance professional is also advisable to review the adequacy of current coverages and ensure understanding of specific requirements that relate to disaster prevention. For example, there may be a requirement to implement specific preventive measures to minimize the possibility of fire in the event water is shut off to a building during rehabilitation or other construction work.

OTHER CONSIDERATIONS: EXPENSES, LIABILITY, AND STAFFING

It's important to keep in mind that there are costs involved in emergency planning and implementation. The amount of time you spend will depend in large part on how comprehensive a plan you develop. There will be upfront costs for emergency equipment and printing of emergency procedure manuals, in addition to costs incurred for the amount of time your staff spends creating the plan. Further costs may be incurred if professional consulting services are solicited as part of development.

It may also be necessary to purchase reference or training materials. Depending on the complexity of the building's tenancy, a need for an emergency planning consultant might be present.

Capital expenses may also be incurred to upgrade existing systems (e.g., sprinklers, fire doors, alarm systems) or to install new equipment that is compliant with local codes. Consider establishing specific accounting codes categorized for the specific expenses related to developing the emergency plan and emergency procedures manual.

There are also potential liabilities to consider. Actions taken in an emergency may cause or result in injury despite someone's intention to be helpful. Inadequate or improper training may render an emergency plan ineffective. These are among the reasons to clarify insurance coverage and to seek guidance from proper authorities, such as local police and fire departments and federal agencies. Also, an attorney can advise whether there are laws regarding public access or other issues that might affect your actions and/or liabilities in an emergency. Liabilities may also arise if you do *not* have an emergency plan in place or do *not* implement a plan to protect people and property.

Just as an emergency plan will only work if the information in it is current, staff assignments to the emergency management team will change as employees are promoted or leave the organization. The same factors affect lists of tenant contracts in commercial buildings. If equipment is changed or relocated, the particulars in the emergency plan must be updated accordingly. The plan may also need to be revised from time to time at the direction of the fire department or other authorities.

Also discuss the types of drills available for practice, including tabletop exercises. The test of an emergency plan is how it works in actual practice. After an emergency has passed, real estate managers should assemble the emergency management team and review their response to the emergency, not only to determine which emergency procedures worked successfully and which did not, but also to identify needs that had not been anticipated. This will allow the team to respond to future emergencies more efficiently, possibly minimizing the extent of bodily injury and property damage.

SECTION 1:

The Basics of an Emergency Plan

CHAPTER 2:

The Emergency Management Team

Assembling an emergency management team is critical to emergency planning, as the emergency management team[1] will be called upon to carry out the property's emergency procedures plan. The team members are appointed to protect and safeguard your property and the occupants by performing their assigned responsibilities before, during, and after an emergency. This team should be equipped to respond to various life- and property-threatening crises and help restore normal operations as soon as possible. Since your emergency management team will be comprised of property staff, they will already be familiar with the property, which will empower them in their understanding of how to respond quickly to unexpected and dangerous conditions.

ASSEMBLING THE MANAGEMENT TEAM

Before establishing and assigning responsibilities, create a team mission statement to reinforce the company's commitment to emergency management. The mission statement should define the team's strategic intent. An effective mission statement provides the directional framework for formulating a solid plan. Most mission statements are two to three sentences that articulate why the emergency management team exists, what its purpose is, and for whom.

Designate a team leader, someone who should be available to the team at all times and have an understanding of the property's layout and emergency procedures plan in order to be able to provide clear and decisive direction at a moment's notice. An assistant to the team leader should also be designated, especially if there are cases when the team leader is not available.

---

1. For additional guidance, information, and training in structuring an emergency management team refer to the Incident Command System (ICS) developed by the National Fire Service. The ICS has been adopted for use by business and industry as well as the government, and is built around five major management activities—command, operations, planning, logistics, and finance. A brief description of the ICS can be found in *"The Incident Command System: A Proven Tool for the Management of Emergency Operations,"* published online by the International Foundation for Protection Officers (IFPO) at *www.ifpo.org/articlebank/incident_command.html.*

In some cases, there may be a crisis management team at the executive or corporate level who can manage a broad response. This team can provide support to the emergency management team, where applicable. When it comes to assigning appropriate duties and responsibilities to the team members, it's important to establish that the team will carry out the emergency plan and take immediate action to assist occupants, lead them to safety, and help secure the property. Depending on the size and staffing of your property, this team should consist of (at least) the following:

- Onsite management staff
- Administrative and maintenance staff
- Occupants of the property (depending on the property type)

It's important to understand the importance of having an evacuation procedure in place. For instance, in a high-rise office building, the tenants' employees might be involved in some or all of the following:[2]

- *Fire warden* or *area captain*—coordinates the evacuation process for a particular floor or a specific area of the building. An assistant fire warden or area captain may also be appointed so there will be a backup if the primary person is not available.

- *Floor leader*—ensures that everyone on their assigned floor knows the location of stairwells and leads the orderly evacuation of their designated work area. The floor leader represents a single tenant on a floor or an entire multi-tenant floor. There may be more than one floor leader for a tenant or floor. In some cases, the floor leader and fire warden functions can be combined.

- *Searcher*—checks that all areas of a floor, including restrooms, have been evacuated. The emergency procedures manual may require those who work in private offices to close their doors as they leave, but this responsibility may be assigned to the searcher. They might, for instance, indicate that a room or area has been checked by placing a Post-it® note or adhesive label on a closed door about one foot above the floor.

- *Stairwell monitor*—ensures that people evacuating a floor stay close to the exterior walls of the stairwell, leaving a clear path along the interior of the stairwell for firefighters and emergency personnel. Stairwell monitors should prevent people from entering a stairwell

---

2. This list provides recommendations specific to high-rise buildings. These suggestions are meant to function as a guide and are not considered a standard practice. Responsibilities and recommendations for staff will need to be customized to fit the needs for different types of properties.

that is filled with smoke by directing them to another way out.

- *Elevator monitor*—directs people *away from* the elevators in an emergency. During an emergency, elevators may not work at all or could become a hazard. Elevators may stop on a burning floor because a heat-sensitive call button could be activated. During an emergency, elevator service should be stopped immediately and returned to the ground floor for use by firefighters (if applicable). In a building with multiple banks of elevators, consider assigning a monitor to each bank of elevators on each floor.

- *Aid Assistant*—helps move disabled workers to safe areas in stair-wells or designated areas of refuge so they can be rescued by firefighters. Real estate managers should ask tenants to provide information about their own and/or their employees' restrictions—names, location of their work space in the premises, and nature of their disability—to assist in emergency evacuation planning for the tenant and the building.[3] A tenant that employs a number of disabled workers may need several aid assistants, depending on the number of workers with disabilities present.

Designate alternative and secondary roles for team members, especially in situations when the primary person is not onsite:

- *First Responder Coordinator*—focuses on specific needs and questions and to communicate directly with the property owner.
- *Media Liaison*—handles all media communication. It is advisable to designate one media liaison to ensure an accurate flow of information.
- *Evacuation Assembly Point Coordinator*—takes a head count and relays information about any unaccounted people.
- *Insurance Coordinator*—takes notes and maintains records to report incidents.

Assembling the Special Emergency Evacuation Team

After a mission statement has been officially created and a solid team of dependable people have been chosen as the emergency management team, the next step is to gather the special emergency evacuation team, which will consist of individual tenants, residents, or employees of tenants. Creating a list of the individuals who have been given emergency response

---

3. Since privacy laws apply, information about disabilities should be considered confidential and made available only to members of the emergency management team.

assignments should be provided in an organized form (Figure 2.1).

Consult your local fire department to identify the roles and responsibilities of the support team that will be involved with the emergency evacuation of a specific building. The fire department may recommend additional or alternative roles.[4] Tenant employees who are assigned to specific roles will need to be trained—and periodically retrained—so they will be prepared to respond when evacuation is necessary. They also need to be clearly identified as team members during an evacuation.

All doors to the common or core areas are normally kept locked for security reasons, such as stairwell doors, and must remain open when the fire alarm is activated. Typically, this is achieved by electromagnetic locks that are wired directly to the fire alarm system. The locks will open when electric current to the locking mechanism is disrupted in case of a power outage. Stairwell doors, lobby doors, and sometimes corridor doors to tenant suites are required to remain open even during a power outage, but the interior office doors and locks are the tenant's responsibility. The evacuation process is explained in more detail in *Chapter 3*.

Identifying Backup Assistance

The emergency plan should identify a support team that comprises of certain specialists who may be called upon for backup assistance. This team may include some or all of the following:

- Contractors and suppliers—electricians, plumbers, elevator and HVAC contractors, board-up services, and glass companies
- Disaster recovery contractors specifically trained and equipped to minimize loss and fast-track restoration of the building and contents
- The building's architect and structural, mechanical, and electrical engineers
- Utility company representatives
- Police and fire department representatives—including hazardous materials and bomb/arson specialists when applicable
- Representatives from the local building department
- Contract security services
- Representatives from the property's insurance company
- Attorneys for the property owner and real estate manager

---

4. This approach is more likely to be used in a high-rise office building, but the same principle may be applied at a large or high-rise residential property where resident volunteers might assume specific roles.

Figure 2.1
BUILDING EMERGENCY RESPONSE TEAM ASSIGNMENTS

Floor	Tenant Name	Area Captain	Asst. Captain	Searcher(s)	Stairwell Monitor	Elevator Monitor	Aid Assistant

- Resident and/or commercial tenant representatives
- Government and charitable agencies
- Humane society or animal shelter representatives
- Consultant or representative from a disaster restoration firm
- Professional public relations representative
- Representative of the communication systems and equipment that are used in the building
- Onsite staffs of adjacent properties
- Certified industrial hygienist
- Corporate purchasing agent

Large properties may employ security personnel directly in which case additional (outside) security may be needed during an emergency. If, however, the security personnel employed at your property are contract workers, it's important to consult your contract to ensure these workers are permitted to hold an emergency-response role. It's also important to check if the contract prohibits you from contracting elsewhere for additional security personnel in an emergency situation. If after-hours janitorial services are provided by contract workers, those workers will need emergency evacuation training for their own safety, as an adjunct to the emergency management team. It might also be necessary to call upon after-hours services to help ensure that any tenants' employees working in the building after hours are safely evacuated.

DUTIES OF TEAM MEMBERS

Each team member should be assigned and trained on specific duties, which should be explained in the property's emergency procedures manual. Remember that not all team members will be available when an emergency arises, so each person should understand the entire emergency plan. Depending on the situation, one member may direct the action during an emergency until the team assembles.

Some of the most important duties include managing evacuations, cooperating with public agencies (fire, police, etc.), communicating with building occupants, or providing first aid to injured parties. Key team members should not only know their own duties, they should also be familiar with the duties of other team members in case they need to assume a secondary role when an emergency occurs.

The team leader will direct the actions of the entire team and will need to know what actions to take for each type of emergency, including what tasks need to be assigned to various team members. During an emergency, all communications should flow from the leader, with all team members remaining in contact with the team leader for instructions. In addition, the emergency management team should include assignments of alternates for each team member and role. Make sure your emergency procedures manual states who is in charge—if the team leader is unavailable—and assign alternates for each position on the team.

TRAINING THE TEAM

After the emergency procedures for the property have been written and the team has been assembled, train the team to carry out the plan, which should be reviewed, studied, and practiced by the members of the team in order to enable an effective response to emergencies. Begin the training by leading a tour of the property alongside the building engineer. Team members may know the property well, but it is unlikely that they will know it to the degree needed in some emergencies. During the property tour, encourage team members to think of the building and its systems through the lens of a crisis situation.

While touring the property, focus on the following relevant features prominent to emergency situations:

- Overall layout of the property
- Configuration of individual floors
- Location of stairwells, entrances, and exits
- Roof and basement access
- Mechanical equipment
- Emergency equipment
- Stored chemicals and hazardous waste, which are listed on the material safety data sheet (MSDS)
- Location of essential keys
- Telephones and other communications equipment
- Life-safety equipment

All utility shutoffs should be clearly labeled for easy identification. Team members should also know where each shutoff is located and how to use them in an emergency. Additionally, ensure your team members know where to locate and how to operate fire extinguishers, fire alarms, emergency telephones, and other emergency supplies. In buildings with elevators, indicate where elevator controls are located and how to manually shutdown elevators to return them to the lobby level. Be sure to indicate any areas that may house hazardous materials, making a point of informing team members who to contact for disposal of hazardous materials, along with the general knowledge of the area surrounding the building—streets, parks, and alternate access routes.

When training the team, invite representatives of the fire and police departments to provide information on evacuation procedures in detail, including how to safely move disabled and senior citizens and how to keep children calm and cooperative during a crisis. Training should also be provided on specific emergency procedures—that is, how some procedures, including evacuation, may differ because of the type of emergency. There may be specific seminars and courses offered by outside entities that can be considered as well. For example, first aid training from the American Red Cross and employee health and safety through the Occupational Safety and Health Administration (OSHA). In order to maintain a constant sense of mission and ensure that procedural instructions are current, it's important for the emergency management team to meet periodically to review and discuss any changes to the emergency plan and specific emergency procedures.

To ensure easy access to written emergency response procedures, provide two copies of the plan to all team members and onsite personnel—one copy to be kept in their work areas and one at their homes. Make the information portable and universally accessible. Create a digital version so that team members and onsite personnel can view the emergency response procedures on Smartphones, laptops, or tablets. Go a step further; create wallet-sized cards with key emergency procedures information, evacuation routes, and points of assembly for building evacuees. In cases when properties might not have onsite personnel, the emergency procedures information should be shared with all residents and tenants on the property.

Post links to emergency procedures on the property's website, and also on bulletin boards or newsletters to promote emergency awareness. The frequency of such communications depends upon many factors, including the size, type, and location of the building. For instance, the management staff and occupants of a high-rise building may need more frequent training than the real estate manager and tenants at a small strip shopping mall. Emergency procedures and preparedness materials can be made easily available to all building occupants for complete awareness of who the emergency management team is, what they do, and how to react in the face of an emergency.

PRACTICE DRILLS

Scheduling practice drills enables team members to instinctively respond to emergencies and builds confidence within the emergency management team and among the building's occupants. Practice drills provide the opportunity to evaluate the emergency plan, identify weaknesses, and correct any problems before an actual emergency arises. Practice drills should be announced in advance to give team members a chance to walk through their roles. Later, the leader can schedule surprise drills to evaluate the team's performance—separate drills can be scheduled for building occupants and the emergency management team.

Many municipalities have ordinances covering practice evacuations and other safety procedures—including how and when drills should be conducted. These ordinances may only apply to buildings of a certain size or height, such as mid- and high-rise buildings. Local ordinances should be checked to ensure that evacuations and practice drills for your managed property are compliant. Requirements for emergency procedures are usually posted on a city's website as a reference.

Safety is a community concern, so it's important to meet with residents and tenants to explain the significance of practice evacuations and other drills. Only you and the leader of your emergency management team have the ability to make these practice drills a valuable part of a building's emergency procedures plan. Leaders provide basic encouragement, along with an established emphasis on what could happen if occupants are not prepared for emergencies.

Drill Performance Review

Immediately after a practice drill, the emergency management team should be assembled to critique the plan and the team's performance. When evaluating the performance, consider asking the following questions:

- Do members of the emergency management team understand their respective responsibilities?
- Have new team members been adequately trained?
- Are there problem areas and resource shortfalls? If so, they must be identified and addressed.
- Does the plan reflect structural changes in the facility (including the leased premises)?
- Are photographs, blueprints of the property, and other records and documents up to date?
- Are the names, telephone numbers, and responsibilities of the team members up to date?
- Does the plan consider ongoing changes in the occupant profile?

When reviewing the team's performance, encourage everyone to speak freely by pointing out areas that need improvement, while also applauding good performance. If parts of the plan did not work effectively, the plan should be revised and the staff should be retrained accordingly. It's also beneficial to have a suggestion box for others in the building that participated in the drill but were not members of the emergency management team—they could have observed something that might be valuable for the team.

In addition to evaluating and possibly modifying the emergency procedures plan after each training drill, it is imperative to evaluate it after each emergency and under the following circumstances:

- When personnel responsibilities change (e.g., via promotion or reassignment)
- When the layout of the facility changes
- When policies and procedures change
- When annual audits of the property's maintenance and emergency equipment are conducted

23

Some cities stage mock disasters with mass casualties to test their emergency response capabilities—for instance, fire department, police department, 911 system, paramedics, or trauma centers—and help work out problems with responses. Encourage residents to participate as volunteers, or mock victims in staged emergency situations. When participating or observing these mock disasters, it might provide a better idea of how different types of emergency situations are handled, especially in terms of evacuation and communicating orders.

CHAPTER 3:
Evacuation

Evacuation of a building needs to be carefully planned. Evacuation plans should be designed to quickly move occupants out of the building using stairwells rather than elevators. Your emergency management team must be prepared to evacuate the premises at any time, whether as part of a practice drill or in response to an actual emergency. The evacuation procedures for a property will depend on the following variables:

- Property type
- Property size
- Number of occupants
- Occupant profile
- Number of visitors

As a rule, larger and more complex buildings require more detailed evacuation plans. For example, a four-story residential building will be easier to evacuate than a high-rise building, just as an open-air shopping center will obviously be easier to evacuate than a multi-level enclosed mall. Depending on the property type, it may require specialized attention, particularly senior housing or assisted living facilities. Every property is unique, so it's important that evacuation plans are prepared to address six significant, but universal issues:

1. Planning the evacuation
2. Communications—how to get the word out
3. Initiating and managing the evacuation
4. Returning to the property after an evacuation
5. When and how to return to the property
6. Staging of practice evacuation drills

PLANNING THE EVACUATION

Evacuation of a building should be carefully planned to quickly and safely move all occupants via stairwells rather than elevators. One of the key considerations to make while devising your evacuation procedures is what to do and who to defer to in the event of a fire. Responders to a fire—firefighters, often including a fire chief—will usually assume authority and order a full or partial evacuation based on what they know. However, a designated person onsite may have to assume this responsibility until the fire department arrives. It's important that in the case of a fire, only the fire department should use elevators to move firefighters and their equipment. An exception to this rule might be to operate one elevator to accommodate individuals with disabilities or mobility concerns—if this practice is feasible.

Train your emergency management team to be familiar with the building's elevator controls so they will know which elevators can be operated independently. During a power outage, the elevators will not work unless there is auxiliary power from a backup generator with sufficient capacity to operate them along with other vital building systems.

A backup generator may only power one elevator—a system failure or an accident may preclude using some or all of the elevators in a building. When forming the emergency plan, especially in terms of evacuating the building, it's important to provide guidelines for deciding whether a partial or full evacuation is appropriate, under which conditions, and who has the authority to do so.

WHEN TO EVACUATE

Any number of emergencies may signal the need to evacuate a building. Fires, floods, explosions, bomb threats, hazardous materials spills, or acts of violence are all justifiable reasons to call for an evacuation. Even a violent storm may necessitate evacuation, depending on conditions. Whatever the emergency, the decision to evacuate should not be made lightly or in a panic.

Many emergencies, however, do not require evacuation of the entire property, but instead a partial evacuation is sufficient. For example, a fire in a janitor's closet on the second floor of an office building may require evacuation of only the first three floors, while the tenants on the fourth floor might be asked to move up to the fifth floor until the fire has been extinguished.

The real estate manager onsite should always consult the local fire or police department to determine the correct delegation of authority during an evacuation. A fire on the premises may require the order to evacuate to be issued by a fire department representative onsite. On the other hand,

EVACUATION ORDERS

Different types of emergencies may require evacuation of part or all of a building. For example, a crime scene may involve the Federal Bureau of Investigation (FBI), the Bureau of Alcohol, Tobacco, Firearms, and Explosives (ATF), or state police in addition to local law enforcement. In civil disturbances or weather disasters, the National Guard may be called on to provide additional security. These authorities may also be empowered to order evacuation of a property.

Local jurisdictions may suggest or require specific evacuation procedures. The type of property or its size and complexity may warrant a specific response pattern. For example, an alarm may be a signal to evacuate, or people may be asked to assemble in a specific place on a floor (e.g., in a corridor) to await instructions on whether or not to leave the building. In some emergency situations, authorities may instruct against evacuation, asking instead for the population to shelter in place. Emergency procedures should provide for evacuation procedures to be modified according to the type of emergency. They should also provide instructions for staff and occupants to shelter in place when that is appropriate.

a bomb threat or criminal activity may require guidance from the police department or bomb squad.[1]

Communicating Evacuation Orders

The most important step in evacuation is communicating to the occupants and management staff that they must evacuate the building. A communications protocol or system should be designed so it can be used to report emergencies to the proper authorities, warn onsite personnel of danger, and keep building occupants—whether they are onsite or at home—informed of the progress and severity of the situation. A building-wide communications system—be it e-mail or short messaging service (SMS) based—is especially important for large properties to coordinate response actions and to keep in contact with all parties affected by an emergency situation.

How you handle an order to evacuate needs to be tailored to the type of property being evacuated. For example, large shopping centers and modern office buildings usually have public address (PA) systems that can be used to broadcast evacuation orders and instructions. It's important to

---

1. The bomb squad will often, but not always, be a part of the police department while any hazardous-materials (hazmat) response team will be part of the fire department. Be sure you know which authority is responsible for these important roles and include that information in your emergency contacts list.

ensure that all staff and occupants are familiar with the property's warning system. Be sure it has a distinct and recognizable visual and audio signal to be used *only in emergencies requiring an evacuation.*[2] Make sure to test it periodically.

If there is no PA system, however, it is important to have an equally effective means of delivering evacuation orders and other emergency instructions.

Alternative Methods of Communication. Consider the impact on a property and its occupants if standard communications systems became inoperable, and then prioritize the alternative methods of communication to be employed in an emergency. Procedures should always be established for restoring communications systems that have the potential to become inoperable. For example, a battery backup can fix some communications equipment problems. Communications equipment vendors can also provide advice about their products' response and recovery capabilities. Potential backup communications systems include:

- Messenger services, including Twitter and mass SMS deliveries
- Smartphones
- Point-to-point private phone lines
- Satellites
- High-frequency radios
- Walkie-talkies (for short distances or within the property)

Some choices may depend on what equipment and services are available and/or workable in the surrounding area. It's important to determine which sources will be used for communications between the onsite manager and the emergency responders, as well as communications with property employees, building occupants, neighboring businesses, and the media and public at large.

Communicating Announcements. Include the building occupants in an emergency communications network or phone tree. A good phone tree might use a "three-call" system, wherein each person calls three people, who in turn call three others, and so on. In this way, all residents or all commercial tenants' employees can be notified in a very short time. Even quicker methods could be through use of an automated system that distributes

---

2. Local fire codes may require alternatives to fire alarms when evacuation is for a non-fire emergency.

e-mail or text messages to all contacts simultaneously. Depending on the type of situation, it might also be a good idea to use social networks to distribute building news through Facebook or Twitter.

Before making the announcement to evacuate, scrutinize the words and phrasing of the message. Specific guidelines on the wording should be included in the emergency procedures. In most situations, the evacuation announcement is simple and straightforward. However, depending on the situation, it may be wise to withhold the reason for the evacuation in cases of a bomb threat, etc. During an actual emergency, the decision to evacuate and the announcement of evacuation directions should be made by a professional emergency responder (e.g., fire chief or police officer) unless the outside response has been delayed.

Local Emergency Contacts

Maintain an updated list of outside emergency contacts such as the fire and police departments, local hospitals or trauma centers, private ambulance services, the American Red Cross, and the Salvation Army. Also include larger organizations, like the Federal Emergency Management Agency (FEMA), in the surrounding area. State and local governments may have their own emergency management departments or agencies, and these entities should be included as well. Be sure to always make an immediate notification to the appropriate agencies within the local government when any emergency poses a potential risk to public health and safety.

In an emergency, effective communication with the families of staff members and building occupants is essential, so it's important to encourage individuals to consider how they should communicate with their families and each other in case of separation. Some properties arrange for an out-of-town contact for everyone to call in case of an emergency.

INITIATING AND MANAGING THE EVACUATION

During an actual evacuation, it's important to establish a nearby location where people can gather. This could be outdoors, but an indoor location may be advantageous depending on the property, surrounding area, and circumstance leading to the evacuation. When managing a commercial property, discuss with individual tenants where their employees will assemble after an evacuation to minimize confusion and avoid overcrowding of limited space.

Real estate management companies that oversee more than one building in a close proximity may prefer to use one of their managed properties as the place for evacuees to assemble. Communicate with management at adjacent buildings to find out if they have a large space that can be used for evacuation purposes, which might be easier to arrange by offering a reciprocal agreement. Regardless, it's a good plan to designate an alternate gathering place for an evacuation that ensures a specific location for evacuees to assemble. After an emergency, if people cannot get into the building, there should be a primary and an alternate place for people to report if they have not been advised to stay at home.

Orderly movement away from a building requires careful planning along with the participation and cooperation of everyone involved—requiring a clear chain of command that identifies personnel with the authority to order an evacuation. The property's trained floor monitors and emergency management team will help coordinate the evacuation. At a large commercial property, they may be assisted by tenants' employees who are assigned specific roles in an evacuation. If this is the case, the floor monitor may fill the role of the fire warden or area captain as described in *Chapter 2*.

Floor monitors play a key role when ensuring safe evacuation because they monitor the evacuation, make sure all people leave their areas and reach the proper destination, and may be assigned to safeguard against building re-entry until the danger has passed.[3] The following sections could be helpful when applying the property's evacuation procedures.

Evacuation Routes

Have floor monitors and building occupants become familiar with evacuation routes and procedures. These routes and procedures should be explained in the emergency procedures manual, and evacuation routes should be posted and highly visible. They may also be given to each building occupant on paper or electronically. In multistory buildings, selected stairwells may be reserved for use by firefighters, police, and other emergency personnel while the remaining stairwells are used for evacuations.

In most situations, however, stairwells are used by both emergency responders and evacuees—the evacuees are asked to descend along the exterior wall of the stairwell so that responders may move up the stairs more easily along the interior. It's also important that floor monitors

---

3. Some buildings actually require floor monitors to sign in each day so that management knows if an area is covered for an emergency.

encourage occupants to move quickly and calmly during an evacuation and to be sure that evacuation routes are unobstructed at all times. The doors to apartments or offices should also be closed to help prevent the spread of fire.

Evacuating Residents and Tenants with Special Needs

If there are two stairwells available for evacuation, designate one for evacuation of persons with disabilities or mobility issues and the other stairwell for evacuation of everyone else. This, however, may not always be possible or practical in an actual emergency. It may be necessary for persons with special needs to assemble, preferably near or in a stairwell, to await assistance. Specific members of the emergency management team should be assigned to assist disabled and non-English-speaking occupants.[4]

Taking a Head Count

Establish a system to account for all evacuees and staff. One or more persons should be assigned to take the names of evacuees to ensure that everyone has left the building, which can be done by matching evacuee names to an updated list of residents or commercial tenant employees. Once everyone has gathered in the designated location, they should remain at that location until the appropriate authorities say they may leave. In a small property, a head count may be sufficient. An alternate approach would be to have the floor monitors account for the occupants in their assigned areas.

Establishing a Designated Area

When appropriate to the evacuation, have building occupants evacuate outdoors, moving to an established waiting and debriefing area away from danger and out of the way from emergency crews. Evacuees may need to be debriefed by law enforcement officials before leaving the waiting and debriefing area in case they have information relevant to the emergency.

Regardless of the location, evacuees should always congregate in one place, and then separate into small groups after their names have been checked off the occupant list. In most cases, evacuees go directly to their cars after exiting the building, but this can sometimes cause congestion and

---

4. If tenants' employees have assigned roles, the aid assistants would assist these coworkers. It may also be desirable for tenants to arrange for assistance for their employees who are non-English speakers.

impede the efforts of firefighters, police, and other emergency responders to effectively deal with the emergency. It may also prevent a full accounting of all occupants, complicating the evacuation because of concerns that people may be trapped inside. If garage or parking lot attendants are employed onsite, these personnel may be assigned to control traffic flow of exiting vehicles. Remember to establish one or more pre-determined areas where injured evacuees can receive first aid in the event it is needed.

Designated first-aid stations and assigned personnel should be clearly identified in the emergency procedures manual. Personnel should also be designated to shut down critical operations, such as gas supplies, during the evacuation. They must also be able to recognize when to abandon the operation and evacuate the area.

RETURNING TO THE PROPERTY

Re-entry of the property for search and rescue should only be done by the appropriate rescue or emergency professionals with assistance from the management staff—if they are asked to participate—because of the potential liability to the management company if occupants are exposed to hazardous situations. Occupants should not be permitted to return to the property until the person in charge of the emergency management team, police or fire department personnel, structural or city engineer, or a member of the management staff has confirmed that it is safe.

Depending on the extent of the property damage, and only if authorized to do so, onsite management along with other staff may be required to assist emergency responders by escorting residents and commercial tenants' employees back into the building to identify goods, possessions, or equipment that might need to be retrieved. Before allowing a person to enter an apartment or commercial space, require proof of identification to help secure buildings in compliance with the General Services Administration (GSA)[5] after evacuation drills, as well as following emergency evacuations.[6] Remember that in some cases damaged property presents an opportunity for looting. Engage a guard service to watch over buildings and ensure any unnatural openings have been boarded up once the occupants, staff, and emergency personnel have left the premises.

---

5. The GSA would have jurisdiction for U.S. occupied buildings, but would not be the appropriate authority for all property types.

6. If the damage is extensive, special care should be taken during such re-entry. Unfamiliar odors may indicate hazardous-materials leaks, and unfamiliar noises may signal structural instability and further impending damage to the property.

EVACUATION DRILLS

Evacuation drills are essential to a successful evacuation plan as they help familiarize occupants with evacuation procedures and routes, minimize panic during emergencies, and keep floor monitors and other members of the emergency management team alert. Evacuation drills will also allow you to review the performance of the staff and the building occupants to help you determine if the evacuation plan needs to be fine-tuned.

Some municipalities require evacuation drills—usually once or twice a year—for buildings over a certain height. These drills may be conducted on a floor-by-floor basis or the entire building may be evacuated. Occupants may be given advance notice, but occasional drills should be conducted with no warning. Invite representatives of the local fire department to observe the drills and identify areas that need improvement. Some municipalities require fire department oversight of evacuation drills. Meet periodically with the emergency management team, adjunct floor monitors, and police and fire department representatives to review the evacuation plan since it might need updating as changes are made to the property—or due to changes in the resident profile or commercial tenant mix.

SHELTERING IN PLACE

At times it may be necessary for building staff and tenants to shelter in place as a response to a localized act of violence, such as an active shooter, biological or chemical attack, or simply because evacuation is risky or not an option due to a storm or area control by public safety. Essentially, sheltering in place requires choosing a space within the building that is structurally suitable (i.e., limited openings to exterior elements) to seek refuge. It is wise to choose a room with limited HVAC ducting or vents, as they are difficult to seal thoroughly. In selecting the room or rooms to be used, choose one that allows ten square feet of floor space per person, which will provide sufficient air movement to prevent significant build-up of carbon dioxide for up to five hours.

Emergency shelters should be stocked with essential supplies including food, water, first aid supplies, and blankets to allow staff and tenants to exist for a projected period of time while awaiting notice from public safety personnel that it is safe to leave the building or return to normal operations. If, during the sheltering process, the onsite manager is notified or becomes aware that the environment around the building is contaminated or toxic, it may be necessary to seal the room from the exterior and other interior spaces. To effectively seal the room, FEMA recommends:

- Locking all doors and closing all windows, vents, fans, and make-up air units—anything that could potentially bring outside air into the room or circulate air from other unprotected spaces within the building
- Sealing all openings or airways with plastic and duct tape by eliminating gaps to the greatest extent possible
- Turning off mechanical equipment that provides fresh air to the room

To facilitate rapid containment of the space, measure and pre-cut plastic coverings in advance and store them in the space with other critical supplies. It also makes sense to label each piece for rapid installation, as it will expedite the process by eliminating guesswork. Other critical equipment for the space may include radio and/or internet connection for news in case cell phone circuits are overwhelmed—consider having a land-line phone in the room. Sheltering in place for a protracted period of time in the face of a contaminated external environment is a risky business. The ability to effectively preclude seepage of outside air into the space for an extended time span is very difficult.

The following list of supplies has been recommended by the Centers for Disease Control and Prevention (CDC) for sheltering in place:

- Water—at least three gallons for each person
- Food—a three-to-four day supply
- Items for infants—formula, diapers, bottles, pacifiers, powdered milk, and medications that do not require refrigeration
- Items for seniors, disabled persons, or anyone with serious allergies—special foods, denture items, extra eyeglasses, hearing aid batteries, prescription and non-prescription medications that are regularly used, inhalers, and other essential equipment
- Kitchen accessories—manual can opener; mess kits or disposable cups, plates, and utensils; utility knife; sugar and salt; aluminum foil and plastic wrap; and re-sealable plastic bags
- A portable, battery-powered radio or television and extra, fresh batteries
- Several flashlights and extra, fresh batteries
- A first-aid kit
- Blankets or a sleeping bag for each person
- Sanitation and hygiene items—shampoo, deodorant, toothpaste,

toothbrushes, comb or brush, lip balm, sunscreen, contact lenses and supplies (any medications regularly used), toilet paper, towelettes, soap, hand sanitizer, liquid detergent, feminine supplies, plastic garbage bags and ties (heavy-duty) for personal sanitation uses, medium-sized plastic bucket with tight lid, disinfectant, and household chlorine bleach

- Other essential items—paper, pencil, needles, thread, small A-B-C-type fire extinguisher, medicine dropper, whistle, and the emergency preparedness manual

CHAPTER 4:

Operations Emergency Response

After an emergency is over, and control of the property is once again in the hands of building staff, the process of restoration will begin. While restoration may not seem like a vital aspect of emergency preparedness from a tenant or occupant perspective, as a real estate manager, it's as important as response planning. Recovery encompasses far more than the disaster itself. When considering a fire, the blaze itself damages a property; after the fire the property sustains damage not just from the fire itself, but also from the water or other agents that were used to extinguish it. Floods, windstorms, and earthquakes can also involve tertiary damage caused from or by other elements.

PREPARING FOR RESTORATION

Immediately following an emergency, assemble the members of your emergency management team who have been assigned responsibilities related to recovery, such as ensuring safety of personnel on the property, assessing remaining hazards, and identifying any potentially dangerous areas in the building. These employees and building occupants should be briefed on recovery plans and cautioned about potentially hazardous areas. Tasks and duties assigned to your recover team can help ensure that everything has been done to minimize the risk of further loss and include:

- Protecting the property by closing building openings to prevent unauthorized entry, theft, and vandalism
- Removing smoke, water, and debris to avoid injury and minimize hazards
- Making temporary repairs to prevent further structural damage
- Restoring power and other utilities as soon as it is safe to do so, and also consulting utility providers for additional guidance
- Conducting an investigation into the cause of the emergency with your insurance representative, an appropriate government agency, or a restoration consultant

HIRING CONTRACTORS FOR CLEANUP SERVICES

While your property staff may be qualified to perform some types of cleanup, some particular emergencies may warrant having this work done by outside contractors. Contracting recovery tasks might give some managers pause, but recovery can often be expedited in the process as some emergencies will require a contractor's specialized knowledge or equipment needed for some jobs. As a precaution, meet with local contractors before an emergency occurs, perhaps while assembling your emergency procedure manual. Doing so can lead to an informed decision on recovery tasks after a disaster, as arrangements for a wide range of services and costs may need to be negotiated or formalized prior to an emergency. The property's insurance carrier may also be contacted for recommendations.

Working with vendors that have a prior service relationship with the insurer can save considerable time and effort in restoring the property after an emergency. A restoration contractor's objective is to return severely damaged property to its original or near-original condition. The contractor's employees are trained and educated in the specific strategies and technical applications required to restore the property and contents after fires, floods, storms, and other major disasters. Contractors are helpful resources owing to the sheer number of services and skill sets they're able to provide, such as:

- Securing the site against further damage
- Estimating the cost of repairing, renewing, or replacing items of personal property
- Packing and transporting damaged or repaired property from and to the premises and storing it offsite during construction
- Estimating the cost of and repairing structural damage
- Cleaning and restoration of interior finishes and mechanical equipment
- Cleaning and restoration of office furniture
- Cleaning, restoration, or replacement of telephones, computers, and other electronic equipment
- Data retrieval and recovery
- Cleanup of mold, asbestos, and other environmental hazards;[1] smoke and odor removal

---

1. This work should be done only by appropriately licensed companies.

WORKING WITH INSURANCE COMPANIES OR PUBLIC INSURANCE ADJUSTERS

The property's insurance carriers should be notified immediately that an emergency has occurred. Consultation with the management's attorney may be necessary. When working with insurance companies, two approaches[2] are possible: (1) Either the property management staff can work directly with the insurance company, using the expertise of the provider's insurance adjuster to represent the property, or (2) the management company may hire a public insurance adjuster who evaluates the financial loss of property due to damage, and acts as your "agent" in negotiating the settlement.

A public adjuster functions much like a standard insurance adjuster. They inspect properties, work with real estate managers to ensure that insurance claim paperwork is complete, and work with the insurance company to reach a mutual settlement. The principal difference in a public

---

2. The approach and costs of services are very different. Develop a specific plan catered to the needs of your property.

WHAT IF THE WORST HAPPENS TO THE BUILDING?

Emergency planning should consider the worst-case scenario for the property. Fire, earthquake, or weather-related disasters can leave a building uninhabitable. Beyond a certain level of damage, it may not be feasible to make repairs. Construction costs may be only part of the equation. Building codes may require restoration to meet safety or other requirements that were not in place when the building was originally constructed. These requirements and their retrofits may substantially add to the restoration costs. In such a situation, the property owner may decide not to restore the property.

The decision not to restore the property has consequences for the occupants. Leases may include language stating that if a certain percentage of the building is destroyed—as solely determined by the owner or management agent—the lease will be cancelled, relieving occupants of their financial obligations under the lease. However, not having a place to live or conduct one's business is a serious issue for residents and commercial tenants.

A management company may be able to relocate displaced commercial tenants to another property in its portfolio if there is space available and the size of the space and the terms of a new lease are agreeable to both parties. It may be possible to offer a similar relocation arrangement to residents who are displaced. Residents who need assistance finding temporary shelter can be directed to the Salvation Army or the American Red Cross—or to the Coordinated Assistance Network (CAN) in which both agencies participate. Contact the local humane society to assist tenants with pets.

adjuster is that they are not necessarily the employee of a property or real estate management firm's insurance provider. In most situations, it's a fairly rare occurrence for real estate managers or owners to hire their own insurance adjuster. It usually happens for very large insurance claims or when there is, or is anticipated to be, a large difference between the amount the owner is claiming and the amount the insurance company is offering to pay. The most important difference is that a public adjuster represents the interests of the real estate manager and the property owner, as opposed to the insurance company's interests.

The objectives of restoration are to secure the area, prevent further loss, and return the building to normal operation as quickly as possible. Throughout the restoration process, it is necessary to keep all interested parties informed by carefully documenting the cost and nature of all work done to the property.

SECURING THE AREA

A disaster can make a building uninhabitable for an extended period of time. In such instances, one of the management's most important tasks is to keep people out of the building. An evacuated or empty building poses a lucrative opportunity to would-be looters and thieves, who may prey on occupant's personal property and equipment, as well as the building's materials (e.g., copper and aluminum). Potential intruders may not only cause further damage, but also present a liability to the management company, should an injury occur. As a safeguard, consider the following suggestions as supplements to your emergency procedures plan:

- Prevent trespassing by having security personnel patrol the property as needed. As an additional interim preventive measure, arrange for board-up of windows and doors. Install fencing around the perimeter of the building or the property. Designate specific points of entry for use by contractors and others and barricade the remainder of the perimeter.

- When appropriate, ask a structural engineer or other suitable professional to declare the building safe before allowing property staff, vendors, or occupants to enter. Do not allow free access to the property until its safety has been verified.

- Make arrangements for occupants to retrieve their personal property. It is only natural that people will want to get back into the building as soon as possible to collect their belongings—such as valuable, personal possessions, files, computers, or other business essentials. Management staff or security personnel should accompany occupants while they recover personal property to ensure that they do not wander into dangerous areas or enter another occupant's space.

- Require occupants to show identification before allowing them into their units or work spaces in order to prevent theft and vandalism. Keep a record of who entered, when they entered, and how long they stayed.

PREVENTING FURTHER LOSS

Preparing for an emergency is only half the battle. In order to minimize damage after disaster strikes, actions must be planned to address the prevention of additional loss beyond the damage caused by the disaster. In particular, an emergency plan should address debris removal, structural damage, cleaning and salvaging items, and preservation of property records. It should also include procedures for documenting damage before restoration efforts begin.

Documenting Damage

Once it is safe to enter the building—before beginning any cleanup—enter the building with a camera to carefully document the damage to the building and its contents in both photos and videos (if possible). Should an occupant bring a lawsuit against the management company or owner as a result of the disaster, this documentation will provide an important safeguard. As a legal precaution, make sure the video is dated and has a proper introduction before recording.

Removal of Debris

The first step in preventing further loss is to protect the property from debris and trespassers. Call maintenance restoration contractors and utility companies immediately after a disaster to remove debris, repair any damage to utility supply lines, and prevent any further damage. If property staff have the requisite skills, they may be assigned to perform some of the cleanup.

Be advised that the emergency, or the response to an emergency, may create environmental hazards—any materials containing asbestos may crumble when insulation on piping or inside walls is damaged. Damage to walls or ceilings may expose toxic mold that might not have been previously detected. Hazardous chemicals, ordinarily safely stored, may have spilled or become exposed. Not only is exposure to these types of hazardous elements potentially harmful to humans, in the aftermath of a disaster, asbestos fibers, mold spores, and other types of particles may be spread throughout a building by air currents, from open doors and windows, or when the HVAC system is turned on. As a result, salvageable items, as well as debris and damaged goods, may become contaminated. If environmental problems are suspected, a qualified professional should determine whether or not there is contamination and what should be done to mediate it before debris and salvageable items are removed.

In any major emergency that is not a natural disaster, the cause or source of the incident must be determined. The affected area should be closed off pending an investigation by the appropriate authorities and the insurance company. Cleanup should be deferred until the area has been thoroughly documented and the authorities have released it.

Protection from Further Structural Damage

Secure the property from further damage resulting from any structural problems caused either by the emergency or by rescue efforts by pumping out and extracting water. Promptly begin to dehumidify all walls, carpets, and floors. Mold thrives in most environments. In addition to eliminating a serious health hazard, it may be possible to avoid thousands of dollars in damage to the building. Structural damage should be identified by a structural engineer, although the building's engineer or a qualified contractor may make a preliminary assessment. It may be necessary to stabilize joists—horizontal supporting beams that run from wall to wall—that have been weakened due to fire or the weight of water, and to build a temporary roof to protect the building's interior. Temporary plumbing or electricity may need to be installed. These tasks usually require qualified professionals. In some areas, additional permits may be required before various and specific types of restoration work may begin. Weather conditions in the aftermath of a disaster may also be a consideration, as extremely cold temperatures may freeze exposed water pipes, causing them to burst.

Cleaning and Salvaging Items from the Property

The next step is to secure and clean all salvageable items from the property that have survived with little or no actual damage—carpeting, appliances, hardware, fixtures, plumbing fixtures, light fixtures, telephones, or computers. These items should be held in storage until structural repairs have been completed.

If there was a fire, it may be appropriate to open windows for ventilation; clean and coat metals with petroleum jelly or oil to prevent corrosion; brush smoke particles (i.e., soot) from dry furnishings, draperies, and carpets; and dispose of canned goods that were exposed to excessive heat.

Occupants should avoid using electronic equipment and appliances until they are cleaned and checked by experts, and *under no circumstances* should smoking be allowed in or near the building.

Make a detailed inventory of damaged goods, listing and visually depicting each item, and separate them until an insurance adjuster has visited the premises. This is usually performed with the insurance adjuster or the adjuster's salvager. Damaged goods may be moved outside, provided they will not be damaged by external conditions. If you release goods to a salvager, be sure to obtain a signed inventory stating the quantity and type of goods removed—provided the insurance adjuster has inspected and documented the transaction.

Records Preservation

Preserving property-related records is necessary for efficient restoration of operations. Management staff should determine *in advance* which records should be given special protection. First, identify the minimum operating information, that is, the information that must be absolutely accessible to perform essential functions during and after an emergency. This would include important emergency phone numbers and floor plans of the property.

You may want to classify other information into functional categories, such as management records and reports, finance, insurance, and administration. Once classification is completed, identify the equipment and materials needed to access and use the information.

Next, establish a plan to protect and access these records. Options include standard data backup of all software, databases, and documents relevant to business operations, making copies of paper records and storing them in a separate building or in fireproof cabinets, preserving

DOCUMENTING THE RESTORATION

The restoration process should be documented. Photographs and videos can be taken at different stages to show progress over time. As with any construction project, it is important to keep track of construction plans, change orders, directions to contractors, information received from them, and costs. Separate accounting codes should be used to account for construction and other restoration costs. It is also important to keep track of employees' time spent working on restoration activities, including overtime, as these constitute costs from the loss and may be covered by insurance. Accurate records of construction work and costs of employee time are needed to receive reimbursement from the insurer. Include a daily record of activity by personnel and activity.

digital records, increasing security for computer facilities, arranging for evacuation of records to backup facilities, backing up systems handled by service bureaus, and arranging for backup power. Historical records that are accessed infrequently should also be considered for offsite storage, especially if onsite storage is using space that might be rentable.

If the information is considered crucial, some real estate managers store periodic backup drives to offsite locations, such as a safety deposit box or regularly transmit software images to third-party data repositories. If a disaster should strike, it is not difficult for a real estate manager to resume business, provided this data persists either on physical hard disk or as part of a cloud storage system. Data preservation is an issue that real estate managers should weigh carefully. There are a number of options that exist to safely preserve or remotely store core data.

Commercial tenants should have their own plans for backing up and retrieving business records and for resuming operations after an emergency. Residents should store vital personal and financial records in a safe place offsite, either through an online storage service, leased storage unit, or safety deposit box.

RESUMING OPERATIONS

Your emergency procedures plan is a long-term strategy that begins as soon as disaster strikes. It must, therefore, include arrangements for the continuation of critical functions immediately following a disaster and during the recovery process. The hallmark of a successful restoration effort is to have the building returned to normal operation as soon as possible. Otherwise, there is the risk of additional damage to the property and additional expense.

KEEPING OTHERS INFORMED

In order to assess the damage and amount of financial loss, the insurance agent and adjuster should be among the first people called to the scene before restoration efforts begin, unless health and safety issues must be addressed before they can arrive. Real estate managers should consult with the insurance company in the selection of an appropriate restoration contractor. This should be done prior to a loss occurring; the contractor should have visited the property to determine how to approach restoration after different types of emergencies. A pre-selected contractor can also submit their pricing to the insurance carrier in advance to expedite the settlement process.

The following lists additional suggestions regarding dissemination of information after an emergency:

- Keep occupants informed of the condition of the property and progress of the restoration. As soon as possible, occupants should be given the facts as conferred from the authorities or experts, what is being done in response, and when they can enter the building to retrieve their property. Occupants may also be told how long it is expected to take for the total restoration to be completed when that is known.

- Tell residents and tenants when the building can resume operation. Periodic updates allow the real estate manager to provide occupants with progress reports to let them know if the restoration's scheduled completion is on target.

- Consider keeping the media informed of the restoration's progress. Be as ethical in media representation as you would with another client. Media representatives can be valuable allies at this time. A designated corporate employee who is trained and rehearsed should have the media contact. A real estate manager should supply a basic property fact sheet to control this basic information. For extra insight, see *Chapter 5* for a primer in public relations.

- Keep the public informed of the restoration progress. Depending on the incident and the property type, a series of advertisements in local newspapers that inform the public that the building is operational may benefit both the building and its occupants. This can be especially worthwhile when a shopping center or other service-oriented property has been put out of commission by an emergency situation. If there is a fire or police investigation on the property, the media should be referred to the fire or police departments so information is not provided that could impede any investigation.

Don't let media relations distract from the most important interest group in the recovery process—the residents and tenants. Consider how beneficial a website with updated information on the restoration can be. Periodic updates with news on major progress or a setback may warrant changing the status daily or more often. This can save the time and hassle of having a person answer repetitive phone inquiries directly. It may be desirable to give the website or message phone number to others as well (e.g., vendors and the media). An advantage of a website is the opportunity to include photographs showing how the restoration is progressing.

CLOUD STORAGE: AN ALTERNATIVE TO STORING RECORDS OFFSITE

A disaster not only poses risk to life and property, but also to critical business information. For real estate managers, records may be equally as important as the physical asset itself.

Previous advice has always been to keep copies of crucial data offsite, secured in a safety deposit box or storage facility. Some real estate managers may have kept daily, monthly, or yearly records on magnetic tape or discs. While these methods are perfectly sound ways of preserving data, more efficient and automatic methods have become the norm.

Cloud storage automates the backup process by saving critical data—documents, databases, etc.—to an online server. Cloud storage services frequently perform regular backups, ensuring that any data is copied on a regular basis (sometimes hourly).

Storing information in the cloud can help real estate managers remove a lot of the worry and energy from maintaining a manual backup routine. Should a disaster strike, it's likely that a cloud service will have an almost identical version of the data lost when a computer system went down.

Because the information is online, real estate managers may have the ability to access and edit their data from any computer—eliminating a degree of downtime before regular business operations can resume.

A variety of cloud storage services and techniques can be found online. Several exist with the business and commercial market in mind, offering price tiers based on the size, frequency, and type of data being preserved—free options also exist and are worth exploring as an alternative option for preserving property-related records.

CHAPTER 5:
Public Relations

Questions will always follow an emergency. In the case of a major disaster, the onslaught of questions and demands of a real estate manager's time might seem endless. Building occupants want to know when they will have access to their belongings, when they can reoccupy the premises, and how the emergency will affect them. The building's owner will be calling to either ask or answer questions. And, in a large scale disaster, it's not out of the question to suddenly have representatives from the media asking what's happened and what's being done to recover. One of the last things any real estate manager will want, or need, directly following a disaster is an inquisitive reporter, notebook in hand, asking lots of questions to which the manager does not yet have answers. What should the reporter be told? What if the reporter is accompanied by a film crew? How should one respond to the media?

A strong, transparent commitment to public relations is an important component of business as well as emergency planning. With a large property portfolio, it's possible that a real estate manager may spend millions of dollars promoting their properties and image, yet they sometimes fail in working with the media in crisis situations. Whatever the situation—fire, flood, criminal incident, or even loss of human life—a crisis of any kind, if mishandled, can quickly negate the positive image that years of good management and well-planned public relations efforts have created. Conversely, a negative impact can be reduced or even used advantageously after a disaster if the real estate manager plans and prepares for emergencies.

ESTABLISH RELATIONSHIPS WITH LOCAL MEDIA

Having established relationships with local media representatives can also be helpful. A real estate manager who writes about real estate issues for a local newspaper or is available as an industry resource for print and broadcast reporters may receive more cooperation from the media in a crisis than one who is not known to them.

Just as the occupants of a building should be kept fully informed as much as possible during and after an emergency, the public as a whole should also be informed, not only to satisfy public curiosity, but because the public might be affected as well. An astute real estate manager will use the media to relay information and to instill public confidence in the property and its management. The real estate manager should be prepared and have a specific public relations plan in place that outlines the steps for dealing with the public and the media during and after a crisis.

NEVER AVOID THE MEDIA

The first rule in any crisis communications plan is not to avoid the media. Real estate managers must recognize that the media may choose to cover the story with or without their cooperation. It is far better to take an active role in the process, using the press to tell the right story at the time and the place it should be told. Working with the media can be difficult and frustrating at times, but with proper planning, you may be able to use the opportunity to your advantage. Some members of the press take great pride in their objectivity, but the slant they give a story may be affected by the manner in which they are treated. Moreover, if the property does not provide a public relations representative, the media will seek statements from people who are less well informed about the incident or emergency.

The media should not be brushed aside with such statements as "I'll talk to you later," or "This isn't the time," or "We have no comment." The appearance of a cover-up will only create skepticism, maybe even animosity, on the part of the media and the public. It is best to deal with the media honestly and openly. An organized crisis communications plan prepares you to do so.

RESPONDING TO THE MEDIA

A crisis communications plan will include instructions on how to respond to the media, appointing a spokesperson, and timing of the response to media inquiries. This is not as easy as it might sound and is why some management companies solicit the services of public relations firms to handle their crisis communications. Since such firms are experienced in dealing with the media, they can help develop media statements and sharpen the real estate manager's speaking ability and other required skills. The real estate manager can either hire an advertising or public relations firm that specializes in crisis public relations or appoint someone on the staff who is capable and comfortable in dealing with the media.

Because of the importance of accurate and timely written press statements in crisis situations, an emergency procedures manual should include sample statements in the form of generic news releases. These releases—or "fact sheets"—may incorporate specific information about the property. Then, when an emergency arises, only the particulars of the incident need to be inserted. The basic property information is already in place. Following are typical contents of a property fact sheet:

- Building or property name
- Street address
- Real estate manager's name
- Building age—when it was built
- A general description of the building and its occupancy

If the owner wishes to respond to media requests, their name may be included in the fact sheet as well.

Who Should Speak?

Media relations is a delicate skill. It demands openness and honesty and the ability to keep a calm demeanor in the face of probing questions, while also maintaining the owners' and occupants' confidentiality and privacy rights. Only accurate, verified information should be provided to the media at the appropriate time. Finding the right person for this job can be difficult. A person from the property owner's or the real estate management company's public relations firm may be assigned the responsibility of serving as the property's spokesperson. In serious matters, it may be best left to experts if no one in the firm has the expertise.

To maintain consistency in communications with the media, one person should be designated to act as a spokesperson for the property. Only that person would be permitted to speak to the media on behalf of the property. This may be the same person who is the property contact for police, fire, paramedics, and other outside responders—a person dedicated to communications regarding the emergency.

The real estate manager must make it clear to the rest of the staff that only the spokesperson has the authority to interact with the media, and all media inquiries must be referred to that individual. This way, the spokesperson can establish a relationship with media representatives, the rest of the staff will not be burdened with calls at a time when other demands are greater, and the risk of giving out conflicting information is eliminated. To accommodate this procedure, the spokesperson's name and phone numbers—home, work, and mobile number—should appear on all news releases and other media communications as the sole point of contact.

What Should Be Said?

Information given to the media should be as complete as possible, answering all the questions a reporter may ask. Press releases vetted to the media may frequently serve as the strong backbone of a story. Providing the media with the necessary information gives them a solid starting ground for a news piece. Example 5.1 provides a sample template for a press release. Example 5.2 illustrates a completed press release. Regardless of the format, be sure to answer the following questions in your press release or fact sheet:

- What happened?
- Where did it happen?
- How many occupants does the building have?
- When did it occur?
- Who was involved?
- Were there any injuries? Be sure that you *do not* list the names of those injured or report any injury that has not been proven by a medical professional.
- What caused the situation?
- What is being done for the building's occupants?
- Is the situation under control?
- When will the property be restored to normal operating conditions?
- Have there been hazardous material leaks as a result of the incident?

Provide as much *confirmed* information and its sources as you can—avoid speculation. After the property's credibility has been established, the real estate manager can more readily fulfill his or her responsibility to the building occupants and the public by allaying rumors, fear, and panic. In short, never lie or cover up.

More than likely, some information will not be available when questions are being asked. When you do not have all the answers yet, say so and do not guess or provide unconfirmed reports. Statements given to the media must be accurate. Providing inaccurate information, which later must be corrected, can cause untold damage. When answers are not yet available, the real estate manager (who is in control) will reassure the media that more information will be provided as soon as it is known. You should follow through on that promise. It should also be noted, however, that release of certain information may depend on the local authorities. If there is a police

EXAMPLE 5.1
INTRODUCTION TO CREATING A PRESS RELEASE

Company Logo/Letterhead
[Management Company Name]
[Management Company Address]
[City/State/Zip Code]

[Release Date. If not a specific date, use "For Immediate Release"]

First paragraph: What happened?
Give a brief description of the emergency or incident, which may include the authorities that responded (e.g., fire, police, hazmat team). Include when and where the incident took place.

Second paragraph: Why?
If known and verified by proper authorities, state a cause for the incident, citing the source of the information. If no cause is known at the time of release, indicate what is being done to determine a cause.

Third paragraph: Injuries and Damage
Describe any damage or disruption of use to a property. Where injuries to occupants, tenants, or customers are concerned, use discretion. If verified by medical professionals, a number of injuries may be included at the real estate management company's discretion. Do not reveal specific medical conditions, as this is a violation of privacy.

Fourth paragraph: Recovery
Use this paragraph to detail or outline recovery steps to be taken. How long (if applicable) will it take to resume operations as usual? Are parts of the building still able to be used?

Fifth paragraph: Brief Background
Provide a brief profile of the property and its real estate management. This paragraph will vary depending on the property type, but may include the number of units in a residential setting or the date, occupancy, and historical use of a commercial or industrial property. Include a statement providing details on who manages the property to ensure accurate information to the press.

###
(Three pound signs denote the end of the message,
and are typically seen on press releases.)

EXAMPLE 5.2
SAMPLE PRESS RELEASE

XYZ Management
123 Smith Street
Townplace, IL 12345
Contact: John Smith
johnsmith@xyzmanagement.com
(555) 555-5555

November 12, 2012

For Immediate Release

A fire broke out in the kitchen of The Coffee Shop at the Cedar Plaza shopping center at 10:00 a.m. this morning. All Coffee Shop guests and staff were safely evacuated.

Fire department officials are presently investigating the cause of the fire, which did not damage or affect other businesses in Cedar Plaza.

Restoration of the damaged kitchen is underway, pending the close of fire department investigation. The Coffee Shop will resume business by Saturday.

The Cedar Plaza shopping center at 100 Cedar Avenue was built in 1976 and has been managed by XYZ Management Company since 1985.

###

or fire department investigation, some questions may have to be referred to their representatives to preserve the integrity of the investigation.

As previously mentioned, when meeting with media representatives, real estate managers could provide news releases that not only explain what happened, but also provide facts about the property. These "fact sheets" can save valuable time for both reporters and the real estate manager. To help safeguard the property against fraudulent claims or potential litigation, it is important to maintain prudent records of all information that is released to the public.

Estimating the Time of Disclosing Information

Public relations professionals agree that public perception is formed within the first 24 hours after an incident. This means that any delay in communications during this critical period—taking too long to meet with the media, appearing overwhelmed by the emergency, or avoiding the media altogether—is likely to result in a poor or negative public opinion. Once the public's respect is lost, a real estate manager will miss the chance to show who is in command of the situation and assure the public that the property will be back in operation as soon as possible.

Communication with the media begins as soon as reasonably possible during or after an emergency. In highly sensitive situations, the spokesperson should first discuss the release of information with law enforcement officials so as not to jeopardize an investigation. He or she should maintain media contact at regular intervals.

ALLOWING THE MEDIA ON THE PROPERTY

Reporters may want to see the property to get a firsthand look at the damage. Reporters should be allowed on the property, but only under close supervision by the real estate manager, and only after officials have stated that the area is safe. It should be made clear that access to the property will be controlled in the interest of safety and that areas where police or fire officials are conducting an investigation will not be accessible until the investigation is concluded. Instead of letting reporters and camera crews wander freely around a property after an emergency, the property should be closed off and secured until management is ready to allow media representatives on the scene. The real estate manager should then conduct the tour, showing reporters samples of the damage and examples of cleanup efforts. Access to potentially dangerous areas, if allowed, should be limited.

If the media cannot be allowed on the property, arrangements should be made to meet with reporters at the command center that will be set up for the emergency to review the status of the property. In some situations, press conferences may be appropriate. In such settings, many questions can be answered at one time. If possible, reporters should be asked to submit their questions in writing, which provides an opportunity to research the answers and respond with more complete information. Many reporters, however, will refuse to do this, and if it is a fast-breaking story, they simply will not have time.

FOLLOWING UP WITH THE MEDIA

Good media relations continue when the crisis has passed. Even after the emergency is over, channels of communication with the media should be kept open. The media may be used to keeping the general public informed of the progress being made to repair the building and make the occupants feel more secure. Media representatives should be invited back to the property to observe cleanup and repair efforts. Above all, the real estate manager should not pass up the opportunity to let the public know when the property is back in business. A media open house for a restored property can be especially worthwhile, where applicable.

Keeping your eyes on the horizon will help you realize that crises will always arise. Having good rapport with the media as a result of a previous incident may make coverage more favorable in the future.

CHAPTER 6:

The Emergency Procedures Manual

After learning the basic components of an emergency plan, the emergency management team will be better equipped to create an emergency procedures manual that meets the needs of their property. The emergency procedures manual should always contain necessary information to safeguard residents, commercial tenants and their employees, property management staff, and visitors during and after an emergency. The emergency procedures manual should address:

- How to make the property more secure and prevent emergencies and/or minimize impact
- How to prepare for an emergency
- What to do during an emergency
- How to protect people and mitigate damage to the property
- How to restore the property after an emergency
- How to create relevant, standardized forms for quick and easy use

The emergency procedures manual should include a list of the members of the emergency management team and the specific roles each member has been assigned, along with a detailed list of the responsibilities for each team member and instructions for carrying them out. This should differentiate the role of the team leader and identify a clear chain of command for members of the team, along with an alternate chain of command if those members are not available. A good emergency plan provides for periodic review of the emergency procedures manual. Focus your plan on answering the following four questions:

1. Has the building structure or its mechanical systems and equipment changed in such a way that could affect the response to an emergency?

2. Has occupancy changed in any way that can affect the emergency response? Consider the senior and child population. Are there more disabled or restricted individuals than previously accounted for?

3. Have there been significant changes in the staff size or responsibilities that could impact the plan?

4. Have local emergency services or medical care providers changed? Do they still have the capacity to assist in case of an emergency? Be sure to check that all emergency numbers are current and up to date.

Update the emergency procedures regularly to incorporate new requirements established by local, state, and federal regulations. Frequent updates will also keep emergency procedures current with the service level of local emergency services.

For commercial properties, consider interior modifications for tenant improvements. How has the neighborhood changed? How is your property being used? How are nearby properties being used? Consider that commercial properties could be in use as residential property and vice versa. Assess these items when updating any emergency procedures manual. Consider outside elements such as criminal activity, new construction, or new industrial activity nearby, as these factors may warrant modification of emergency procedures.

CREATING THE MANUAL

Putting together relevant and custom-made emergency information in an easy-to-follow format requires thorough planning, research, and a capable writing team. Delegate specific responsibilities for development and documentation of emergency procedures to staff members, who will also serve on the emergency planning team. Consider involving the same group in implementing emergency procedures, especially since they play a vital role of sharing their experiences and expertise. Working as a team creates opportunities to develop an objective perspective while also allowing members to brainstorm and propose more efficient plans and procedures. Consider the following to assist the emergency planning team in creating a tailored emergency procedure manual:

- Decide who will be on the emergency management team, since they are closely involved with the day-to-day operations of the property. Team members should be encouraged to supply input regarding the manual's contents.

- Next, schedule a series of meetings for designated staff to brainstorm ideas and begin to develop emergency procedures.

- Ask team members to research and identify emergency needs with regard to the property and immediate surroundings to develop a property profile.

- Determine which sections of the manual apply to your particular property, recognizing that not all the aspects will apply.

- Use the fill-in-the-blank forms that accompany this book to assemble information for the property's emergency procedures manual (see pg. 305 for instructions to access the emergency forms). Include other relevant information as necessary and appropriate— site plan and building layout, local building codes, etc.

- Appoint the individuals who will assist in writing the manual.

- Create a good organizational structure and solid outline that separates individual sections and allows for integration of replacement pages when necessary.

- Decide on a format for presenting the emergency procedures manual. Consider how important it is for everyone to have easy access to the manual—online access is essential.

- Update and revise your manual as local codes or structural changes dictate. Inform manual users of those changes. Consider setting up a system of user requirements for maintaining up an up-to-date plan.

- Encourage periodic meetings on emergency procedures since they provide a forum for presenting emergency concerns and problems that need to be addressed, while reassuring the team's preparedness for times of crisis.

Developing the emergency procedures manual requires a commitment and a budget. Initially, there will be indirect costs—staff time for planning, writing, and training staff to respond appropriately. There will be direct costs for preparing multiple copies of the manual—printing, binding, and other production costs. Ultimately, having an accessible, electronic version of the manual is extremely important, allowing team members to easily read the manual at their convenience, or view its contents with a Smartphone or other device.

CONTENTS OF THE EMERGENCY PROCEDURES MANUAL

Generally, an emergency procedures manual includes or is comprised of three main sections: (1) Reference information, (2) directions for the management staff and emergency management team to follow for each possible emergency (such as evacuation procedures), and (3) directions for building occupants.

Reference Information

The emergency procedures manual should contain information that might be needed in the event of an emergency. Suggestions include:

- An extensive, updated list of phone numbers to reach team members, management personnel, the building owner, emergency assistance (fire and police departments, etc.), restoration companies, and other outside resources

- An up-to-date list of phone numbers of all occupants (residents and/or commercial tenants' employees), including specialized equipment and need for assistance—this should include extensions at individual desks or workstations at commercial properties

- A designated spokesperson to provide information to the media and examples of news release formats for this purpose (see *Chapter 5* on public relations for more details)

- A general one-page description of the building's statistics—ownership, occupancy, age, construction materials, plans and specifications, mechanical systems, and equipment that is immediately available

- A list of the building's current safety features and equipment, their locations and operating instructions (fire extinguishers, alarms, etc.), along with other supplies available onsite (first aid kit, list of medical supplies, etc.), including quantities and where they are stored

- Floor plans and as-built drawings that show all equipment, systems, and exits to which access may be needed during an emergency

- Insurance information, including the insurance agent's name, business and after-hours phone numbers. Document the type of insurance coverage, policy number, and name of carrier for each policy. Create a current inventory of property possessions.

- The material data safety sheet (MSDS) that lists any hazardous materials or chemicals on the property and where they are stored.

Emergency Team Directions

The emergency procedures manual should include emergencies that could happen on the property and procedures that should be followed in response to them. For each emergency, the manual should address the following specific areas:

- Detailed descriptions of the duties of the emergency management team during the emergency
- A flow chart depicting the chain of command during the emergency
- The person or persons responsible for communications with the media and with emergency responders (police, fire department, paramedics, etc.)
- A copy of the emergency public announcement for the particular emergency
- Procedures to account for all management personnel, residents, and commercial tenants' employees
- Procedures for notifying families of management employees about the status of personnel on the premises—tenants should always assume this responsibility for their employees
- Evacuation and re-entry procedures as they apply to each emergency, including specific instructions for guiding disabled individuals and elderly residents to safety—anyone with mobility restrictions
- Reporting, documentation, and regulatory procedures as they apply to each emergency
- Restoration procedures

Include information about administering first aid to injured persons as they wait for medical assistance to arrive. The manual should also include assignments for emergency management team members in the recovery process.

Directions for Building Occupants

Consider how the property's occupants could prevent and respond to emergencies by educating them on basic emergency procedures and precautions. Information they need would include:

- How they will be notified of an emergency
- How to identify members of the emergency management team and its leadership
- Directions for evacuating residential units or work spaces and leaving the building

Management staff can also help building occupants become aware of safeguards they can employ to protect themselves and others in the building. The following list provides additional options:

- Post emergency directions throughout the property in a prominent location where they will be visible to occupants—for example, a laundry room or other common area of a residential property, common corridors, and stairwells.

- Promote safety guidelines from police, fire officials, and others in a newsletter directed to occupants. These may include holiday safety tips and reminders to drive and walk carefully on icy surfaces in winter. Other frequent reminders include keeping doorways, corridors, and stairwells clear of obstacles.

DISTRIBUTION OF THE MANUAL

The emergency management team members and onsite mangers should each have a copy of the manual. Additional copies should be stored in a safe place—onsite or off—in case originals are misplaced or destroyed. If the owner, an emergency management team member, or an emergency professional needs to access the manual, but are away from the premises, the emergency procedures manual should be accessible online or in another digital form.

Whenever a manual is given to a new employee, the onsite manager should emphasize the confidential nature of the material in the manual, particularly the phone numbers, security systems, and insurance information. If a team member leaves the property, their copy of the manual should be retrieved and reissued to the person assuming their position as part of conducting a thorough review and training where needed. It may also be appropriate to post occupant emergency procedures on the property's website if it has one. Posting emergency procedures online allows the document to become dynamic, corrected, or replaced without the need to distribute paper copies with each update—major or minor.

Encourage occupants to periodically check emergency information on the property website to ensure the information is always up to date. Never underestimate the benefit of e-mail when it comes to getting the word out. Notify occupants electronically when critical changes have been made to the emergency procedures. Promote emergency preparedness at regular intervals throughout the year by timing more general e-mails or notices to the start and end of daylight-saving time, when many fire officials recommend testing smoke alarms.

EMERGENCY PROCEDURES FOR OCCUPANTS

Whatever the property type, occupants should be educated in emergency procedures and safety precautions, which can be accomplished by creating an emergency procedures guide. While not as detailed or complex as the emergency procedures manual used by staff, the guide provides building occupants with instructions to help them facilitate the larger emergency procedures plan as devised by the emergency management team. Giving occupants a resource for evacuation can go a long way in making sure emergency procedures run as smoothly as possible. Points to discuss in an occupant guide include:

- Evacuation directions and procedures, especially note that elevators are not to be used during an emergency
- Recommended assembly areas to be used during an emergency, which can be used as staging areas for a drill
- Guidelines for maintaining personal safety and security for residents and for commercial tenants' employees, such as navigating smoke filled corridors, etc.
- Consideration for pets in residential buildings and for assistance animals at both residential and commercial properties

If there is a large amount of information for the occupants, it might be appropriate to incorporate emergency procedures information into a resident guidebook or commercial tenant handbook along with other property rules and instructions so that occupants have all emergency procedure information in one place.

Contents of an Occupant Emergency Guide

An emergency procedures guide for occupants should include lists of safety precautions that occupants can follow to avoid certain emergencies, which include:

- Proper use of in-unit appliances
- Best practices for storage of potentially dangerous items
- Proper use and maintenance of smoke and fire detectors
- Safe smoking practices
- Proper use of office equipment

Many times, a building's occupants will be the first to notice an emergency situation. Therefore, residents or commercial tenants should be given instructions on how to report emergencies such as fires, assaults, bomb threats, chemical spills, and explosions. Generally, occupants should contact the onsite manager, the fire department, and/or the police department. Other potential contents of an occupant emergency handbook may include:

- An explanation of building-wide communications, if appropriate, and how they will be used in emergencies
- Locations of all building entrances and exits
- Diagrams of evacuation routes
- Explanations of evacuation and safety procedures
- Items to have immediately available to facilitate evacuation (e.g., flashlight and batteries)
- Location of emergency supplies including bottled water, first aid kits, etc.
- Tips for prevention of theft and assault
- 24-hour phone numbers of management staff
- Information on the building's safety features
- Telephone numbers of police and fire departments and government, social, and charitable agencies
- Lists of safety precautions or actions that could be taken during specific emergencies, including storms, earthquakes, fires, bomb threats, and medical emergencies on the premises

Commercial tenants should be encouraged to develop additional emergency procedures for their staff and their businesses as may be necessary or appropriate. Likewise, guide residents into developing emergency plans for themselves and their families. An occupant emergency guide might include information to help them make certain preparations, along with potential sources for disaster assistance, such as the American Red Cross and the Salvation Army—both of which participate in the Coordinated Assistance Network (CAN), as well as state and local agencies that provide emergency assistance.[1]

Distribution of the Resident/Tenant Guide

For residential properties, each resident should be given a copy of the property's resident emergency procedures guide at the time of move-in and a new copy or replacement inserts whenever revisions are made. Copies should always be available to residents upon request.

---

1. The official website for contacting U.S. government agencies is *www.FirstGov.gov.*

SOURCES OF INFORMATION FOR CREATING AN EMERGENCY MANUAL

Government Publications:

Floods: The Awesome Power (NOAA)

Hurricanes: Unleashing Nature's Fury (NOAA)

Thunderstorms, Tornadoes, Lightning: Nature's Most Violent Storms (NOAA)

Winter Storms: The Deceptive Killers (NOAA)

Surviving the Storm: A Guide to Hurricane Preparedness (FEMA)

Are You Ready: A Guide to Citizen Preparedness (FEMA)

Emergency Management Guide for Business and Industry (FEMA)

How to Plan for Workplace Emergencies and Evacuations (OSHA)

Most of these publications can be downloaded from the respective government agency websites:

www.fema.gov
www.ready.gov
www.weather.gov
www.redcross.org

For commercial properties, tenants should be given enough copies to share with their employees. Emphasize the need to incorporate emergency procedures training into the orientation program to commercial tenants for their new employees. Ask commercial tenants to assign at least one employee to an emergency response leadership role to facilitate evacuation. Tenants with large staffs should have one or more employees assigned to monitor stairwells and elevators to ensure that everyone leaves their premises, and provide assistance to co-workers with special needs.

DOCUMENTATION

As a safeguard for the property's reputation, to serve as insurance records, and as protection against legal liability or financial loss, a thorough and accurate system for recording the events surrounding an emergency should be in place and regarded as a central part of the emergency plan. The insurance company will want to know details about the emergency, so you will need a complete report of what happened and what steps were taken in response. It is also important to maintain accurate records of costs incurred as a result of an emergency.

Emergency Report

Emergency reporting and documentation should begin with a form that allows anyone on the management staff to quickly report an emergency. During and after an emergency, management personnel will be busy and will not have time to prepare exhaustive reports. For this reason, the emergency report form should be designed so that accurate and necessary information can be provided simply by filling in blanks. This is preferable to requesting detailed descriptions of events. The emergency report should include:

- Name and address of the person reporting the incident
- Date and time the report is made
- Name and address of any witness
- A brief description of what happened, when, and where
- Name and address of person(s) involved
- What authorities were called and when
- When the authorities arrived
- Actions taken by the authorities

The description of what happened should include any observed injuries or property damage, as well as the nature of the emergency or other incident. An example of an emergency incident report form is shown in Example 6.1.

Insurance Report

The insurance adjuster can be your guide as to what level of detail the insurance company requires. If no requirements are offered by the insurance adjuster, asking early can save time later. Generally, the more comprehensive the information the real estate manager can gather before meeting with the insurance adjuster, the better the chances are of receiving a rapid and equitable settlement. This information should include:

- A brief written description of the events that transpired prior to the loss
- Appropriate police or fire department reports
- Documentation of the extent of the loss, including inspection reports, photos, and videos
- A record of all emergency repairs and expenses
- A prepared inventory of property contents

EXAMPLE 6.1
EMERGENCY INCIDENT REPORT

Reported by:
Name _____
Address _____
Date _____
Time _____

Witnessed by:
Name _____
Address _____

What happened: _____
_____
_____
_____

Injuries (describe): _____
_____

Property damage (describe): _____
_____

When did it happen: _____
_____

Where did it happen: _____
_____
_____

Person(s) involved:
Name _____
Address _____

Authorities: _____
_____

Authorities called:
Time called _____
Time arrived _____

Actions taken by authorities:
_____
_____
_____
_____

The insurance inventory should include a description of each item, the brand name, model number, serial number if applicable, age of the item, and number of similar items if more than one. Specifications for built-in components of the building should be available so that materials and equipment of a similar kind and quality will be used for restoration or replacement.

This information will be used in conjunction with a physical inspection by the insurance adjuster, restoration contractor, and real estate manager to determine the scope and cost of the damage and loss. It can also serve as proof of loss for possible deductions from income taxes. To supplement the insurance report, photographs or video recordings can be extremely valuable in documenting the damage. Your insurance agent may be able to provide more specific reporting guidelines for inclusion in the emergency procedures manual.

Have examples of claim forms from the various companies on hand that provide insurance coverage on the property. This can facilitate compilation of information, as well as expedite submission of individual claims. The real estate manager should be familiar with the insurance coverage and its requirements.

Expense Report

It is important to maintain a record of all expenses resulting from emergency response and recovery. Separate accounting codes should be established for allocating the costs of repairs and replacement. Create specifications that define the scope of work for outside contractors so they can accurately estimate costs of labor and materials as well as replacement equipment. The following expenses are easy to overlook when accounting for emergency costs:

- Employees' time (including overtime worked)
- The real estate manager's time
- Contractors' invoices
- Materials and supplies purchased specifically for this purpose
- Materials and supplies taken from other properties in response to the emergency
- Materials and supplies already onsite that were used for the emergency

When calculating employee costs attributable to the loss, be sure to add the payroll burden (taxes, overhead, etc.) and costs related to having the employee on the payroll.

There may also be incident-related costs incurred separately from construction and restoration contracting to be accounted. For example, board-up service, removal and storage of salvageable items, business relocation fees, and consulting fees (e.g., for environmental reports).

It may be appropriate to include specific procedures for providing written reports to the property owner in the emergency plan. Also be aware that some documentation may be requested in the event of litigation regarding the emergency, so it may be desirable to check with the owner or an attorney before adopting any specific forms or formats for documenting emergencies.

SECTION 2:

Emergency Planning by Property Type

CHAPTER 7:

Residential Properties

An emergency plan is specific to one property. The emergency guide-book, therefore, should reflect the needs of the specific property for which it has been designed. It should communicate specific policies, rules, and regulations, including safety tips and emergency procedures that residents will need to know in order to successfully evacuate. Residents should know when to evacuate, where to assemble after an evacuation, and who to contact during an emergency. If possible, periodic evacuation drills and emergency equipment testing should be performed. Since the resident profile influences how emergency evacuations will be conducted, a chain of command should be established to facilitate onsite emergency responses. Most importantly, specific communication with residents is needed to ensure awareness on how to respond to emergencies.

EVACUATION PROCEDURES FOR SMALLER RESIDENTIAL PROPERTIES

Evacuation procedures that are directed for mid- or high-rise residential buildings with multiple floors in an urban environment will require the evacuation plan outlined in *Chapter 3*. When dealing with multiple low-rise apartment buildings, a special evacuation process would be required—for example, it might be a 260-apartment development in a rural area that is spread among 30 buildings and covers 16 acres of land.

In this instance, to evacuate in case of a fire, the evacuation process would obviously start at the closest building to the fire and then spread out. The real estate managers or site managers would need to coordinate which building they will oversee and the specific directions that would need to be made for each location.

If evacuation is ordered because of a property-wide emergency, such as a gas leak, and the specific locations and buildings are unknown, there should be a planned route to check each property. For example, members of the emergency management team could help evacuate the entire property in a clockwise direction from the main office. Regardless of the direction, everyone on the team should have exact guidelines and orders so that they are prepared in cases of emergencies. The evacuation process for different types of residential properties will always need to be customizable so that it fit the needs of its residents.

CREATING THE RESIDENT PROFILE

Emergency procedures for a residential property must take into account the residents who live there. By creating a resident profile during the emergency-planning process, you will get answers to specific, essential questions about the residents that help impact the effectiveness of your emergency procedures. Creating this profile before starting the planning process is essential, but privacy laws, disclosure, and permissions will apply when questioning residents about health concerns or other medical conditions. When deciding what questions to ask while creating the document, consult with an attorney. Residents should be asked to sign an agreement acknowledging that their information will be kept on file and only disclosed to emergency personnel. The following addresses some of the questions to possibly consider:

- Are any residents disabled or have mobility challenges?
- What is the type/extent of the disability or restriction?
- Do any residents have assistance animals?
- How many children and senior residents live on the property?
- Do any residents have skills that may be helpful in an emergency situation, such as trained firefighters, police officers, or active in the military or National Guard?

Although creating a resident profile from information in residents' leases and lease applications is possible, the information relevant to a resident profile is only useful if it's current. To collect this information, consider using a form or letter, such as the resident emergency information request that is depicted in Example 7.1.

A special section asking whether anyone has had training in first aid, cardiopulmonary resuscitation (CPR), or use of an automatic external defibrillator (AED) could also be added, along with a request to indicate whether the person would be willing to act in an emergency, and if they can fluently speak other languages. An alternate approach would be to compile information and ask the residents to confirm or correct it—bearing in mind that the information must be current. New residents might be asked to provide emergency information at the time of move-in, and established

EXAMPLE 7.1

SAMPLE RESIDENT EMERGENCY INFORMATION REQUEST

Dear **[Resident]**:

[Management Company or name of real estate manager] is preparing to **[develop/update]** emergency procedures for the building at **[street address]**. In order to be certain that every occupant of the building is accounted for in the event of an emergency, we need to know the first and last names of every person living in your unit, along with age and gender, and if they need any special assistance. This information will be used by management only in developing specific emergency procedures. It will be made available to the fire department and other emergency services personnel in the event the building must be evacuated.

Please complete the form below and return it to the management office by **[due date.]**

Apartment Number _____

Name(s)	Phone No.	Gender	Age	Special Assistance*
_____	_____	M / F	____	Yes / No
_____	_____	M / F	____	Yes / No
_____	_____	M / F	____	Yes / No
_____	_____	M / F	____	Yes / No
_____	_____	M / F	____	Yes / No
_____	_____	M / F	____	Yes / No

*If an assistive animal is used, please include the type of animal.

Do you have any skills that might be helpful in an emergency? If yes, please describe.

May we call upon you to help us in an emergency?

Thank you for your assistance.

[signature]

[Management Company or name of real estate manager]

residents should be asked at least once a year to update their information—such as at the time a lease ends or goes into automatic renewal.

The information requirement applies to any type of multiple-occupancy residential property. If the property is professionally managed, the real estate manager would likely have the primary responsibility for compiling the resident information. Members of the board of directors of a self-managed condominium or homeowners association should be familiar with the profile of their residents so they can take appropriate action in the event of an emergency. Regardless of the type of residential community, emergency procedures should always include specific provisions for evacuating and caring for children, special-needs residents, and senior residents.

Including Children in the Resident Profiles

Because children require special attention and consideration during an emergency, be sure to include them on resident profiles. Depending on the emergency, children may experience a degree of panic or trauma. Parents should help by teaching their children how to respond to emergencies, including whom to call (i.e., 911 or poison control) and how to get to safety. Management should also encourage parents to practice the response with their children.

One of the best ways to prevent emergencies at a residential property is to help children avoid hazardous areas—containing machinery, cleaning equipment and supplies, swimming pool maintenance equipment, and chemicals. These areas should be kept secure at all times by keeping doors and specific areas locked. Playground equipment should be regularly inspected and maintained. For communities with drive-through areas, it may be appropriate to install speed limit signs or speed bumps. Consider requiring children under a certain age to be supervised by an adult while using playground equipment or other recreation areas—for example, swimming pools or exercise facilities.

If a daycare or education center is operated anywhere on the premises, management should require the operator to develop an emergency plan for the center, including specific evacuation procedures. The daycare or education center could possibly be staffed by a few adults—each responsible for several children. In an emergency, it may be necessary to provide additional supervision as well as evacuation assistance. If that is the case, the property emergency procedures manual should include this information and assign personnel to provide such assistance.

Profiles for Special-Needs Residents

A temporary illness or other condition of impairment, such as broken bones, might prohibit an individual's ability to escape from or avoid an emergency situation. Although difficult to track, onsite managers should try to be aware of these conditions and record them—with permission—in the resident profiles. Other nonpermanent disabilities could also impair a resident's ability to react to an emergency. Size and agility, but also conditions like arthritis can affect one's ability to escape and avoid danger, often precluding rapid movement. Therefore, real estate managers should attempt to foresee any conditions that will hamper a smooth evacuation.

Long-term disabilities often require advanced emergency planning and consideration. Residents with visual, hearing, and mobility impairments may benefit from having a "buddy"—someone on their floor to provide personal assistance. Each emergency management team member should have a list of disabled residents whom they may need to assist. Mental disabilities pose further points of consideration as they might impair emergency response. The Fair Housing Amendments Act of 1988 extended fair housing protection to mentally ill individuals, rehabilitated alcoholics, and drug abusers, as these individuals might have difficulty understanding directions or the reason for evacuation.

Do not forget that residents with illnesses or special needs may need regular, specific medical treatment. Drugs kept in refrigerators, oxygen machines, and other medical needs may be a concern addressed to emergency personnel following an emergency.

Profiles for Senior Residents

As more and more senior residents choose to remain in their rental units instead of relocating, additional challenges are raised for real estate managers of conventional residential properties. Senior residents may have limited mobility, impaired vision or hearing, or difficulty understanding due to their age. Some of these residents may rely on medical equipment or assisted devices such as walkers, portable oxygen tanks, or motorized wheelchairs. Emergency procedures should include provisions for evacuating, not only the resident, but also medical or assisted equipment. Encourage residents to arrange for auxiliary or alternative power sources for electrical devices in the event of an emergency. Information on which units are occupied by senior residents and their individual needs is invaluable in emergency evacuations, and should be readily available to fire and police personnel.

During practice evacuations, senior residents should function as independently as possible. If special assistance is needed, it should be indicated as part of the individual's senior resident profile. If there is more than one stairwell, it may be desirable to direct senior residents to use a separate stairwell from the other residents to allow for their slower evacuation.

When assisting seniors, it's important to have a personal communication with them, maintaining a clear and respectful tone. As always, residents' pride and dignity should be considered at all times. When personal attention is required for assisting senior residents, it should not appear as an inconvenience—such behavior may discourage them from asking for help when it's needed. Real estate managers of senior housing should seek planning assistance from appropriate sources to ensure safe evacuation of their residents. Additional information may be found in a publication from the American Red Cross titled, *Disaster Preparedness for Seniors by Seniors.*

ESTABLISHING AN EMERGENCY CHAIN OF COMMAND

Properties With Site Managers

While planning for emergencies in residential properties, it may be advantageous to alter the normal chain of command and appoint the site manager, rather than the real estate manager, as the "team leader." The site manager is more familiar with the residents, vendors, contractors, and other people involved in the daily operation of the property. The real estate manager's role should be one of oversight, allowing the site manager to direct the emergency response. If the site manager is to have primary responsibility for overseeing emergency procedures, they should be involved in developing those procedures and trained to implement them.

Properties Without Site Managers

At smaller residential properties where there are no site managers, the residents often report emergencies, and emergency phone number lists become a higher priority. In this scenario, residents become integral members of the emergency management team. In such situations, real estate managers must work closely with the residents by letting them know that they are responsible for a good part of the emergency response, and by clearly explaining the potential dangers of neglect. Meet with residents to explain the property's emergency procedures and consider appointing residents as floor or building monitors—with alternates. These monitors would be responsible for directing residents to safety until management or fire or police personnel can arrive on the scene.

In established condominium and homeowners' associations, members of the board of directors are often long-term homeowners. Work with them in communicating emergency procedures information to owner-residents and appointing monitors. In a new condominium development, one of the key questions to ask of those running for office is, "What experience have you had in coping with emergencies?"

For condominium developments without onsite staff, the need for owners to be responsible for certain emergency duties must be clearly understood.

COMMUNICATING WITH RESIDENTS

Residents need to be made aware of emergency procedures planned for the property, in particular, evacuation procedures that should be regularly reinforced. The emergency procedures for a property should be fully explained to every new resident. They may also be included in a resident guidebook along with property rules and regulations. Otherwise, a handout listing emergency procedures for residents can be prepared.

Resident newsletters are ideal to communicate information about safety and security. A resident bulletin board can serve the same purpose, as can an occasional flyer or e-mail distributed to each resident. Communication can also take the form of holiday safety reminders about the danger of fire from improperly used candles, decorations, fireworks, or barbecues, as well as occasional reminders about personal safety in parking lots and garages. Reminders to use door locks properly and not to leave entrance doors unlocked are also appropriate.

Development resources for safety information include your local police department, which can provide information and tips on security and crime prevention. Local fire departments usually have outreach programs covering smoke and fire alarms, fire prevention strategies, and life-safety tips. Consult the National Fire Protection Association (NFPA) for a variety of printed brochures promoting fire safety and awareness. Don't forget about the online resources available from the Red Cross, who maintains emergency preparedness guidelines for individuals and families.

Residents might be encouraged to participate in a community-watch program sponsored by local police. Residents should certainly be encouraged to look out for their personal safety and the security of their dwellings and personal property. Depending on property size, management might consider scheduling "safety days" in which local authorities come to the property to answer residents' questions. Activities could even include safety games or custom presentations for children.

DEALING WITH DEATH IN A UNIT

In some situations, you may experience or deal with a death of a resident or tenant in a unit. The nature and circumstances of the death will determine what action is warranted. The death may be due to natural causes following a serious illness or result from unnatural causes, such as an injury, accident, suicide, or foul play.

Upon the discovery of a death, immediately contact the proper authorities. The family of the deceased usually assumes this responsibility. If there are no other family members in the unit, it may be necessary to arrange to have the body properly removed. In all instances, it is essential to contact the police, coroner, next of kin, and then seek direction from the appropriate authorities on how to proceed.

Because many residents live alone and may have no family nearby, it may often be a real estate manager or staff member that discovers or is notified of a death in a unit. When this occurs, it is essential that the body is not moved or touched until after the police and other authorities have examined it. If the identity of the deceased person is known, the next of kin should be notified by the authorities. Therefore, it's necessary to provide contact information to the authorities so they may make the notifications. Depending on the circumstances surrounding the death, the real estate manager may want to contact the property's attorney and insurance agent.

Apart from arranging for removal of the body, be prepared to restore the unit in the event that the death has had some adverse physical effect on the property. Odors and damage from exposure to bodily fluids associated with the presence of a dead body will have to be mitigated. Death following an illness may mean that infectious agents, such as bloodborne pathogens or other contaminants are present. These problems may not arise in all incidents, but are likely if the death was violent or self-injurious, or if the body was not discovered for an extended period. It may be appropriate to hire professionals with special services to restore the unit's interior—especially if bodily fluids are present and/or to ensure that stains and contaminants are properly removed.

In any death, the real estate manager will be asked many questions by other residents and should be prepared to answer them tactfully, with respect for the deceased and other family members—the same rule applies to inquiries by the media.

While not a definitive sign that a resident has died, the following lists some visible factors that could suggest a death or serious health problem:

- Accumulated mail, newspapers, etc.
- Unanswered phone calls
- Lights, televisions, or radios left on day and night
- Neglected pets
- Cars not moved
- Failure to attend events as expected
- Inquiries from family, friends, neighbors, employers, creditors, etc.

CHAPTER 8:
Office Buildings

When planning emergency procedures for office buildings, it's important to realize that though they may share similar evacuation or readiness procedures with residential properties, they have a distinct set of new challenges for consideration. Office buildings may accommodate different types of businesses, with the onsite equipment ranging from computer systems, building-wide HVAC, and even cooking systems.

What is more, the amount of activity in a commercial or office building can be heavy. A steady flow of customers or clients could be coming or going throughout the business day and into the evening. Office buildings are generally closed overnight, but will usually be active 12 or more hours a day. Given the large window of time in which an emergency could arise, plan your emergency procedures carefully.

CREATING THE TENANT PROFILE

Equip yourself and your management staff with profiles of building occupants in order to ensure safety and proper emergency planning, response, and evacuation. An occupant profile may include:

- Type of business conducted in order to assess potential threats
- Number of tenants in the building, including the number of people each tenant employs
- Work, home, mobile numbers, and e-mail addresses of key tenant personnel or business owners
- Type(s) of equipment or materials (with a specific emphasis on hazardous materials) tenants use or store in the building
- Hours that tenants operate their business—normal business hours, peak hours of traffic, and after hours
- Amount of cash that tenants keep on hand
- Detailed list of access codes for all tenants

Be sure to know when outside contractors for services such as cleaning, security, or construction will be working in the building. Since these people are not considered occupants of the building, they may be required to sign in and sign out as a security precaution and wear identification name tags.

Nontraditional Tenants: Medical and Education Tenants

Carefully tailor the level of detail in a tenant profile such that it closely examines the needs and restrictions of each tenant's staff and premises. For example, consider the level of detail that might be needed when one of your tenants is a daycare center on your property. In particular, the daycare center's procedures for evacuation and assembly should be coordinated with the building's procedures so that parents in the building can be quickly reunited with their children. In some cases, parents might have to report to the company's assembly so they can be accounted for, and then move to a designated area to find their children. Daycare centers, like other forms of residential communities, require special planning. Refer to *Chapter 7* for information on planning emergency procedures for children in residential properties.

Be aware of other non-traditional commercial tenants, such as physicians or other medical professionals, who often lease space in office buildings that may not be specifically designed to house medical offices. A healthcare-related tenant requires a specific level of planning with regard to emergency procedures, as exposure to bloodborne pathogens, hazardous-medical waste, or disease may become a concern in an emergency. Be sure to keep the tenants' current floor plan on file, regardless of their industry, to ensure that emergency access remains possible to specialized equipment (e.g., servers, computers, wiring) and potentially sensitive or dangerous materials (e.g., hazardous materials or medical waste). Additional steps for addressing the added considerations of medical office buildings and healthcare professionals are outlined in *Chapter 9*.

Consider the needs of disabled individuals that may be part of your tenant's personnel. The tenant profile should include who these workers are and what (if any) special assistance they will need in case of an emergency. In compliance with the Health Insurance Portability and Accountability Act (HIPPA), be sure to get written permission to collect this information from tenant personnel.

WORKING WITH OFFICE TENANTS DURING EVACUATION DRILLS

The success of commercial building emergency procedures depends on the cooperation of the property's occupants. The attitude of the occupants regarding emergency response and preparedness, and their willingness to cooperate during a disaster, can make the difference between a successful program and a catastrophe.

Unfortunately, some people view emergency procedures and evacuation drills as a time-consuming inconvenience. As a real estate manager, convince them otherwise. Before a new tenant moves into the building, meet with the tenant's office manager or other designated representative to review and emphasize the building's emergency procedures. All tenants should be informed of their responsibilities in this regard, including the responsibility to inform their employees about the building's emergency procedures. Put these procedures in writing and include a provision in the lease agreement noting that the tenant's representative was made aware of the tenant's obligations regarding building emergency procedures.

After the tenant moves in, schedule a meeting with all of the tenant's managers and/or employees to review the building's emergency procedures. If possible, a representative from the local fire department may be invited to discuss the life- and property-saving benefits of emergency plans. Stress to the tenant, again, the importance of keeping floor plans current as a way to protect both the property and themselves in case of a disaster.

Give tenants their choice of floor monitors to assist their employees during the evacuation of the building for both drills and emergency situations. Tenants should choose employees who are both enthusiastic and respected by their coworkers, since they will likely listen to someone they trust. Once floor monitors have been designated, meet with them and explain their duties, distribute the printed emergency procedures, and train them in their roles regarding evacuation drills.

ESTABLISHING AN EMERGENCY CHAIN OF COMMAND

The emergency plan will benefit the property only if a clear chain of command is established and understood between the site manager and commercial tenants. Ask that a representative from each office is designated as part of the emergency management team to ensure that everyone plays an active role in performing their assigned duties. In addition to floor monitors, tenants' employees may serve as floor leaders, searchers, stairwell monitors, elevator monitors, or handicap aides. Some tenants may have several employees in each of these roles—those with only a few employees may only designate a floor monitor.

It should be made clear that, although some offices may occupy one or more floors, they must still adhere to the directions set by property management or the designated team leader as head of the emergency management team. Keep commercial tenants' representatives up to date regarding changes in the building structure, emergency equipment, planning, and policies. Commercial tenant representatives, in turn, should periodically keep you abreast of changes to their business activities, personnel, and steps they are taking to prevent emergencies. In doing so, a list with tenants' emergency team members' names, business phone extensions, and mobile numbers should be maintained.

SECURITY IN THE WORKPLACE

A scenario that may be overlooked in developing emergency procedures is an instance of violence in the workplace. While it may not be the most destructive kind of emergency in terms of property, it's a serious concern to consider for tenant and building security. According to the U.S. Department of Justice's Bureau of Justice Statistics (BJS), simple assault is one of the most common workplace incidents, followed by aggravated assault, robbery, rape or sexual assault, and homicide. The BJS compiles statistics on the numbers and types of incidents, which finds that simple assault is actually one of the most common workplace incidents followed by aggravated assault, then robbery, rape or sexual assault, and homicide. Because violence in the workplace is a possibility in any type of commercial property, encourage security staff to monitor stairwells, parking lots, and other areas that may function as hiding places for intruders.

Coach maintenance personnel and other management staff on how to monitor interior areas of the building as they go about their day-to-day duties. A high percentage of the instances in which violence occurs in the workplace result from the actions of angry former employees who were fired or feel they had been mistreated by their former coworkers or employer. While not an absolute safeguard, basic security precautions can go a long way in preventing a violent incident. Keep security personnel abreast of employee turnover. Require that all previous employees return their office keys, access devices, or employee identification to their former employer before they exit the building. Establish a protocol for collecting

DEFINITIONS OF CRIMES COMMITTED IN THE WORKPLACE*

Simple assault: An attack without a weapon that results in either no injury, minor injury—bruises, cuts, or scratches—or an undetermined injury requiring less than two days hospitalization, and also includes attempted assaults without a weapon.

Aggravated assault: A completed or attempted attack with a weapon, regardless of whether or not an injury occurred, and an attack without a weapon in which the victim is seriously injured.

Robbery: A completed or attempted theft of property or cash directly from a person by force or threat of force, with or without a weapon and with or without an injury.

Sexual assault: A wide range of victimizations distinct from rape and attempted rape and including unwanted sexual contact between the victim and the offender. It may not involve force, but it includes such things as grabbing or fondling and verbal threats.

Homicide: The willful unlawful killing of one human being by another.

*Adapted from definitions published by the U.S. Department of Justice, Bureau of Justice Statistics.

these items as part of the documentation of an employee's departure. Tenants should always follow up with management if an employee leaves, under any circumstance, without returning building access cards, keys, or building ID.

A growing trend among real estate managers of office buildings is reaching out to tenants' employees as part of their tenant-retention strategies. Real estate managers sometimes sponsor health fairs or other types of informational educational or enrichment presentations. They may use periodic newsletters to announce activities in the building and the local area, which may also function as a way to disseminate safety tips that include safeguarding personal belongings in employees' work spaces, protecting themselves in parking lots and while driving, and family at-home safety during the holidays, along with reminders regarding building evacuation procedures. For more information on crime and violence in the workplace, refer to *Section 5*.

EVACUATING THE OFFICE BUILDING

Given the variation in size, nature, and use of an office building, there is a strong necessity for thoughtful planning that must go into these evacuation procedures. No matter the size or scope of an office building, an evacuation plan is a necessity to ensure the safety of others. Tenants' employees must know where all of the building's exits are and the closest one to their workplaces. Evacuation route maps should be prominently posted on each floor. Employees must also know where they should congregate once they leave the building—which is especially important during violent storms and earthquakes—and how they will be informed when it is safe to return to the building (see *Chapter 3*).

Conduct regular announced and unannounced evacuation drills to keep tenants of office buildings prepared for emergencies. In cities, fire drills are often mandatory, and some cities require a set number of drills each year. As office building tenants often experience a high turnover of employees, these periodic drills serve the dual purpose of introducing new employees to evacuation procedures and keeping long-term employees familiar with the routes. Post-9/11, many cities across the U.S. have instituted an "all hazards plan" protocol that maintains certain requirements for larger office buildings.

CHAPTER 9:

Medical Office Buildings

Medical office buildings have unique features designed to handle the diverse needs of medical professionals and their patients. These environments deal heavily with sensitive material, particularly in regard to the drugs, medical equipment, and patient information on the premises. Occupants of medical office buildings must adhere not only to basic building policies set by the real estate manager, but also to strict sanitary and medical compliance guidelines prescribed by the medical profession, local and state health and safety codes, and the guidelines of the Occupational Safety and Health Administration (OSHA).

Like residential and office spaces, it is important to create a tenant profile for medical offices. Security and evacuation planning could also share similarities with the commercial and residential sectors. In fact, the largest difference between a medical office and a commercial tenant is likely the amount of hazardous medical waste that could be present. Medical waste is a particularly important consideration, given the potential for outbreak of disease from factors such as bloodborne pathogens.

CREATING THE TENANT PROFILE

While possible, it is probably unlikely that a medical office building will be occupied by a single type of healthcare professional. Owing to the sheer volume of medical and dental specializations that abound in the healthcare industry, the typical medical office building could include anything from podiatry and optometry offices to chiropractors, psychologists, and physical therapists.

Building a tenant profile for medical office tenants helps you, as the real estate manager, understand the specific needs, risks, and vulnerability of each tenant in case of an emergency.

Medical office spaces take multiple-use to a new level. Spaces may be leased to consult and examine patients, collect specimens of bodily fluids or tissues (e.g., blood, urine, plasma), perform laboratory tests, or administer treatments. Sometimes, all of these functions could be operating within the same leased space. Furthermore, given the nature of the work being done, healthcare professionals often require the use of specialized medical equipment, which will likely be installed or housed in leased spaces. Depending on the scale and scope of the practice of medical office tenants, these may include imaging centers for X-ray services and MRI scanning, or are as complex as outpatient surgery centers, medical laboratories, or pharmacies.

Given the necessary degrees of specialization, medical office tenants will often have employees who are trained to provide and assist in specific treatments—in addition to equally specialized administrative staff. It's important to also consider the people working in the space. When creating the tenant profiles for a medical office space, you should consider:

- The type of medical services being provided, including the hazardous waste and specialized equipment that may be involved. How much medical waste is stored? How is it disposed of?
- What specimens or samples are collected from patients? How are those stored for pick-up and analysis?
- The categories of medicines and materials that may be stored in practitioners' offices.
- How is the space used? Are patients with an illness sitting alongside healthy patients? Are areas that could house medical waste or specialized equipment located at a safe distance from high-traffic, public areas?
- Who are the tenants' patient base? Adults? Children? Senior citizens? Those with disabilities? Pets?
- How many patients do the tenants serve on a yearly, monthly, and weekly basis?
- When are healthcare providers and patients going to be in the building? When are patients seen? Are there certain days of the week the office is closed?
- What is the typical staff size for the tenants?

ESTIMATING THE DAILY USE OF SPACE

The size of a patient population is of particular importance to planning emergency procedures in a medical office setting. Compared to office and other commercial properties, medical office tenants tend to lease smaller spaces—usually no larger than 3,000 square feet compared to 10,000 square feet in an average commercial building. Additionally, medical offices, by their very nature, will see more visitor traffic than their commercial counterparts, who might see other visitors (vendors, potential clients, etc.) per day. The average medical professional might see 15 to 20 patients per day, while others might see even more—usually four patients per hour.

In comparison, commercial buildings may have ten tenants—each leasing and doing business in 10,000 square feet of space—while medical office buildings may have as many as 30 or 40 tenants occupying spaces, which is a quarter of the size used for typical commercial tenants. Ultimately, this means that more people will use smaller spaces. At 15 to 20 patients a day per tenant, a medical office building could quickly see between 450 to 800 visitors each day. In an emergency situation, this factor could make evacuation more precarious, along with the existing health of those being evacuated.

Population aside, consider the other factors and risks associated with each tenant in regard to the types of equipment they use. X-rays, laser equipment, and certain categories of drugs can pose a health and safety issue if misused. Along with equipment, security is also another issue. Burglary might result in more than lost property, but potential loss of confidential medical information. Damage to sensitive medical equipment may also result in a leak of hazardous materials.

MEDICAL WASTE DISPOSAL

Of hazardous materials, medical waste is an especially important consideration for preparing medical office buildings for emergencies. If not properly handled, stored, and disposed of, hazardous medical waste can threaten the safety and health of the entire building. Medical waste, such as used syringes and needles, can pose a critical risk of infection that may cause serious illness to an unsuspecting staff member, janitor, or patient. OSHA requires medical offices to segregate their medical waste into three general types—(1) soft medical waste (gauze, bandages, etc.), (2) "sharps" (needles and syringes), and (3) other medical waste. Be sure that medical office tenants have properly marked containers for the relevant types of medical waste.

As the real estate manager, it is advisable to educate yourself on the proper handling and disposal of medical waste. In general, needles and syringes are commonly disposed by inserting them in a sealed receptacle that includes, in the opening, a device for destroying these items. The container is replaced when it has been filled. Soft and other medical wastes are commonly disposed in heavy-duty red plastic bags. Ensure that occupants of the building you manage keep hazardous medical wastes separate from regular trash and use the appropriate, designated containers for disposing of them.

It is likely that tenants will directly contract state-approved and licensed medical-waste disposal services, which is usually mandated in their lease. These licensed contractors commonly provide appropriate containers for disposal of medical waste. If these are not supplied by the waste disposal service, medical professionals can usually obtain appropriate containers from their existing medical supply vendors.

As most medical-waste disposal companies provide only monthly pickups, encourage tenants to store their medical waste in proper containers in a locked closet or other secure area. Once retrieved by the contractor, the materials may be scanned for potential radioactive material before being incinerated. Janitors should also be advised to never touch or retrieve medical waste containers.

Be sure to document each and every case in which medical waste has either been disposed of improperly or spilled. Record each incident in a letter to the occupant, keeping a copy in the tenant's correspondence file. Proper documentation may protect you and the property from potential lawsuits. Where applicable, contact the proper authorities to inform them of a hazardous-materials spill.

SECURITY FOR MEDICAL OFFICE BUILDINGS

The demands, materials, and nature of work that medical office tenants entail—in particular, drugs kept onsite for treatment—can be a temptation for burglars, trespassers, or intruders. It's important to stress that all medical facilities store their prescription drugs in safe and secure areas. Another security consideration to address in the lease is the physician's after-hours access to the building for medical emergencies.

EVACUATION FOR MEDICAL OFFICE BUILDINGS

In addition to the sheer amount of patients that may be in a medical office building at the time of a disaster, an equally important concern for you and your medical office tenants is how to evacuate during a critical medical procedure or treatment.

Meet with each tenant to review the specific services provided and to prepare an appropriate response plan that adapts to the occupants and their patients' needs. Keep in mind that evacuations of medical office buildings may take longer than other occupancies, due to the physical restrictions or afflictions of some patients. You may wish to consult with a local hospital and use their evacuation plans as a model. Work with your tenants to make special arrangements for patients who have not fully recovered from out-patient surgery, or who otherwise need special attention to be transported to the hospital in the event of an emergency.

To better understand the potential risks that an emergency situation may pose to tenants performing outpatient surgery or providing other critical medical treatments, ask tenants the following questions:

- Are you likely to have patients under anesthesia? If necessary, how could you evacuate them?
- Are you likely to have patients connected to equipment that would need to be transported along with the patient in an evacuation? If so, what type of equipment would be involved? Is it portable? Have you made provision for its removal in an emergency?
- What is the range of ages of your patients and their general medical profile?
- Do you have special Medicare or other formalized guidelines that impact your emergency requirements?
- Do you have certain days defined as surgery days?
- How many members of the building staff are required to assist patients who are unable to evacuate on their own?
- Do you need wheelchairs/gurneys for evacuating patients? If so, how many might you need, and how many do you have access to?
- Do you have staff members who are disabled? If so, what are their specific needs?

Tenants should also be asked to list the names of at least two key people from their office who will be the emergency contacts for the building evacuation plan.

Consider having tenants identify hazardous materials they have in their premises and indicate how they are stored, and whether they are labeled for easy identification. Of particular concern would be flammable and combustible materials.

A SPECIAL ISSUE: BLOODBORNE PATHOGENS

Bloodborne pathogens are pathogenic microorganisms that are present in human blood and can cause disease in humans. These pathogens include the hepatitis B virus (HBV), hepatitis C virus (HCV), and human immunodeficiency virus (HIV).

Risk of Exposure

Occupational exposure to bloodborne pathogens is a major employee safety issue. The industry with the greatest exposure to and risk from bloodborne pathogens is without a doubt the healthcare industry. However, there is also potential risk of exposure for those who come into contact with medical wastes as part of their work, including janitorial and cleaning personnel in medical office buildings. Because of this potential exposure, professionals who manage medical office buildings need to be aware of ways to protect their employees.

To protect workers who may be potentially exposed to bloodborne pathogens, OSHA published a specific standard (29 CFR 1910.1030) that became effective March 6, 1992. The OSHA standard covers *all* employees who could be "reasonably anticipated" to come into contact with blood and other potentially infectious materials, as the result of performing the duties for their job. However, "Good Samaritan" acts, such as assisting a co-worker with a nosebleed, would not be considered "occupational exposure."

The OSHA definition of occupational exposure to bloodborne pathogens is "reasonably anticipated skin, eye, mucous membrane, or parenteral contact with blood, or other potentially infectious materials that may result from the performance of an employee's duties." Medically, the term "parenteral" means by injection into muscles or veins or under the skin. Potentially infectious materials include body fluids and/or tissues other than blood.

Exposure to bloodborne pathogens may occur in many ways, but needle-related injuries are the most common. Bloodborne pathogens can also be transmitted through contact with open wounds (e.g., cuts, abrasions) or cultures of body fluids and tissues or organs containing such pathogens. Specific requirements of the OSHA Bloodborne Pathogen Standard are outlined in *Chapter 13.*

The Real Estate Manager's Responsibilities

Currently, only real estate management personnel, who are assigned first aid duties in case of an accident or emergency, would be covered by the OSHA standard. However, management employees responsible for any type of cleanup duties (e.g., maintenance and janitorial personnel) may be at risk of exposure, particularly in a medical office building. Requirements of the OSHA regulation that may apply include the following:

- Development of an exposure-control plan
- Taking precautions to protect workers from exposure
- Providing medical evaluation and follow-up for exposed workers
- Use of biohazard labeling to communicate the type of hazard
- Provision of specific training regarding bloodborne pathogens
- Maintaining records of exposure and training

Although most real estate managers would not "reasonably anticipate" that they or their employees would face occupational exposure to blood, it is prudent that they have policies and procedures regarding cleanup of blood and other bodily fluids. Because there is potential for liability in the event of such exposure, you may wish to seek guidance from a qualified professional regarding development of policies and procedures related to bloodborne pathogens and compliance with the OSHA requirements. Also, it may be possible or preferable to contract for janitorial services with a company that specializes in medical office buildings, or has specific experience with this type of property.

Preventing Employee Exposure

Although only operators of medical facilities are required to provide vaccinations for hepatitis-B virus to their employees, who may become occupationally exposed, you may encourage the same with any "at-risk" employees. In addition, occupationally exposed personnel should take the following steps to reduce their risk:

- Wear protective clothing and equipment such as gloves, gowns, laboratory coats, face shields or masks, and eye protection when necessary. In particular, employees must wear appropriate gloves when in contact with blood or infectious fluids or materials that can be reasonably anticipated. Employees should wear appropriate eye and mouth protection (e.g., goggles, masks) when dealing with splashes.

- Remove protective clothing and equipment before leaving the work area or when it becomes contaminated.

- Place used protective equipment in appropriately designated areas or containers to ensure proper storage for decontamination, washing, or disposal.

- Decontaminate utility gloves for reuse if their integrity is not compromised. Discard gloves when they show signs of cracking, peeling, tearing, etc.

- Never wash or decontaminate disposable gloves for reuse.
- Consult the material safety data sheet (MSDS) for appropriate treatment to any exposure. Treatment may instruct the person exposed to wash the exposed skin with soap and water, and to flush eyes with water as soon as possible. Liquid antiseptic or moist antiseptic towelettes may be utilized if soap and water are not immediately available, followed by washing with soap and water as soon as possible.

It is the responsibility of the tenant to ensure that they're using proper preventive control and personal protective equipment when dealing, storing, and disposing of potentially hazardous medical materials. To underscore the fact, it may be wise to include the OHSA standard requirements for these matters in the tenant's lease as follows:

Labeling. The OSHA standard requires fluorescent orange or orange-red warning labels to be attached to containers of regulated waste, refrigerators, and freezers containing blood or other potentially infectious materials, and for containers used to store and transport blood or potentially infectious materials. Where orange or orange-red labels are absent, red bags or containers may be used. Ensure that janitorial workers, especially, are aware of such labels and the potential hazards they warn against.

Housekeeping. In compliance with the OSHA standard, each place of employment must be kept clean and sanitary. Tenants must develop and implement cleaning schedules that include appropriate methods of decontamination based on their location within the facility, type of surface to be cleaned, the type of contamination present, and the tasks or procedures being performed in the area.

HANDLING EXPOSURE TO BLOODBORNE PATHOGENS

As the real estate manager, you, as well as the tenants of a medical office building, should consider developing a written exposure control plan based on the requirements stated in the OSHA Bloodborne Pathogen Standard. The following list includes specific training for employees:

- The contents of the OSHA standard
- Types of bloodborne diseases and its transmission
- Response to emergencies involving blood
- Use of personal protective clothing and equipment

- Safe work practices
- What to do in the event of exposure
- Use of biohazard labeling

The tenant will be required to provide treatment and post-exposure medical evaluation to an employee who may have had an exposure incident. Employees should immediately follow special procedures to clean the exposed area of the body, report the incident to their supervisor, and seek medical treatment.

Should you introduce these programs, maintain training records that include dates of all employee training sessions on handling bloodborne pathogens, including the names of employees who attended each session, the trainer's name and qualifications, the method of training, and the topics discussed. Tenants are also required to maintain records of employees who are exposed to bloodborne pathogens.

Contact OSHA regarding regulations and educational materials. Information about the OSHA standard and related fact sheets are available on the OSHA website (*www.osha.gov*). It is also advisable to check with state regulations, which are often more stringent than those at the federal level. Information about bloodborne pathogens may also be available from your insurance company.

CHAPTER 10:

Shopping Centers and Other Retail Properties

Retail properties can frequently be broken down into five categories: (1) freestanding stores, (2) strip malls, (3) open-air malls, (4) enclosed malls, and (5) mixed-use developments. While their size, scope, and needs vary, they feature similar guiding principles. In this chapter, most of the discussion is catered to both types of shopping malls (enclosed and open-air malls), but much of the information could easily be scaled and translated to freestanding stores or retail space within a mixed-use development, such as a store on the ground floor of an office building.

ANTICIPATING CROWDS: SAFETY IN THE HUM AND BUZZ OF RETAIL

A retail building—be it an enclosed shopping mall or freestanding store—is visited daily by hundreds to thousands of shoppers. It's easy to think of shopping centers as places of commerce or places where teenagers, young adults, or families spend their extra time—whether it's during weekend hours or weekday afternoons. Regardless of time shoppers visit the property, it's easy to lose sight of the workplace safety concerns that directly affect retail employees. Tenants should be policing their own internal safety requirements in regard to workplace safety. However, it is advisable to consider working with retailers to ensure that safe conditions are maintained. For example, consider promoting proper upkeep of a neatly organized, maintained stockroom. Although typical stocking of merchandise in retail spaces are not the responsibility of real estate managers, it would become an issue if merchandize in the stock room is stacked so high that it blocks fire sprinklers.

Many concerns of industrial warehouses have come into play for members of the retail sector. Stores such as home improvement warehouses must now deal with not only employee safety, but also the safety of its guests. (For more details on industrial properties, see *Chapter 11*.)

SECURITY FOR SHOPPING CENTERS

Retail properties, especially shopping centers, are characterized by their large floor spaces and high level of visitor traffic. When building a security plan for your retail property, the first step may be to conduct research on the incidence of crime in the surrounding area in order to evaluate the security needs for your property. This level of research involves obtaining statistics on the types of crimes and the number of incidents from local police or other experts on crime in the vicinity.

Added security equipment may include special lighting systems, surveillance cameras for parking lots, garages, and corridors, or conveniently located land-line telephones so that shoppers can easily contact the security office. For both open-air and enclosed malls, parking lots may be patrolled by security personnel in vehicles or may have uniformed security personnel patrol on foot. Shopping strip centers may arrange for a private security service to drive by the property on a regular schedule, or increased police patrols may be requested.

As the real estate manager, you can provide retailers with information and tips on security issues, while other programs (e.g., community relations) may provide shoppers with safety tips or escorts to their cars.

RESPONDING TO CRIME AND VIOLENCE

When it comes to safety, it's important to differentiate between the responsibilities of the real estate manager and the retail tenant. As the real estate manager, your security responsibility is generally for security in the common areas such as the parking lot, the corridors, unoccupied lease space, and restrooms. Retail tenants are responsible for security within their leased premises. Since a retailer's company policy dictates what action can be taken within a store, the store managers must decide how their employees will respond to criminal incidents or other offenses. The shopping center may employ or contract a security force that retail tenants can call for assistance, but retail tenants must keep in mind that their stores are ultimately liable for damaged or stolen property within the premises.

To increase shopper confidence, malls may offer some or all of the following services:

- A lost and found area where lost items may be stored for 30 to 90 days until claimed
- A telecommunications device for the deaf—a text-based messaging machine that allows deaf or hearing-impaired people to communicate

- Vehicle jump starts for visitors whose cars have stalled or lost battery power
- A specially appointed roving security guard may be assigned to escort shoppers to their cars—a similar service may also be extended to employees of the retail tenants
- Medical emergency services—security may assist with minor medical emergencies in which they are trained or may contact local authorities as needed

TEEN PRESENCE ON RETAIL PROPERTIES

According to ongoing research by Teenage Research Unlimited (TRU), American teens spend more than $170 billion per year, and the amount continues to grow.[1] Teens are responsible for a significant percentage of sales in shopping centers.

While teens can be a huge economic boon to a mall or retail center, they can also present risks of vandalism and occasional criminal activity. As a real estate manager, you and your security personnel should be concerned if teens begin taking part in behavior or activity that frightens other shoppers away. Gangs can also become a problem for retail centers, exposing the property to vandalism, shoplifting, robbery, and occasional assault.

Graffiti or increased incidents of shoplifting may indicate gang or teen crime on the premises. Parking lots are often a good barometer. Check to see if there have been any acts of larceny (purse snatching, etc.) or loitering near the shopping center. Should you grow concerned about unsupervised, unruly teens or fear the presence of gangs, consult with your security team on the following suggestions:

- Cooperate with the police department and community organizations that work with youths and gangs.
- Hire security officers who reflect the demographics of the neighborhood to encourage a sense of community.
- In large open malls, a mobile security force can closely watch parking lots, mall plazas, or isolated restaurants.
- Provide seminars on shoplifting, credit card fraud, response tactics, and arrest procedures for retail tenants' employees. Proper training creates more awareness and confidence among retailers' employees so that they can help combat gang-related activities.
- Try to place similar retail stores at different ends of the mall to discourage large gatherings of gangs.

1. For more information about TRU, visit *http://www.tru-insight.com.*

Additional information on how to detect gang presence on managed properties and how to address gang activity is presented in *Chapter 22*.

POLICE SUBSTATIONS IN MALLS

The presence of local police in a retail space can provide a sense of reassured safety and comfort to consumers while inviting further connections to the local community within the culture of the shopping mall. Real estate managers of both enclosed and open-air shopping malls can sometimes provide local police with a designated substation on the property's premises, which provides a sense of security for patrons and retail tenants, and may serve as a meeting place for uniting parents with lost children. They also allow for a stronger security presence, which discourages civil disruption and criminal activity.

If you invite police to operate a substation in a shopping center you manage, be sure the mall's insurance and the substation's insurance provide adequate and appropriate coverage since the mall ownership is allowing a formal police presence on private property.

CUSTOMER AWARENESS PROGRAMS FOR RETAIL PROPERTIES

In order to create the culture of safety, fun, and family, post your security policies and standards of conduct in visible locations throughout the store or mall. Some mall managers encourage weekly family nights for patrons to build a strong sense of community. Others work to establish relationships with local high schools by offering special discounts, gift cards, or other award programs to students who present satisfactory grade reports. They may frequently allow high school or youth groups to stage fundraising events at the mall, which helps to build a sense of community, respect, and trust.

Negative perceptions based on actual or attempted criminal activity drive patrons away from malls, stores, and other retail centers. To combat this, consider starting a mall- or store-watch program. The idea behind this program is to create a proactive initiative in which customers, merchants, security personnel, and law enforcement agencies work together to fight crime, control store losses, and protect a positive shopping experience. Such programs may help reduce activities leading to a commercial loss, including shoplifting, the passing of bad checks, and credit card fraud, but also criminal activities, such as car theft and personal assaults. Your local police crime prevention unit may be willing to provide information and training to mall management personnel and retailer's employees. Mall-watch programs may combine elements of neighborhood-watch programs to create awareness with educational seminars.

Customers are an important component of a mall-watch program because they can report any suspicious behavior observed in parking lots or inside the mall to the nearest mall security guard or store employee, who can then contact the appropriate persons in the mall-watch network. As a more effective way to report suspicious behavior on the mall's premises, real estate managers should encourage the store's employees to always have a watchful eye. By helping make the retail spaces unfriendly to criminals, customers will have a more enjoyable shopping experience.

EVACUATION FOR ENCLOSED AND OPEN-AIR SHOPPING MALLS

Much of the general principles and procedures that retail properties follow for evacuations are established in *Chapter 3*. However, there are specific issues that should be considered when preparing for evacuation.

Evacuations for properties of this scale can be tricky. Like the medical office buildings (outlined in *Chapter 9*), retail spaces are likely to have a large number of people inside at any given moment—many of whom may not know where to go, how to act, or what to do during any given emergency. It's imperative to create clear evacuation procedures that patrons may follow with a minimal amount of questions.

Consider the size of the retail space—the larger the property, the more complex the evacuation plan. The difference between a large, enclosed mall versus a strip mall is clear. Strip shopping malls require much simpler plans since they open right into the parking lot. Outdoor, open-air shopping malls may find similarly less restrictive evacuation options.

Large multistory centers and enclosed malls, on the other hand, require detailed, meticulous thought behind their evacuation procedures. As larger retail spaces will have more tenants, you and your management staff will need to rely on merchants and their employees to assist in the communication of the evacuation or shelter orders. Training in emergency and evacuation procedures poses several challenges within a retail setting. Unlike apartment residents and employees of office building tenants—who can be trained to evacuate the premises by conducting drills—the majority of the people in retail spaces are customers who will likely spend a few scant hours on the property. Therefore, much of the emergency and evacuation preparedness falls upon the real estate management staff and the tenants. Encourage tenants, especially large anchor tenants, to devise an evacuation plan that dovetails or functions in addition to the larger center's procedures. Involving tenants in evacuation procedures, particularly large anchor tenants, will help to reinforce preparedness in seasonal, part-time, and temporary employees throughout the property.

Notifying tenants and patrons of an emergency may be done in a number of ways. Loudspeakers or public address announcements can be utilized. Messages may be displayed over televisions or displays where applicable. When determining a notification protocol, it should be thorough.

A more recent trend with enclosed and open-air shopping malls is to generate a branded, customized mobile application for Smartphones and tablets. While these may have a primary function to notify users of sales, they may be configurable to post emergency announcements via push notification or text message. Regardless of how the evacuation notice or emergency announcement is made, be sure to repeat it on a continuous basis by telling retailers and customers what they should do and where they should go. Scripted templates of announcements for different situations requiring evacuation may be an effective tactic, and prevent errors or omissions during public announcements.

Be conscious of the tone and wording of your evacuation announcement. It should be worded in a way that will avoid causing panic for mall patrons and tenant employees. Proper judgment and good taste should be utilized. For example, if the shopping mall receives a bomb threat and the real estate manager decides to evacuate the mall, the announcement should be nonspecific, stating that the mall is being closed. Should a reason be stated, keep it vague but plausible in such a way as to avoid inciting

THE FOLLOWING IS A BASIC SCRIPT THAT CAN BE USED DURING AN EVACUATION FOR VARIOUS COMMERCIAL PROPERTY TYPES:

"ATTENTION, ATTENTION. This is the Building Management. There is an emergency situation in the building. Please evacuate the building immediately using the nearest exit stairwell. Move slowly down the right side of the stairs, out of the building, and into the parking lot. Follow the directions of the Floor Wardens. DO NOT USE ELEVATORS."

panic. Once the announcement has been made and the property is evacuated, retailers' employees should conduct storewide searches to make sure no customers are lingering. Security staff and other mall staff should search common areas for customers.[2]

The real estate manager has the responsibility for determining whether or not the center should be evacuated, but should defer and take input from local, state, and national organizations or authorities. In turn, security and maintenance staff should be notified. Special considerations should be made depending on the nature of an emergency. It may be the police, for instance, that order the evacuation of a center during a bomb threat or discovery of a suspicious object. Defer to the orders of authorities in similar situations such as hazardous-materials spills. When there is an immediate threat to life, *always* evacuate.

Mall staff should be assigned specific duties for evacuation, taking cues from the emergency response team outlined in *Chapter 3*. Consider having the team start at the center of the mall on each level and move outward, instructing shoppers to move toward the exits, advising store managers to close immediately. Additional staff members should also be stationed at each end of the mall, assisting in the evacuation of patrons, facilitating a calm, organized process.

SPECIAL LEASE PROVISIONS

Like other types of properties, retail properties experience a considerable amount of damage beyond that inflicted by the disaster itself. For retailers, a blow to established shopping and business habits can be as destructive as any disaster. A store closed for any length of time can lose customers to competitors—even loyal shoppers.

Facilitating Recovery

Rebuilding and recovering quickly is key to protecting a business's reputation following a catastrophe. Beyond your business interests, it is as important to consider the interests of tenants. Other than a sound insurance policy to allow the real estate manager to rebuild the damaged property, no document may be more important than a shopping center lease. As part of your emergency preparedness plan, it may be worth considering

---

2. *Shopping Center Management and Leasing,* published by the Institute or Real Estate (IREM®), includes information on emergency procedures that may be helpful to real estate managers and retail tenants.

the following types of emergency recovery clauses and precautions that can be offered to tenants in their lease possibly during the negotiation process:

- *Continuation of rent.* In most situations, tenant payments and other lease obligations should remain in full force while damage is being repaired. The lease should also require the tenant to maintain business interruption insurance coverage (to pay for rent, salaries, and other costs while they are out of business until the damage is repaired).

- *Responsibility for repairs.* The landlord is generally responsible for repairing damage to the building's structural elements, such as the roof, walls, and common areas, while retail tenants must restore leasehold improvements such as built-in furnishings and wall and floor coverings.

- *Time frame for repairs.* The lease may specify a time frame in which the owner is obligated to complete repairs.

- *Escape clause.* This provision makes it possible to release tenants without penalty if the landlord fails to finish the building repairs within a required time period, or if the damage exceeds a predetermined limit. This can be beneficial for retail tenants during unexpected repair delays.

You should make every effort to encourage positive relationships amongst tenants, the building's insurer, and yourself as management. A strong, healthy commitment to restoring the building as quickly as possible will help retailers get back into business, while ensuring that your business continues its rapport with consumers.

CHAPTER 11:
Industrial Properties

Industrial properties often have a specialized functions just as both retail and medical office properties. They also come in different form factors. Properties in older urban areas are likely to be multistory buildings, while those in suburban areas are more likely to be a single-story facility with a large parking area. Industrial sites with several buildings are often landscaped to create a park-like setting—hence the term industrial park. Industrial tenants may have less interaction with the real estate manager and tenants at nearby industrial properties, as they frequently have specific responsibilities to provide a safe work environment mandated by the Occupational Safety and Health Administration (OSHA). The internal responsibilities and protocols for tenants are often complete with their own emergency plans that are tailored to their needs. This, however, does not supersede the need for a real estate manager's emergency plan for the entire property.

Industrial properties typically fall into the following categories:

1. Owner-occupied plants or manufacturing facilities
2. Single-use bulk warehouses
3. Multi-tenant warehouse and light manufacturing facilities
4. Research and development buildings and parks
5. Office service and showrooms
6. Flex space and call centers
7. Distribution buildings and truck terminals

CREATING THE TENANT PROFILE

As the real estate manager of an industrial property, you have a responsibility to keep first responders to an emergency aware of potentially hazardous processes and materials stored in finished or unfinished areas. Work with tenants to build a tenant profile of the types of industry, equipment, and materials that will be taking place or stored in the leased space. Some real estate managers fear sharing this information with public officials, but this is typically a misplaced fear. Officials are better able to protect employees, neighboring businesses, and residents with up-to-date adequate information.

Although emergency planning issues may not be as obvious as in residential or office uses, inspection with public safety, code officials, or risk management professionals will significantly improve the planning efficiency for industrial properties.

Emergency planning for industrial properties must also consider the type of activity in the leased space, materials and equipment being used, and number of tenant employees. Actions being taken to prevent emergencies are especially important, and site managers should seek assurances that tenants provide a safe work environment for their employees.[1]

EMERGENCY PLANNING CONSIDERATIONS

One primary focus of emergency planning for industrial properties will be on the processes and materials used on the property. Site managers should request a copy of the material safety data sheet (MSDS) information for each tenant, as well as a copy of their site safety plan.

Given this data, site managers, tenant representatives, and other risk and safety professionals should determine the adequacy of hazard detection, notification, and suppression systems. The potential hazards in the industrial setting are many, varied, and not always obvious. However, good liability management may require consulting beyond the site manager. In fact, the site manager should be certain that processes and storage areas are acceptable within zoning and building codes.

The scale of industrial properties demands special attention to the adequacy of power and water supplies for both normal operations and emergency demands. Access to the property and property resources for first responders is another important consideration. Determine where fire, police, and emergency medical technicians can stage their response, while also taking into consideration the location of fire hydrants and utility entrances. In regard to hydrants, utility shut-offs, etc., layout is an important consideration that may present hazardous issues. For example, consider adjacent bodies of water that may be impacted by an emergency on the property, as well as neighboring properties, and natural surroundings.

---

1. The safety information presented in this chapter relates primarily to responsibilities of individual industrial employers. However, many of the rules also apply to management staff and emergency management team members as these individuals have need to enter a tenant's premises—whether in response to an emergency or otherwise.

SPECIAL CONSIDERATIONS

Industrial uses present numerous challenges because of the size of the space for materials and equipment used in tenants' operations. As previously stated, industrial tenants have a primary responsibility for safety in their leased premises, but as the real estate manager, you should make yourself aware of the requirements of the specific tenants leasing your property. Building an accurate tenant profile for an industrial property, like other property types, will help better prepare for emergencies.

Warehouses

Management concerns about warehouse space generally pertain to ensuring safe, normal operation that is free from obstruction. This means scrutinizing to ensure the space has clean workspace areas, proper storage of chemicals, functioning safety devices on loading dock doors, clearly marked exit routes, and proper clearances. Stored materials should only be stacked to prescribed heights to allow sprinklers and fire suppression systems to work properly. Tenants and their employees are responsible for keeping work areas free of materials and debris that cause trip-and-fall accidents. OSHA regulations and standards provide guidelines for recognizing these types of hazards and preventing accidents. For instance, pallets and forklifts left in aisles can slow evacuation in emergencies and should be kept out of the way when not in use.

Multistory Structures

Manufacturing processes rely on complex, specialized, and often heavy equipment typically set up in production lines that include conveyor systems and/or complicated pipelines. Industrial tenants who overload floor slabs in multistory structures can unknowingly put excessive weight on a structural support that might eventually collapse. The collapse of an upper story can obviously affect supporting walls and cause them to collapse as well. Since industrial machinery might weigh more than floors in the building, the lease should stipulate the weight capacity for each floor level, which should be stated on a square foot basis.

Hazardous-Materials Storage and Disposal

Since industrial tenants may have numerous chemicals and other hazardous materials in or on their leased premises, proper storage and disposal should be a priority. Public walkways and heated rooms should be kept clear of hazardous materials to avoid spills, accidents, or heat-related explosions. Encourage your tenants to adhere to proper storage guidelines for chemicals they use. Storage guidelines are provided on product labels and the MSDS from the chemical source, along with information on specific hazards and recommended protections. Specific information can also be found in the *NIOSH (National Institute for Occupational Safety and Health) Pocket Guide to Chemical Hazards*, available for download from the Centers for Disease Control and Prevention (CDC).[2] Guidelines for first responders to hazardous materials incidents can be found in the *2012 Emergency Response Guidebook* from the U.S. Department of Transportation.

Leaking containers or spilled chemicals have the potential to generate deadly fumes. If the chemicals are flammable or combustible, these fumes may cause fires or explosions, which in an enclosed space can lead to devastating damage in loss of both property and life. All chemicals should be clearly labeled with the chemical name and specific hazards, as required under the Toxic Substances Control Act (TSCA) in compliance with the Environmental Protection Agency (EPA). More information on hazardous-materials incidents can be found in *Chapter 16.*

Industrial tenants should also understand and comply with guidelines for the storage, security, inventory, and disposal of their chemicals and hazardous materials. Disposal of such wastes is closely regulated by the EPA under the Resource Conservation and Recovery Act (RCRA), which is also known as the Solid Waste Disposal Act. Numerous lawsuits have been filed against tenants and owners of industrial sites for improper disposal of hazardous wastes. As such, be sure to thoroughly research local, state, and federal waste disposal laws and regulations in addition to making sure industrial tenants are aware of their responsibilities and liabilities. This issue should also be addressed in the lease to safeguard the property's management and ownership against potential liability resulting from an industrial tenant's negligence.

Proper Ventilation

In fully or partially enclosed buildings, such as factories or industrial plants, the industrial employer must ensure that proper ventilation exists to accommodate a large group of workers. Improper ventilation can result

---

2. To download a copy of the NIOSH Pocket Guide to Chemical Hazards, please visit *http:// www.cdc.gov/niosh/npg/.*

in poor indoor air quality, which can impair the health and performance of those exposed, especially if chemicals release fumes when in use.

The local OSHA office can be contacted for a free onsite consultation regarding the safety of the property, which should especially be coordinated with commercial tenants. Congress has authorized a joint federal-state activity whereby a state consultant can visit the site and give practical advice on a property's job safety and potential health problems without issuing citations, proposing penalties, or reporting workplace conditions to authorities. The program is explained in the OSHA publication titled, *Consultation Services for the Employer.*

Fire Suppression

Different equipment and material types will require different fire suppression materials, chemicals, and system designs based on the type of work and processes taking place. Unlike other property types, one size or type of system does not fit-all in industrial use. Prior to initial leasing and with each annual inspection, you must be assured that the current use and storage demands are properly protected by the building's life safety systems.

Confined Spaces

Some emergency situations may necessitate entering confined spaces to rescue workers overcome by a lack of oxygen or toxic fumes. Such spaces may include tanks, pits, vaults, sewers, and pipelines. Entry into these spaces can expose the rescue team to toxic gases, explosive atmospheres, oxygen deficiency, and electrical hazards. A person should never enter a confined space unless the atmosphere has been tested for lack of oxygen, toxic substances, and potential combustibility. It's also critical to ensure that an open line or method of communication is possible with onsite backup personnel. People who may be involved in confined space rescue must obtain approved OSHA training and certification for this procedure.

If there is a possibility that management personnel may be called upon to assist in a rescue from a confined space, the real estate manager may wish to seek out more specific guidelines. Such information may be found in the *NIOSH Criteria for a Recommended Standard: Working in Confined Spaces,* produced by the CDC.

Personal Protection

Reliable protective equipment and clothing is essential for employees exposed to workplace hazards, which could include:

- Personal injury from equipment or materials used
- Chemical splashes or contact with toxic materials
- Falling objects and flying particles
- Hazardous atmospheres that may contain toxic gases and vapors or insufficient oxygen to sustain life
- Fires and electrical hazards

OSHA mandates the use of special protective gear by industrial workers in compliance procedures that must be enforced on the premises during industrial operations. Manufacturing supervisors should check with their state and local OSHA offices to ensure that industrial procedures and safety rules and equipment meet state and local guidelines.

In an emergency situation at an industrial property, members of the management staff may encounter the same types of hazards if they are required to provide assistance in a tenant's premises. They will need the same types of personal protection that the tenant's employees use. Protective safety equipment may include the following:

- Safety glasses, goggles, or face shields for eye protection
- Hard hats and safety shoes for head and foot protection
- Proper respirators for breathing protection
- Whole-body coverings, gloves, boots, and hoods for body protection from hazardous chemicals
- Body protection for extreme hot and cold temperatures, respectively, in environments that include industrial furnaces or refrigeration

Chemical plants should have multiple eyewash stations, as well as basins for hand washing, so they are readily accessible by workers in the event of a spill or splash.

Industrial operations often generate noise at levels that can be harmful. Workers in noisy environments should be provided with earplugs, earmuffs, or other protective devices to prevent hearing loss.

Selected equipment should be approved jointly by the Mine Safety and Health Administration (MSHA) and NIOSH, or comply with the standards set by the American National Standards Institute (ANSI). Consultation with health and safety professionals is encouraged before choosing specific protective equipment.

RESPIRATORY PROTECTION

Respiratory protection is necessary for potentially toxic atmospheres including those laden with dusts, gases, mists, or vapors or which are oxygen deficient. There are four basic categories of respirators:

1. **Air-purifying devices (particulate filters, gas masks, and chemical cartridges):** These devices remove contaminants from the air but cannot be used in oxygen-deficient environments.

2. **Air-supplied respirators (airline respirators and hose masks):** These should not be used in atmospheres that are immediately dangerous to human health.

3. **Self-contained breathing apparatus (SCBA):** Required for unknown atmospheres, oxygen-deficient atmospheres, or atmospheres immediately dangerous to life or health (positive-pressure type only). SCBAs should have a minimum service life of 30 minutes.

4. **Escape masks or respirators.**

It is critically important that the correct type of cartridge is used in a respirator to protect the user in a specific situation. Different cartridges, used individually or piggybacked in combination, provide protection against very specific airborne hazards.

Before assigning or using respiratory equipment, it is up to the industrial employer to ensure that each employee has a medical evaluation to determine if the employee is physically able to use a respirator; a fit test is performed to verify a secure match between the face piece and the wearer; written use guidelines are posted; a regular maintenance program is in place to keep equipment safe and sanitary; and distribution areas for equipment used in emergencies are readily accessible.

Some types of equipment may require specific training to ensure proper use. Professional consultation is necessary to ensure adequate respiratory protection for specific work environments. Information on different types of respirators and their applicability can be found in the *NIOSH Guide to Industrial Respiratory Protection*.

DETECTION AND NOTIFICATION FOR EVACUATION

During a major emergency involving a fire or explosion, it may be necessary to evacuate tenant offices in addition to their manufacturing areas. Normal water, telephone, and electricity services may be disrupted or nonexistent. It may be necessary to establish an alternate meeting place for industrial workers and other employees to assemble in order to communicate with the fire department and other local authorities.

Alarms should include both visual and audible cues, distinct above the noise common on industrial sites. The tenant plant manager should explain to employees the methods for reporting emergencies—PA systems, pull stations, telephones, etc.

Since 1994, OSHA has mandated that all employers are required to establish hazard communication programs to transmit information on the hazards of chemicals to their employees. This should be done by means of labels on containers, the MSDS, and other training programs. For specifics on a wide range of chemicals, consult the *NIOSH Pocket Guide to Chemical Hazards*. Implementation of these hazard communication programs assures compliance with employees' right to know the hazards and identities of the chemicals they work with, and will reduce the incidence of chemical-related occupational illnesses and injuries.

EVACUATION

Evacuation plans for industrial sites will be dictated by specific tenants' uses. Often the flow of a production line—from raw materials to finished product—will determine where aisles are positioned and where workers performing specific tasks will stand or sit. It is important for exit signs to be visible, especially since there may be a limited number of exits for a very large space. Workers may have to travel a long route to reach exits. Additional directional signs may be needed to ensure that directions to exits can be seen from all areas of the plant.

Tenants should be advised to take care in designing production lines and be considerate in their placement of equipment so that there will be multiple clear paths to all exits. The same applies in warehouses where pallets are stacked in multiple layers, limiting sight lines.

It may be necessary or appropriate to include loading docks as evacuation exits if they open to the outside and include stairs or walkways that would allow for such an exit. As with all property types, practice evacuations are a must.

SECTION 3:

Preparing for Specific Emergencies

CHAPTER 12:

Managing Power Outages

Unforeseen power outages caused by faulty wiring, utility blackouts, thunderstorms, hurricanes, floods, or earthquakes can be devastating to both humans and property. Real estate managers must pay attention to their property's power needs and be ready to respond to power outages in emergency situations.

THE TYPES OF EMERGENCIES TO EXPECT DURING A POWER OUTAGE

In the event of a power outage, all electrical systems in the building will shut down. The total darkness—except for any supply of flashlights—will greatly inhibit evacuation unless a backup lighting system is in place. Elevators could stop between floors, leaving inhabitants trapped. Electrically operated security doors, garage doors, and gates might not operate, impeding evacuation. Desktop computers and server equipment may experience a degree of data loss.

HOW TO PREPARE FOR A POWER OUTAGE

The emergency procedures manual should include a plan to prepare for and respond to power outages. It is beneficial to have an up-to-date diagram showing where the building's power transformers, generators, circuit breakers, and standby electrical supply systems are located, which will enable the emergency management team to track the source of partial or full power outages, and restore service as soon as possible. A detailed diagram showing which switches serve which areas in the building and to what transformers they are connected will allow a real estate manager to direct the contractor or repair person to the source of a localized outage. This preparation also reduces hourly contractor billing costs.

During an actual incident, the real estate manager should ask the following questions:

- How extensive is the power outage?
- Which floors and voltage loads are affected?
- Does the outage require an evacuation of the building?

The Blackout Two-Step: Knowing What Goes Out When

The real estate manager should also be familiar with municipal building and fire codes, which stipulate whether emergency power backup equipment is required on the premises.

Regularly check the property's backup equipment, such as battery-powered lighting systems and emergency generators. Some municipal codes require periodic maintenance of emergency generators.

Become familiar with all equipment on the premises that could be affected by a power outage. Consider the two-step approach of (1) identifying all critical operations and (2) establishing preventative maintenance schedules for all systems and equipment.

When identifying all critical operations, be sure to include:

- Utilities such as electric power, gas, water, hydraulics, compressed air, municipal and internal sewer systems, and wastewater treatment services
- Security and alarm systems, lighting, elevators, electrical distribution systems, and heating, ventilation, and air-conditioning (HVAC) systems
- Communications systems, both internal and external
- Business equipment necessary for business continuity (computers, fax machines, copiers)
- Electronic access controls (exit doors, computer rooms, or vaults)

In California—and other regions in the U.S.—intentional power outages are activated by the utility on a predetermined schedule. Often called "rolling blackouts," a local utility may reduce electrical output in an area for a set period of time to prevent a disruption or failure of the larger grid. In areas like southern California and other warm or arid temperatures, the demand for electrical power may outweigh the supply, goading the utility provider to take preventative action.

Rolling blackouts, sometimes called load shedding, are announced beforehand and are typically mapped to a specific region or numbered power grid. Ask your property's utility provider which zone or grid your property occupies. Having this information will help you alert tenants ahead of scheduled power loss. Many times, these events are announced online and may be part of a state of emergency announcement.

It's important to consider the potential equipment damage that a blackout—scheduled or sudden—can have on equipment. Use surge protectors or surge-protected power strips for computers or appliances. For critical equipment, consider investing in an uninterruptible power supply. Before a scheduled blackout, consider what could be lost; any previously unsaved data will be lost during a power outage.

Install Backup Emergency Generators

Many buildings utilize an emergency generator to provide power for exit lights, stairwell lights, and emergency lighting in tenants' premises. In the event of a power outage, these generators provide critical voltage loads, which are connected to an automatic transfer switch. When the switches sense that voltage from a normal source has been interrupted for a predetermined time, they automatically transfer power to the emergency backup generator. The emergency generator, in turn, transmits the energy to transformers, which convert the power to a usable voltage.

Generators operate on diesel fuel or natural gas, so they must be located in safe, cool areas and properly maintained. The location of generators might be in or next to fire command panels, emergency lighting systems, communications boxes, elevators, or other easy-access locations. Sometimes large generators may be located outside the building, especially in suburban areas.

It is important to know how long the generators will provide backup power in terms of minutes or hours. The emergency management team will need to know how much time and light they will have to attempt to restore operations and safely evacuate building occupants if necessary.

Identify Other Power Sources

If your building does not have a backup emergency generator, determine if it is necessary to have alternative plans in case of power outages. A battery-operated, backup PA system will facilitate smooth evacuation and help avoid panic. Additional emergency lighting with a battery-operated system can be installed in each stairwell.

Floor wardens should have portable lamps or flashlights, and the real estate manager should have a transistor radio to monitor local news updates in the event of an area-wide blackout. Citizens are discouraged from calling 911 for information; the electric utility is usually the primary information source, providing announcements for broadcast to the public.

> ### EMERGENCY ALERT SYSTEM
>
> Created by the Federal Communications Commission (FCC), the national Emergency Alert System (EAS) uses digital technology to distribute messages so that state and local officials can quickly send out important local emergency information targeted to a specific area. The EAS uses the same digital signal as used by the National Weather Service (NWS) and the Federal Emergency Management System (FEMA). The signal is decoded by EAS equipment at broadcast stations and cable systems. Specially equipped consumer products (e.g., televisions, radios, pagers) can also decode EAS messages.
>
> The EAS is tested weekly using an eight-second digital data signal. Monthly tests include a spoken message. This is the source of the "test" messages heard periodically on radio and television.
>
> Because EAS messages may not be broadcast on all available airwaves, it is important to know which local radio and television stations make such broadcasts. Alternatively, one should have a transistor radio that can be tuned to NOAA Weather Radio (NWR).

Safeguarding the Electrical System

Real estate managers should also ensure the following items are in order to safeguard against electrical blackouts:

- Electrical panels, switches, and fuses should be enclosed in metal cabinets that securely close.
- Circuits should be easily identifiable.
- Fuses or circuit breakers should be properly sized for equipment and lighting, and a supply of replacement fuses should be maintained.
- Ensure that the property does not have recurring problems with fuses or circuit breakers that are continually tripped.
- All ground-fault interrupters should be safe to use—e.g., not in potentially damp areas.
- Protect/insulate power connections that are exposed to the elements, which should be inspected periodically to ensure the integrity of the protective material.
- Sound systems, computers, and office equipment should be protected by surge protectors. For some equipment, an uninterruptible power supply may be more appropriate than a surge protector.
- Avoid using extension cords as permanent power sources in lieu of hardwiring or adding an electrical outlet.
- Ensure that adequate clearances or suitable protective layers are provided between recessed light fixtures and insulating materials.
- Regularly inspect and test the emergency generator.

POWER SURGES AND SURGE PROTECTION

Power surges result when the electrical charge carried on power lines is boost- ed. Lightning is probably the most familiar source of power surges. A lightning strike can cause a surge that will overpower almost any system. More common sources that are easily affected are refrigerators, air conditioners, elevators, and other types of equipment that require substantial amounts of energy to switch motors on and off, creating sudden brief increases in demand for power. While not as intense as a lightning surge, these changes in demand can cause dam- age to sensitive equipment. Other sources of power surges include downed power lines, problems with the utility's equipment, and faulty wiring.

To protect electronic equipment from power surges, individual surge protectors are needed for each outlet. Surge protectors are available in varying levels of quality and capacity. The basic power strip is an extension cord with five or six grounded outlets. A better, more expensive version will include an indicator light and separate switches for each individual outlet. (During a lightning storm, a surge protector may be inadequate; it is better to unplug the computer.)

Larger models, called surge stations, offer superior voltage protection and may include input and output phone lines to protect a modem and have built-in circuit breakers. Greater protection is provided by an uninterruptible power supply unit, which converts alternating current (AC) to direct current (DC) stored in a battery. The uninterruptible power supply converts the DC power from the battery to AC power for the electronic components attached to it. While an uninterruptible power supply does give a high level of protection, a surge protector should also be used to protect the former from being damaged by a power surge.

Inventory Emergency Equipment

For insurance purposes and protection against liability, keep an up-to-date list of emergency equipment on hand. A backup generator may qualify the building for additional insurance benefits. Adhere to a periodic mainte- nance inspection schedule to ensure that all emergency backup systems and equipment are ready for immediate use.

PROBLEMS TO ANTICIPATE

While electrical blackouts or power failures are likely to occur during the course of other emergencies, they can also be emergencies themselves. In the event of a power failure, it is essential to determine its cause and extent. Even the smallest power outages should be investigated. The loss of power to a single apartment unit, office suite, or store space may indicate a poten- tially serious problem.

Loss of power affecting the entire building should be immediately reported to the local electric utility to ensure that electric company personnel know the property has no power, and will begin efforts to restore electrical service if such work has not been started already. If the outage affects a larger area, utility personnel or an electric company hotline may provide information on the extent of the outage and when they expect service to be restored.

If power fails as part of another emergency, the emergency procedures for that type of event would likely be implemented as well as those for power outages. But when a power failure occurs apart from another emergency, it is wise to keep building occupants from unnecessarily moving around the building. In a residential property, an isolated electrical blackout is usually no reason to evacuate. Most residents could be encouraged to remain in their units and use flashlights during that type of power failure. (Use of candles and open flames should be discouraged.) For commercial properties, tenants' employees could be escorted from the building by emergency management team members. It may be necessary to implement crowd-control measures if there is an indication of panic among evacuees. If the power failure cannot be easily remedied (i.e., it is not related to blown fuses or tripped circuit breakers), the local electric utility should be called in to investigate and make repairs.

Real estate managers should inform residents and commercial tenants of the cause and extent of the loss of power, the recovery efforts under way, and the expected duration of the outage.

STALLED ELEVATORS AND ELEVATOR EMERGENCIES

Obviously, any building with an elevator is at risk of an elevator emergency. The taller the building, the greater the risk of an emergency arising if an elevator malfunctions.

Areas in the U.S. that are earthquake prone present special risks, and it is appropriate to adopt preventive measures for buildings in these areas (see *Chapter 20*). Any disaster that disrupts electrical power can also impact elevator operation, so it is advisable to implement some general measures to prevent elevator emergencies or, at least, minimize their impact. The following list provides suggestions to prepare for cases of stalled elevators or other elevator emergencies due to power outages or other equipment malfunctions:

- Develop a comprehensive plan of action in cases of fires, earthquakes, or other major disasters.

- Appoint an individual and an alternate to oversee implementation of the plan of action.
- Install a separate communication system for elevators that include emergency signals for passenger use. Have a backup power source for these systems in case normal power is disrupted.
- Install emergency car lighting that will turn on automatically in the event of a power failure.
- Make sure there are emergency work lights in the elevator machine room.
- Train management staff, especially maintenance and security personnel, on what to do in the event of an elevator emergency.

Elevator manufacturers and companies that provide contract elevator maintenance services are the best sources for specific information on elevators and elevator emergencies. In most situations, there will be little that onsite personnel can do, but they should know what can be done while they wait for the elevator service contractor's personnel to arrive.

ELEVATOR SAFETY TIPS

The following lists some basic, daily elevator safety tips for management staff and residents and tenants:
- Do not attempt to enter or exit an elevator while the doors are closing.
- Stand aside for exiting passengers.
- Watch your step while entering or exiting elevators. Look down to make sure the elevator cab is even with the floor.
- Once inside, press the button for your floor and move to the rear of the car.
- Stand next to a wall in the elevator. If there is a handrail, hold onto it. Do not lean on elevator doors.
- When the elevator stops, stand clear so that passengers can exit and enter.
- If the doors do not open when the elevator stops, press the "door open" button. If that does not open the doors, use the built-in alarm, intercom, or telephone to signal for help.

In the event of an elevator emergency, passengers should:
- Stay calm.
- Use the alarm, intercom, or telephone in the elevator to signal trouble.
- Stay put. Never try to pry open elevator doors or climb out of the opening on the roof of the car unless assisted by trained emergency personnel.
- Always use stairways (not elevators) to exit a building in an emergency.

Note: These tips can be shared with residents and commercial tenants' employees in their respective tenant manuals or via a property newsletter.

Modern elevators often have emergency communications and lighting systems built in. If these features are not present in the elevators in an older building, you should explore the practicality and costs of retrofitting them.

Preventive Measures for Elevator Safety

Elevator specifications are highly regulated—they cover construction, operation, and maintenance. At the very minimum, real estate managers should know what federal, state, and municipal codes apply and follow them precisely.

Elevator equipment is complex and specialized because elevators integrate electrical, mechanical, and hydraulic subsystems or solid-state components to transport millions of passengers every day. Preventive maintenance is particularly important for elevator systems because 60 to 70 percent of an elevator's parts are subject to wear. Elevator cables, in particular, should be inspected regularly for wear.

Loss can be minimized or prevented by ensuring that elevators have emergency controls. Though many elevators come equipped with these controls, some of the features can be added later. Basic controls include:

- Smoke detectors that, when set off, signals the elevator to return to the ground floor and shut down
- A switch that, when triggered manually, returns the elevator to the ground floor and shuts it down
- A direct-dial telephone system that is connected to an answering service, the elevator service company, or a 24-hour security station
- A button that triggers an audible alarm—this may not be effective after hours because it does not allow two-way communication

Elevators may also be equipped for firefighter's service, which signals for an immediate recall to a specified landing (usually the lobby) to remove cars from normal use and permit controlled operation by firefighters or other authorized emergency personnel.

To help ensure personal safety of elevator passengers, real estate managers can also implement the following precautionary measures:

- Program elevators to stop at the lobby level before going down to or after coming up from the basement
- Program elevators to bypass vacant floors
- Connect elevator stop buttons to an alarm bell and a security station

- Investigate the appropriateness of installing mirrored walls in elevator cars so a person can see the whole interior before entering

Areas prone to earthquakes increase the likelihood of elevator emergencies and installation and maintenance codes are stricter than areas not as prone. Some additional preventive measures should be implemented in those locations. Here are some suggestions:

- Bolt down the elevator machine room equipment to prevent "migration" due to vibration
- Fasten control room panels securely to the building
- Use collision switches to trigger the interlock mechanism to prevent car-to-counterweight collision
- Use additional reinforcing brackets between normal mountings so guide rails are held in place
- Install a guide on top of hoist motors to hold elevator cables in place on their sheaves

What to Do During an Elevator Emergency

Every building with an elevator should be prepared to respond to an elevator emergency. Emergency procedures should address elevator malfunctions as well as elevator operation (or shutdown) in the context of other types of emergencies such as a fire.

If elevator service is disrupted, the first step to be taken is to immediately contact the elevator service company. As this is highly specialized work, only qualified personnel—for example, elevator service company personnel, fire department personnel, and specially trained building employees—should be permitted to fix elevator malfunctions.

If occupants are stranded in an elevator during a malfunction, they should not be evacuated unless the situation is life threatening. Sudden movements can be dangerous, and evacuating the elevator can actually increase the likelihood of harm. When evacuation from an elevator is necessary, first check for slack in the hoistway ropes; a quick movement of the car could be dangerous with slack or broken suspension. Do not attempt to evacuate an elevator without the assistance of an elevator technician, police, or fire department.

With the best of intentions, untrained people may wish to remove a person from a stalled elevator. However, this could result in injury or loss of life if the elevator suddenly moves. Educating occupants and staff on these dangers could prevent a misguided rescue attempt.

At the same time, management should communicate with passengers trapped in an elevator—installed elevator phone systems are especially useful here. The communicator should assure the passengers that they are safe, caution them not to panic, warn them not to try to force the elevator doors open, and let them know what steps are being taken to free them. Management could ask if they can contact anyone on behalf of the trapped passengers. Communication should be maintained with stranded passengers until they are safely evacuated from the elevator.

It is a good idea to have emergency medical service phone numbers handy in case trapped passengers need assistance. Injuries are not the only concern. Some people may experience panic or anxiety attacks in enclosed spaces—the stress of the incident could even cause a heart attack.

What to Do After an Elevator Emergency

Immediately after an elevator emergency, appropriate personnel should conduct a thorough investigation of the cause of the mishap and corrective steps should be taken.

If elevator service was disrupted because of an earthquake, or there has been damage to the elevator system, elevators should not be operated until the hoistway and machine room equipment have been thoroughly inspected and all necessary repairs have been made.

SECONDARY DAMAGE AND EXTENDED POWER OUTAGES

Major equipment and sensitive electrical equipment such as computers—that may be damaged by a power surge or that may cause damage when power is restored—should be turned off until power has been restored. Tenants who have major computer network installations should have their own backup power for the network; however, individual computer terminals may be turned off as an added precaution.

Another concern during an electrical blackout is the spoilage of food in refrigerators and freezers that could result from a prolonged loss of power. Utilities usually recommend keeping refrigerator and freezer doors closed for the duration. Many retail tenants keep food and other perishable merchandise refrigerated. Some commercial refrigerators and freezers are open all the time. If a power outage is lengthy and risk of spoilage seems likely, real estate managers could encourage residents or commercial tenants to dispose of perishable items to avoid potential health risks.

Disrupted Sewage Lines

Because electricity powers pumps that move water and sewage in many areas, a power outage can disrupt sewage discharges. Include a backup alternative in case your sewage operations are disrupted. Keep an updated telephone number for a local portable toilet service or have plastic liner bags accessible for use in wastebaskets as temporary toilets. Advise occupants to tie the bag after each use to minimize odor, prevent spilling, and avoid spreading infection.

Extended Power Outage

Power outages that last 24 hours or longer require more extensive emergency planning, particularly if the outage is widespread. A severe storm can cause heavy damage throughout a wide area, including downed power lines that take more than a day to repair. Because such events do occur, it may be wise to have plans in place that address these additional considerations:

- **Evacuation will empty a building.** Where do occupants go if it is night and there are no streetlights? Those who drive will have lights in their cars. What if public transportation is compromised by an outage? How do people get home? Do they go home? Should a shelter-in-place program be planned?

- **A power failure may trap people in one or more elevators.** Do the elevators have emergency hatches or trap doors for rescuing people?

- **Electronic door locks will not work without power.** If backup generator power is exhausted, what provisions will be needed to secure the property? Will security personnel be needed? How will they be transported to the property?

- **Essential building personnel may have to remain at the property.** Are there stockpiles of food and water for such personnel? What about sanitation facilities? If personnel are offsite and have to return to the building, what provisions will be needed for them to access the building during a power outage (e.g., identification passes)?

- **Communications equipment may fail.** While battery-operated radios and televisions will allow access to information from outside the property, how can people outside the property be reached?

What if cell phone service is curtailed (e.g., because transmission equipment is knocked out or high traffic exceeds the capacity)? Are there hardwired phone lines available for real estate managers, building engineers, and security personnel? Are similar lines available for occupants' use?

- **Emergency power generation equipment will only run until its fuel is exhausted.** What provisions have been made to ensure a supply of fuel in an emergency? Has consideration been given to having multiple fuel sources in case a supplier is shut down?

- **Extreme outdoor temperatures may cause damage inside a building.** Do water pipes need protection from freezing? Is excessive heat and humidity likely to cause warping (e.g., of wood veneer finishes) or lead to mold growth?

It may be advisable to run an occasional test of the building power system to ensure that established emergency plans and procedures will work during a real power outage. The idea of such testing may raise concerns from commercial tenants about business interruptions. However, it makes more sense to test in advance than to wait for a real emergency to find out that a plan or procedure does not work.

An even more extensive plan may be necessary or appropriate. It may be desirable to install a gas powered, onsite generating system to provide power for the building. While this will require capital investment, the heat generated as a by-product can be used to heat and cool the property, and it may be possible to negotiate a favorable long-term contract with the gas supplier that protects the property against price fluctuations.

Partial Power Outages

A partial outage can occur when a fuse is blown, a circuit breaker is tripped, or when excessive voltage is drawn from the power system—for example, when too many pieces of electrical equipment are drawing energy from one extension cord or electrical outlet. When this occurs, simply switch the appropriate circuit breaker off, then unplug some of the electrical equipment. When you switch the circuit breaker on again, the power should return. If it does not, unplug more equipment until the outlet matches the voltage demand. Before returning to previous conditions, investigate the electrical demand of the property against what the power system will allow—it may be overloaded.

HOW TO RESPOND TO A POWER OUTAGE

Once the emergency generator starts after a power outage, the source of the outage should be immediately located. This is where the diagram of power sources and connections is helpful. Real estate managers should notify the utility company of the source and severity of the building's outage.

In addition, real estate managers should also instruct building staff to call all elevators to the ground floor to let out anyone who may be trapped. If it is safe, all stairwell doors should be unlocked to allow people free access from floor to floor. The freight elevator (where present) could be used to give emergency personnel access to the building and to transport those who may be unable to use the stairwells because they have a physical disability or other medical condition. It is also wise to activate one elevator in any parking garage that is part of the premises.

Building occupants should turn off all electrical equipment in their leased premises to prevent equipment damage from an electrical surge when power is restored. Even short lapses in power quality or a few seconds of electrical deprivation could inhibit use of elevators as well as cause data loss. Emergency generators may only be programmed to route energy to more critical voltage requirements such as elevators, electric doors, and lighting.

Real estate managers may recommend that their commercial or industrial tenants routinely backup their data—onsite or offsite. Inform all of your tenants to the potential damage to appliances or digital equipment posed by power disruption or surge. Laptops, tablets, and Smartphones are immune from surges if they are not plugged in to power or a network cable. For desktop or server systems, a battery backup power system keeps computers from being affected by power surges. Depending on the product, the backup system can provide constant power from three minutes to several hours. These products can be purchased from a local computer supplier.

For general information on the status of a blackout, occupants can send one individual to the real estate manager or onsite security desk (if available). Place a staff person (or a guard, if there is one) at the main entrances and exits to ensure that no intruders enter the building and to monitor removal of equipment from the premises.

Shutting Down Operations

Shutting down a facility is generally a last resort, but it may be necessary in extreme situations, such as a natural disaster or a major threat to a property's occupants. Some facilities require only simple actions, such as turning off equipment, locking doors, and activating alarms. Other facilities may require intricate shutdown plans. Real estate managers should work with the emergency management team to prepare for shutdown plans to include in the emergency procedures manual. The procedures should address:

- When and how to shut off each utility
- Who can order a shutdown
- Conditions that could necessitate a shutdown
- Who will carry out shutdown procedures
- How a partial shutdown would affect other facility operations
- The length of time required to complete a shutdown—and for restarting

The emergency management team should be trained in shutdown procedures. Posting shutdown procedures next to the respective equipment/system controls will allow for easy reference.

Restoring Power

If there is a power outage and a property is equipped with a backup power generator, the power will go off for approximately two or three seconds before the emergency system starts to supply electricity to corridors, emergency stairwells, exit lights, elevator communications systems, fire pumps, freight elevators, or wherever it is programmed to supply power.

When full power is restored, all emergency electrical systems will go off for approximately two or three seconds, and then they will draw full power from the utility source. After this occurs, advise your staff to restore permanent elevator service to the building as well as HVAC service. Remember that the air conditioning system will take time to cool the building, especially if the blackout lasted several hours.

The amount of power passing through the building when power is restored may trip circuit breakers. An occupant whose total electrical supply is not restored should be advised to notify the management office. Care must be taken to restore power systematically and not cause additional damage.

CHAPTER 13:
Medical Emergencies

Medical emergencies can occur any time and any place, so real estate managers should equip themselves with guidelines for treating injured or medically endangered people on their premises. A medical emergency can range from a sprained ankle or broken bone, to burns, internal bleeding, heart attack, or even death. They can be the result of a person's poor health, human action, natural or manmade disaster, accidents, or unexpected physical injuries. Real estate managers and the emergency management team should be prepared to respond quickly and effectively to a medical emergency.

AREAS AND PROPERTIES AT RISK

All properties in every area run a risk of medical emergencies. However, medical emergencies may be more likely to occur in certain types of properties. These include properties that house a large number of senior residents, commercial properties where heavy equipment or hazardous chemicals are used, and certain industrial properties.

PREVENTING HUMAN LOSS AND LIABILITY

When developing a plan for responding to medical emergencies, real estate managers should designate members of the emergency management team to be trained in lifesaving and medical treatment techniques. The best people to select are those who have a reputation for being calm, quick-thinking, and level-headed; who perform well in emergency situations, and who are most likely to be on the property when an emergency arises. Certainly, anyone with interest, background, or experience in medical emergency procedures should be considered.

The emergency procedures manual should include medical and first aid procedures. Real estate managers should create and keep current lists of:

- Organizations and phone numbers to call for emergency medical services—local hospital or trauma center and a private ambulance service should be considered along with fire/rescue services, which usually include paramedics and public ambulance services

- The names and phone numbers of property staff and occupants (residents, commercial tenants' employees) who have received accredited training in lifesaving techniques, first aid, cardiopulmonary resuscitation (CPR), and/or use of an automatic external defibrillator (AED)

The emergency procedures manual should also address the following medical emergency information, guidelines, and procedures:

- The first aid kit with a list of its contents
- First aid, CPR, and AED procedures
- Avoiding disease transmission
- Preventing occupational exposure to bloodborne pathogens
- Calling for emergency assistance (e.g., 911 service)
- Treating seniors, disabled persons, and children

Real estate managers should also ensure that management personnel and the emergency management team receive up-to-date training on these subjects.

Maintaining a First Aid Kit

The availability and proper use of first aid kit contents can often be sufficient in treating minor injuries or help sustain an injured person until necessary professional emergency care arrives.

First aid kits come in many sizes and can be purchased from a drug store, medical supply company, or local chapter of the American Red Cross. Retailers that cater to campers, boaters, and sports enthusiasts often sell first aid kits. For a large property, an industrial first aid kit or cabinet may be most appropriate. As an alternative, you can also separately purchase the items needed to make up a first aid kit. Be sure the kit contains all the necessities, remembering to check expiration dates of medicines and previously opened disinfectants. Schedule and log regular inspections of the first aid kit to verify dates and restock as needed.

In anticipation of medical emergencies, every property should have a basic first aid kit that includes an assortment of bandages in different types and sizes, disinfectant solution, pain medication, a tourniquet, soap (to clean the assistant's hands, not the injured person's wounds), and disposable gloves. A separate first aid kit may be kept in a maintenance area specifically for assisting with injuries to building staff. Other specific recommendations can be found on the American Red Cross and Federal Emergency Management Agency (FEMA) websites.

First Aid Procedures

Knowledge and timely implementation of first aid and CPR, when applied correctly, may make the difference between life and death for an injured person. When there is a major injury, first aid should be administered to the injured person until paramedics arrive on the scene. If the injured party is not breathing, or the person's heart has stopped, CPR should be administered immediately in an effort to restore heart functioning and respiration. An AED machine is a medical device used to restore the heartbeat, often installed in commercial buildings and public spaces. Specific training in AED may be needed, but the procedures are easy to learn. Some units provide instructions that include audible prompts for what to do and when to do it.

Application of first aid will depend on the type of injury. Minor cuts and scrapes can be cleaned and bandaged to protect them from infection. Heavy bleeding can be stopped with a tourniquet, but it may be preferable to simply apply pressure to the wound. The Heimlich maneuver may be used to dislodge an obstruction in the throat. More serious injuries—open wounds, internal or severe bleeding, burns—should be treated only by persons properly trained to administer the first aid that is required.

Specific first aid procedures are beyond the scope of this book, but may be found in materials offered by the American Red Cross, which also offers certification and training classes in first aid, CPR, and AED, along with informative pamphlets on responding to medical emergencies. Some classes and publications are available free of charge. Training can also be provided through specially contracted services.

GOOD SAMARITAN LAWS

Are you risking a potential lawsuit when you assist someone in an emergency situation? Most states have enacted Good Samaritan Laws, which protect people who assist victims in medical emergency situations from liability. Real estate managers should contact their local municipality or a legal professional to determine if their state has a Good Samaritan Law. The insurance company that underwrites liability coverage for the property may also be a good source of information in this regard.

According to the American Red Cross, when citizens respond to an emergency and act as a reasonable and prudent person would under the same conditions, Good Samaritan immunity generally prevails. This legal immunity protects the rescuer from being sued and found financially liable for the victim's injury. Keep in mind, however, that states with this law have had lawsuits enforced in which the judge ruled that the rescuer was grossly or willfully negligent or reckless in his or her medical assistance efforts. This underlines the necessity for the emergency management team to be properly trained in first aid and CPR procedures.

The following lists examples of reasonable and prudent emergency medical assistance efforts that should be made by a rescuer:

- Summoning professional help to the scene by calling 911 or other emergency assistance
- Asking a conscious victim for permission before providing care
- Checking the victim for life-threatening injuries before providing further care
- Moving a victim only if the victim's life is endangered
- Continuing to provide care until a medical professional arrives

As a safeguard, real estate managers should keep accurate records of injuries and fatalities occurring on the property, and if possible, take a photograph of the scene. Personal injury reports should include information such as who was injured; when, where, why, and how the injury occurred; names and contact information of any witnesses present; time and date of the incident; and which medical assistance service responded to the call for help. Recording other details such as the weather, lighting, condition of the surface, or the victim's apparel may also be helpful. An example of an emergency incident report form is included in *Chapter 6* (pg. 65).

AVOIDING TRANSMISSION OF DISEASE

Imagine that a person injured on your property is bleeding. You want to help, but you are afraid of catching an infection or disease from the open wound. It is important to know how diseases are transmitted and how to protect yourself when providing first aid.

Infectious diseases can pass from one person to another through transmission of bacteria or viruses from contact with blood (bloodborne pathogens) and other body fluids. In administering first aid, such transmission can take place through touching, breathing, and biting, through contact of one person's body fluids with those of the other person. Germs can be transmitted through breaks or cuts in the skin or through the mucous membranes lining the eyes, nose, and mouth. A primary concern is the transmission of human immunodeficiency virus (HIV), which causes acquired immunodeficiency syndrome (AIDS), and the hepatitis B virus. The following list provides some basic guidelines that can help you reduce disease transmission in the event of administering first aid:

- Avoid contact with body fluids when possible.
- Place barriers, such as disposable gloves or a clean dry cloth, between the injured party's body fluids and yourself.
- Wash your hands with soap and water immediately after giving care.
- Do not drink or eat or touch your mouth, eyes, or nose when giving first aid.
- Do not touch objects that may be soiled with blood or bodily fluids.
- Use the compression-only CPR method.

Remember that the likelihood of HIV transmission during first aid is very low. Always try to give first aid in ways that protect you and the victim from disease transmission.

OCCUPATIONAL EXPOSURE TO BLOODBORNE PATHOGENS: THE OSHA STANDARD

Real estate managers should be aware of the Occupational Safety and Health Administration (OSHA) standard on occupational exposure to bloodborne pathogens—disease-causing viruses and bacteria. The standard applies to employees who could be "reasonably anticipated" to face contact with blood and other potentially infectious materials as a result of performing their job duties. This means that the standard is not limited to workers in the healthcare industry. Property management staff such as security, general maintenance, and engineering personnel who are assigned to apply basic first aid techniques in case of an accident are at potential risk of exposure—especially during a medical emergency. OSHA regulations outline the following employer requirements:

- **Exposure control plan**—requires employers to identify, in writing, tasks and procedures as well as job classifications where occupational exposure to blood occurs—without regard to personal protective clothing and equipment. The plan should include procedures for evaluating the circumstances surrounding exposure incidents, along with a schedule and method for implementing other provisions of the standard. The plan must be accessible to employees and available to OSHA for examination. Employers must review and update it at least once a year—more often if necessary to accommodate workplace changes.

- **Methods of compliance**—mandates universal precautions, treating body fluids or materials as if infectious. It stresses hand washing, requiring employers to provide facilities, and ensure that employees use them after exposure to blood. It requires employers to provide protective equipment such as gloves. It requires a written schedule for cleaning and decontamination as well as handling of contaminated laundry.

- **Post-exposure evaluation and follow-up**—requires employers to make available confidential medical evaluation and follow-up, documenting the circumstances of exposure, identifying and testing the source individual if feasible, testing the exposed employee's blood (if he or she consents), post-exposure prophylactic treatment, counseling, and evaluation of reported illnesses.

- **Hazard communication**—requires warning labels including the fluorescent orange or orange-red biohazard symbol affixed to waste containers and to refrigerators, freezers, and other containers used to store or transport blood or other infectious materials. Red bags or containers may be used instead of the labels. Janitorial workers should be especially aware of such labels and the potential hazards they warn against.

- **Information and training**—training, initially upon assignment and annually thereafter, that includes the text and an explanation of the OSHA regulation, a general discussion of bloodborne diseases and their transmission, the company's exposure control plan, engineering and workplace practices, use of personal protective equipment, hepatitis vaccinations, responding to emergencies involving blood, handling exposure incidents, post-exposure evaluation and follow-up, and the requisite hazard labeling or color coding. The American Red Cross offers specific training in preventing disease transmission from bloodborne pathogens that complies with the OSHA regulation.

- **Record keeping**—Calls for confidential medical records to be kept for each employee with occupational exposure for the duration of employment plus 30 years. Training records must be maintained for three years and must include dates, contents of the training program, the trainer's name and qualifications, and the names and job titles of all persons attending the sessions. Medical records must be made available to the subject employee, anyone to whom the employee gives written consent, OSHA, and the National Institute of Safety and Health (NIOSH). They are *not* available to the employer.

Bloodborne Pathogens Training Program

In order to safeguard employees from exposure to bloodborne pathogens and to ensure compliance with OSHA regulations, real estate managers should contact their regional OSHA office or corresponding state agency to request a professional safety consultation.

Bloodborne pathogens training programs vary depending upon the type of property, tenant mix, visitors to the property, and other variables. A training program includes, but is not limited to, the following segments:

- **Introduction**—The introduction provides an overview of the goals and objectives of the training program. The trainer must explain how people can contract the hepatitis B and HIV and also discuss the importance of universal precautions. The American Medical Association (AMA) provides technical explanations of bloodborne pathogens and ways medical professionals should protect themselves from infection. The AMA also has information on bloodborne pathogens for non-healthcare employees, which helps to relate the issues to the general workplace. Also, consult with OSHA for current and new resources to augment a bloodborne pathogens training program.

- **Discussion of the concept of universal precautions**—The training program cannot emphasize enough that the bodily fluids of all persons and animals should be considered to contain potentially infectious agents and that universal precautions must be practiced. Universal precautions or universal blood and bodily fluid precautions refer to the handling of all types of bodily fluids.

- **Training session records**—A record of all training sessions must be maintained. The record should include the date of the training, who conducted the training session, the session's agenda, and a list of each person in attendance.

- **Hepatitis B vaccine**—Employees who have occupational exposure to bloodborne pathogens should be offered the hepatitis B vaccine.

DURING A MEDICAL EMERGENCY

The emergency procedures manual should state specifically who should be contacted in the event of a medical emergency after 911 has been called. Unless trained and educated in specific medical procedures, real estate managers and other members of the emergency management team are best advised to leave medical treatment, beyond first aid and CPR, to medical technicians, nurses, and doctors.

If first aid and CPR can be helpful, however, those educated and trained in these procedures should administer them immediately to the injured party.

Calling for Emergency Assistance

Calling for help is often the most important step in aiding a victim. A member of the emergency management team, or anyone present at the scene, should call the local emergency assistance number as soon as possible, without leaving the injured party unassisted. Most communities have 911 service that dispatches police, firefighters, and paramedics to respond to emergencies.

Communities that do not have 911 service may have separate emergency phone numbers for police and fire services—it is important to have the correct number to call. Where programmable telephones are in use, the different emergency numbers can be entered so they can be called by touching a single button.

If the victim is unconscious, call 911 immediately. At times, a conscious victim may tell you he or she is "OK," but the 911 number might need to be called regardless. The following lists situations and warning signs of serious injury that might warrant a 911 call:

- Current or impending unconsciousness
- Inability to breath or labored breathing
- Pain or pressure in the chest or abdomen
- Severe bleeding
- Vomiting or passing of blood from nose, mouth, or other body openings
- Seizures, severe headaches, or slurred speech
- Head, neck, or back injuries
- Possible internal poisoning
- Possible broken bones
- The victim cannot be moved easily

Be prepared to provide the following information to the 911 or emergency assistance dispatcher:

- The exact location or address of the emergency, including the name of the city or town, and nearby intersections or landmarks
- The telephone number you are calling from
- Your name
- What happened to the injured party and his or her physical condition
- How many people are involved
- What medical treatment/first aid is currently being administered

The information you provide is vital in allowing the dispatcher to send the specific medical help that is needed. The dispatcher may also be able to tell you how to best care for the injured party until the ambulance arrives. Once the dispatcher hangs up, return and continue to care for the injured party. Do not hang up first because the dispatcher may need additional information. If possible, assign someone to watch for the arrival of emergency medical personnel and guide them to the person or persons needing assistance.

Treating People with Special Needs

Particular groups of people are more susceptible to injuries, and therefore, special precautions should be taken. These include children, people with disabilities, and senior residents.

Children. Accidents are the leading cause of death among children and teenagers. Because of this, real estate managers need to be prepared to prevent accidents and attendant injuries. They must also be prepared to address injuries to children resulting from accidents, most prominently those involving motor vehicles, falls, poisonings, drownings, and fires.

Checking an ill or injured child can be difficult. An injured child may be frightened as well as hurt. Younger children may not be able to communicate about an accident or their injuries. The American Red Cross makes the following recommendations:

- Observe the physical condition before touching an injured child. A child's condition may change when they are touched because they can become anxious or upset, especially with strangers.

- Remain calm. Caring for injured children can be stressful. Showing the child you are relaxed and confident will help keep the child and parent calm.

- Communicate clearly with the parent or guardian of the child. When you can help the adults relax, the child will relax, too. Talk slowly and use simple words. Calmly telling the child what you are going to do to help treat the injury will earn his or her trust.

- Do not separate the loved ones from the child unless necessary. The child will need their emotional support.

Disabled Persons. People who are physically disabled can be just as seriously injured as any other injured person, but if they are paralyzed to any extent, they may not be able to detect their injury. Attempts should be made to observe the victim's external physical condition before administering first aid; in any event, the victim's limbs and torso should be moved as little as possible.

Senior Residents. As people age, they experience a general decline in body functions. The heart rate slows and blood vessels harden, causing the heart to work harder. As a result of weakening bones and slower reflexes, sensory perceptions, and balance difficulties, seniors have a higher chance of falling and injuring themselves.

Because the size of the human brain decreases with age, there is more space between the brain and the skull, increasing the possibility of head injury. Because of this, seniors should always be checked for head injuries by a medical professional.

Seniors are also at increased risk for strokes and diseases as their nervous systems weaken. If care is being provided for a victim who appears confused, the rescuer should try to speak up and be as clear as possible, so to communicate with the victim to ascertain if an injury has been sustained. Also, bear in mind that victims may not recognize serious physical conditions, and may even downplay their physical state out of fear of the loss of independence.

At all times, senior victims—or victims of any age—should be treated with respect and concern. It is helpful to check the victim's medications, if possible, and inform the professional medical assistance team of his or her identity. The medical team should also be informed of any first aid or assistance that was administered to victims before their arrival.

AFTER A MEDICAL EMERGENCY

When a medical emergency is the result of an accident on the property, the area where the accident occurred should be inspected. There may be debris and residual body fluids to be cleaned up. In addition, the practices discussed in *Chapter 4* regarding safeguarding the property from further damage may be necessary, depending on the nature of the emergency.

OTHER WAYS TO PREVENT INJURIES

Also important in preventing human injury or liability is for the real estate manager to ensure that the property is safe and in good physical condition. Management personnel should remove all potentially dangerous items and obstacles that might lead to trip-and-fall incidents and injuries from public areas. Maintenance work that creates slippery floors should be announced with appropriate signage. Crevices and cracks in sidewalks and paved areas should be filled, and overgrown hedges should be trimmed to avoid interference on walkways. Air conditioning and heating systems should be checked and cleaned regularly to avoid illness from air contamination. Accommodations for disabled people should comply with guidelines of the Americans with Disabilities Act (ADA).

Real estate managers can evaluate their property to identify potential accidents that are waiting to happen on the premises and correct them up front through preventive maintenance and preservation of safe building conditions.

CHAPTER 14:

Dealing with Fires of All Types

Fire deaths occur most frequently in multifamily residences and single-family homes when fires are out of control and occupants are unable to escape. These victims have been disproportionally children, seniors, and those who were unable to flee from the home—even if a smoke detector sounded an alarm. It is perhaps surprising that the primary cause of fire deaths is not the fire itself, but smoke inhalation—the carbon monoxide in smoke can be lethal. Smoke can also impede escape by obscuring routes to safety.

The most effective tactic to minimize fire damage is to put out the fire while it is still small. A fire may smolder for hours before bursting into flames and can then consume an entire room within two minutes. Ideally, a fire should be extinguished by an individual that has been trained on proper use of a fire extinguisher—attempting to extinguish a fire without proper training could possibly lead to further disaster. The best advice is to call the fire department immediately whenever there is a fire, unless the fire is small enough to extinguish on your own.

THE TYPES OF PROPERTIES AT RISK FOR FIRES

According to statistics compiled by the Fire Analysis and Research Division of the National Fire Protection Association (NFPA), 1,331,500 fires were attended by public fire departments in the U.S. in 2010. Of that total number of fires, 482,000 (31 percent) occurred in structures, 369,500 of them in residential properties, and 215,500 occurred in vehicles. The remainder—some 634,000 fires—occurred in "outside properties" including brush and timber, farm crops, outside storage facilities, and dumpsters. What these statistics mean is that a fire occurs in a structure every 24 seconds; in particular, a residential fire occurs every 65 seconds.

In 2010, there were a total of 2,665 civilian fire deaths—2,640 (99 percent) were in the home. There were 15,420 civilian fire injuries in 2010—13,350 occurred in residential properties. Nationwide, there was a civilian fire death every 169 minutes and a civilian fire injury every 30 minutes.

Property damage from fires was estimated at $11.6 billion. Structure fires accounted for $9.7 billion of damage, $7.2 billion of which was in residential properties. The latter breaks down into $5.9 billion in one- and two-family residences and $1.3 billion in apartments or multifamily dwellings.

Very few high-rise fires expand beyond the floor or room of origin because many high-rises employ such preventive measures as heat and smoke detectors, sprinkler systems, and fire-resistive construction. If people die in high-rise residential fires, they are much more likely to have been in close proximity to the fire. Statistics on high-rise fires are included in Figure 14.1

Older structures are at great risk. This is due to a number of factors, but most notably, these properties tend to lack:

- Adequate heating systems
- Safe electrical appliances
- Construction in accordance with strict electrical and building codes
- Use of fire stops in walls
- Access for fire-fighting equipment
- Modern fire-resistant building materials

The U.S. Fire Administration advocates the use of automatic fire sprinklers in residential buildings. Advocates also praise the National Residential Fire Sprinkler Initiative, which requires residential sprinkler systems in new construction of manufactured homes, college dormitories, and residential units owned, leased, subsidized, or otherwise supported by the federal government.

Because building and fire codes are subject to change, real estate managers should keep up to date with applicable requirements and be sure that their buildings are in compliance.

PREVENTIVE MEASURES

Every property is vulnerable to fires. To determine what these vulnerabilities are, a real estate manager can arrange a walk-through of the premises with fire department personnel to inspect fire and alarm systems. This type of inspection includes evaluating the adequacy of the current emergency announcer system and the fire control panel. Each sprinkler head and fire hose should have a flow switch monitored at the fire control panel. The fire control panel should be monitored around the clock in case of any after-hour alarm emergencies and should be inspected annually (or as required)

FIGURE 14.1

STATISTICS ON FIRES AND FIRE LOSS BETWEEN 2006 TO 2010

The National Fire Protection Association (NFPA) reported the following statistics:

Building Type	No. of Fires	Civilian Deaths	Civilian Injuries	Property Damage
One- and Two-Family	279,000	2,200	9,400	$5.9 billion
Apartment Structures	90,500	440	3,350	$1,003,000*
High-Rise Buildings	15,700	53	546	$235,000,000
Industrial	42,800	22	300	$951 billion
Office Properties	3,830	4	37	$108,000,000

* Does not include $809 million in damage caused by Southern California Wildfires

Source: *The U.S. Fire Problem Overview Report: Leading Causes and Other Patterns and Trends* (Quincy, Mass.: National Fire Protection Association, 2003).

The NFPA also prepared statistics for the average fires in high-rise buildings that are seven or more stories tall in between 2005 and 2009.

Building Type	No. of Fires	Civilian Deaths	Civilian Injuries	Property Damage
Apartments	6,900	29	320	$44,000,000
Office Buildings	300	0	0	$4,000,000
All Structures	15,700	53	546	$235,000,000

Source: *High-Rise Building Fires* (Quincy, Mass.: National Fire Protection Association, 2011).

for any malfunction or required repairs.

Real estate managers should work with fire officials when developing a fire safety plan. They should also ask whether the alarm system should be connected directly to the fire department. One should not be dependent on a single fire alarm system. If it fails, the building may be unprotected. It is best to evaluate a variety of alarm systems. The following are some fire safety systems that could be employed:

- A supervised automatic sprinkler system.
- A Class I standpipe system.
- A fire alarm system with an approved emergency voice and alarm communication system.
- Emergency lighting standby power and a central control station.

Automatically activated fire alarm systems may have a direct line to the local fire department through a central station (in accordance with NFPA standards). It may be appropriate to consider retrofitting a building with sprinklers. This may have to be done if local fire codes require sprinklers in existing buildings. Standpipes are usually installed as part of new construction. The cost of installing fire sprinklers depends on several factors:

- Proximity to water supplies
- Building and space use
- Degree of compartmentalization
- Building size
- Building construction materials
- Building complexity
- Quickness of response

It is a good idea to consult a fire-prevention expert regarding complex buildings and situations. In complex or specialized buildings, it may be most appropriate to have a single integrated fire system that is monitored 24 hours a day. Real estate managers can develop a three-way approach to fire prevention that includes:

1. A detection system
2. A way to compartmentalize the fire, using code-approved fire walls and floors, UL-labeled doors, or smoke-activated doors that are held open until they are released by fire or smoke alarms and still permit people to exit through them
3. A method of extinguishing a fire using sprinklers and other extinguishers

Fire extinguishers and fire extinguishing systems may use a variety of compounds to extinguish a fire. These include:

- Halon (halogenated hydrocarbon) for computer rooms
- Water
- Wet and dry foam
- Carbon dioxide
- Dry chemical

Fire Extinguishers

Portable fire extinguishers should be installed within easy reach and near a door for easy access, and to ensure a safe escape route for the user. The following lists some other fire and life safety measures to consider implementing:

- Paint floor numbers boldly on the stair side of hall exit doors or the adjacent wall.

> ### TYPES OF FIRE EXTINGUISHERS
>
> Fire extinguishers have several designations, depending on their intended use:
> - **Class A:** Water based; used to extinguish fires in wood, cloth, paper, etc.
> - **Class B:** Chemical based; used to extinguish fires involving gasoline, oil, solvents, and other flammable liquids.
> - **Class C:** Dry chemical; used to extinguish fires in electrical equipment, wiring, etc.
> - **Class ABC:** Multipurpose; can be used on all types of fires.
>
> Other classes of fires require special extinguishing materials. Fire extinguishers are labeled to indicate the types of fires they can be used against.

- Install smoke detectors in corridors, common areas, and elevators.

- Install a speaker system to guide in evacuations.

- Form a fire brigade with help and training from fire officials. The brigade would be responsible for: extinguishing small fires; contacting the fire department in the event of a fire; and evacuating occupants, property employees, and others on the premises.

- Test fire equipment according to local fire codes. Equipment to be tested includes alarm systems, fire extinguishers, sprinklers, exit doors and exit lights, and smoke detectors.

- Consider inviting fire officials to the property for inspections so they become familiar with the property—this could be advantageous in the event of a fire.

- Provide fire-safety education and training for occupants as well as your employees.

- Post all fire regulations and instructions prominently.

- On each floor, prominently post a scale drawing of the floor showing exits and evacuation routes.

- Make sure occupants are always able to exit through designated fire doors and that none of the doors are locked or obstructed. All exits should be mapped and posted.

- Post signs warning people not to use the elevators in case of a fire.

- Learn which fire extinguishers are used for the specific types of fires. Real estate managers, management employees, and occupants (residents and commercial tenants' employees) should know where they are located and how to work them.

- Designate non-smoking areas in the building and enforce them.
- Take special care during the holiday seasons when decorations could create fire hazards.

To combat a loss of power or the presence of heavy smoke, use photoluminescent (glow-in-the-dark) exit signs with directional arrows and self-adhesive tapes that can be used to provide additional visual cues during an evacuation. These types of exit signs are often placed low on a wall (i.e., above the baseboard). The tape may be placed on the floor in stairwells or corridors or around stairwell door frames, preferably in areas that are normally lit 24 hours a day.

Aside from the obvious benefits of implementing fire prevention and safety precautions, having such a program can be a significant marketing tool. A sound fire safety program can encourage safety-conscious prospective residents and commercial tenants to locate in a given property.

Smoke Detectors

The best way to reduce fire deaths is to prevent fires, and fire experts agree that one of the most effective fire prevention tactics is an early-warning

SOME FIRE PREVENTION AND SAFETY TIPS

- Keep storage areas clean; do not let files, empty cartons, waste, or rags collect.
- Keep heating appliances away from walls and combustible materials.
- Encourage occupants not to stack or store items close to fire sprinkler heads, where they may hinder the flow of water when the system is actuated.
- Inspect electrical equipment. Does it work properly? Does it give off an unusual odor? Are cords frayed or cracked? Are cords placed where they will be stepped on or chafed? Is there more than one extension cord per outlet?
- Ensure that deadbolts and other locks work quickly and easily.
- Be sure that windows open and close easily.
- For commercial, office, or industrial properties, specify how cooking appliances are to be used, including what types of appliances are permitted. Typically, hot plates are prohibited, and microwave popcorn is specifically discouraged because it burns easily and sets off smoke alarms. As a general rule, stoves and open-flame cooking are not permitted in office buildings other than in food service establishments.

system to get people out as quickly as possible. The best way to provide the earliest warning is to install an adequate number of smoke detectors.

There are two types of smoke detectors—(1) ionization detectors that activate quicker for fast, flaming fires and (2) photoelectric detectors that are quicker for slow, smoldering fires. Both types of detectors will provide sufficient warning. Smoke detectors emit a very loud audible signal when potentially dangerous levels of smoke are detected in the indoor air. If there are hearing-impaired people on the property, smoke alarms that flash a light or vibrate should also be available.

Smoke detectors should be installed on each floor in residences and buildings. Manufacturers' instructions for installation will often recommend specific locations—local ordinances may specify multiple locations for installation. Smoke detectors may be powered by electrical current or batteries or a combination (hard wired with battery backup). Battery-powered detectors should be tested periodically to confirm that the battery has not expired. Many fires have raged out of control simply because the resident has neglected to replace a defunct smoke detector battery.

Carbon Monoxide Detectors

Carbon monoxide (CO) originates from faulty gas furnaces, gas stoves, automobile exhaust seeping in through attached garages, and fireplaces. Odorless and colorless, CO cannot be easily detected, so victims experiencing symptoms of increasingly intense drowsiness may be unaware of the immediate danger. Due to the high number of deaths in homes resulting from carbon monoxide poisoning, many local building codes require CO alarms in residences that use gas or oil or have a fireplace. Like smoke detectors, CO detectors can be hardwired, battery operated, or hardwired with battery backup. Batteries should be tested regularly and replaced as needed. The sensor element in CO alarms must also be replaced regularly. Real estate managers would be wise to inspect a property for potential pipe breaks or leaks and install carbon monoxide detectors where appropriate. The gas company may also be asked to send a representative to check for gas leaks.

Fire Command Stations

Fire command stations are another option for properties to use in fire prevention and response. The stations are equipped with fire command panels, which display locations and floors where fire alarms and other emergency alarms are sounded. Many are also equipped with handheld microphones, which allow authorities with key access to make building-wide announcements. This enables quick notification of evacuation for specific floors or the entire building. Telephone intercoms allow the person at the control panel to talk to floor monitors to assess fire conditions.

HOW TO RESPOND DURING A FIRE

No matter how small a fire appears to be, the fire department should always be contacted. This should be emphasized as the first instruction in a fire response plan. Moreover, it should never be assumed that someone else has already called the fire department.

The following procedures should be included in the emergency procedures manual in special cases dealing with fires:

- Shut off power to the fire area. Provide specific instructions and assign this task to a member of the emergency management team.
- Close as many doors as possible while escaping from a fire to prevent the fire from spreading; however, do not endanger yourself by doing so.
- Get down, and keep low. Smoke rises; the cleanest air is nearest to the floor.

The following lists special instructions for residents, tenants, and other staff members when leaving a building during a fire:

- Maintain contact with a wall.
- Use handrails while descending stairs.
- Take off high-heeled or awkward shoes.
- Test doors before opening by putting the back of your hand to them. If the door is hot, find another way out. If it is cool, open the door slowly and carefully, and be ready to close it quickly if heat or smoke pours in.
- Walk calmly; never panic or shove others.
- If clothing catches fire, stop, drop, and roll. Do not panic and run; this will only fan the flames. Cover your face with your hands. Never beat at the flames with your hands; rather, smother them with your body.
- Fabric, preferably wet, may also be used to cover your mouth to better respiration.
- After escaping the building and getting to the street, move away

from the building. Do not block firefighters and equipment.

- Be careful of falling glass.

The following lists general guidelines on what to do if you cannot escape:

- Try to find a room with an exterior window, and stay there until help arrives.
- Call the fire department, if possible, and let personnel know exactly where you are.
- Open the window slightly to allow in fresh air and to create positive air pressure to help keep out smoke.
- Keep smoke out by sealing cracks and covering vents with clothing, newspapers, towels, etc.
- If possible, breathe through a wet cloth.
- Wave something brightly colored out the window to attract attention.
- Keep in mind that most fire department ladders do not reach above six floors, which means that other methods will be used for a rescue on higher floors.

Where appropriate, members of the emergency management team and other specially trained personnel should administer first aid and tend to people who are injured. Use only water to soothe burns; never apply salve or butter. Professional medical attention is needed for serious injuries or burns. Those victims should be immediately transported to a hospital or trauma center. (See *Chapter 13* for more information on medical emergencies.)

RECOVERY AFTER A FIRE

The fire department has jurisdiction until the fire is put out. They must release control or give permission to re-enter before anything can be done. Real estate managers may be overwhelmed with responsibilities after a fire. There may not be time to think about exactly what must be done and in what order. That is why the duties in the aftermath of a fire should be detailed in the emergency procedures manual.

Identifying the Needs of Occupants

One of the first actions to take should be dealing with the needs of tenants or residents. Does anyone need medical attention or emergency services? Is everyone accounted for? Remember that tenants and residents are impacted just as much as management staff, especially if a disaster forces them out of their home or business.

Notifying the Proper Contacts

Notify the building owner, insurance company, and—where necessary—disaster recovery services or contractors. Follow instructions provided by the building owner and insurance company with regard to preparing for recovery. For insurance purposes, be sure not to disturb anything at the fire site before proper authorities have investigated the site to determine a cause.

Recovery and Response Procedures

Your emergency procedures manual should come in handy here, as it outlines the steps that should be taken for the property following a disaster. *Chapter 4* explains the importance of securing the area and preventing further loss or damage to the asset. Begin by covering broken windows with plywood or plastic, fixing doors that have been burned or broken by firefighters responding to the emergency.

It's important that all action is done in compliance with all fire department requests, particularly as investigations into the cause of the fire may be ongoing.

Arrange to have power restored to areas of the property damaged in the fire. This may require assistance from the utility company. As power is restored, arrange for a certified electrician to thoroughly check the electrical system—provided you have been cleared by the fire department to do so.

Communicating with Cleanup Crews

Cleaning and restoring a property is no small feat, particularly after a disaster. Devise a cleaning schedule and cleanup crews. Inspect the property in waves, being aware at all times of the potential material hazards in the building. Following a fire, materials such as friable or burned asbestos or loosened lead paint can become hazardous materials. It's possible that structural elements of the building may also be impacted. Wear proper safety gear such as protective glasses, gloves, and hard hats while restoring a property.

Begin your restoration efforts with common areas of the property so that they may be used by the remainder of the building's occupants. While restoring an area, focus on restoring an area to a safe, clean condition before focusing on detailed work. It's more important to dehumidify, remove water, soot, glass, and debris than to ensure the floor surface has its normal level of polish. Do not attempt to wash walls, ceilings, or porous surfaces. This work should not be undertaken without supervision, as many cleaning techniques can actually worsen the damage.

Contacting Specialists

Several aspects of the recovery plan may need to involve outside contractors. Some of these include:

- Elevator technicians to verify the elevator is safe for use, as well has having elevators cleaned to prevent redistributing soot and odors to other floors
- Disaster restoration contractors, if appropriate, to evaluate the damage and provide specialized clean-up services
- Professionals to ascertain if mold has begun to grow in the walls
- Account for all expenses related to damage caused by the fire.
- Notify affected occupants of the damage and the status of restoration; it is important to keep residents or commercial tenants apprised of progress with the cleanup

FIRES AS A RESULT OF OTHER DISASTERS

Fires can accompany other disasters as part of an event or in its aftermath. An earthquake can damage natural gas pipelines, propane containers, and gasoline tanks in vehicles causing leaks of materials that could explode or ignite. Alternative heating devices used during winter storms, tornadoes, hurricanes, or floods can pose fire hazards if they are not used properly. Generators used during power outages can also be hazardous unless they are properly used and maintained. Pools of water from floods or storms can be electrically charged, which can lead to an electrical fire. Fire safety should be a consideration in planning for other types of disasters. The U.S. Fire Administration has published a series of fact sheets on fire during and after different types of disasters.

DEALING WITH WILDFIRES

In certain parts of the U.S., forest and brush fires—i.e., wildfires—pose a particular threat to properties. Susceptible regions have been known to yield thousands of acres to raging fires that have started in open prairies, fields, or forests, or on properties on which the flames spread by contact with dry grass or vegetation. This devastation has occurred within days. The National Interagency Fire Center (NIFC), reports that 74,126 wildfires occurred in 2011—these fires affected more than 8.7 million acres. The number of wildfires is ultimately not as severe as the amount of land that they impact. For instance, 2000 remains one of the worst years for wildfires in the U.S. by volume with 122,827 fires. However, those fires involved approximately 8.4 million acres.

While they often begin unnoticed, wildfires spread quickly, by igniting brush, trees, and buildings in their path. Drought conditions contribute to wildfires, but most are started by people who are careless with fire.

Areas and Properties at Risk for Wildfires

Wildfires occur in chaparral regions—areas characterized by hot dry summers, cool moist winters, and dominated by dense growth of mostly small-leaved evergreen shrubs. Such regions in the U.S. are predominantly in California and the western region. Although brush, canyon, and forest fires can occur at any time, the principal fire season is usually from May through October.

Preventive Measures

A number of measures can be implemented to minimize human and property loss attributable to wildfires. Obtain local building codes and weed abatement ordinances that apply to structures built near wooded areas and take steps to comply with them as appropriate.

It might also be advisable to use elements of the property landscaping as a fire prevention measure. Consider the following in your landscaping design:

- For at least 30 feet—or to the property line, whichever is nearer— trim any brush that could catch fire to a maximum height of two inches.
- For another 70 feet—or to the property line, whichever is nearer— trim all brush to a maximum height of 18 inches.

OTHER WILDFIRE PREVENTION TACTICS

How you design your landscaping is only part of what can be done to prevent the spread of wildfires. Consider the following suggestions that can be made to your property's exterior.

- Screen chimney openings, using one-half-inch-thick mesh, to prevent sparks from escaping.
- Keep piles of firewood away from combustible items.
- Keep long garden hoses hooked up and ready to use around the property to squelch fires if necessary.
- Keep lawn chairs, wicker and canvas furniture, and patio umbrellas away from buildings on the property.
- Coordinate with adjoining properties to take preventive measures.
- Use caution when clearing open spaces, especially if electrical or gasoline-powered equipment is being used. Sparks generated when equipment runs into rocks or other foreign items can cause a fire.
- Keep hoses connected and ready to extinguish any fire that starts.
- Have a cell phone available to expedite calling the fire department.

- Prune trees away from roofs. Clip trees and shrubbery that over-hang adjoining properties.
- Prune branches to a height of 8–10 feet and keep trees adjacent to buildings free of dead wood.
- Plant fire-resistant ground cover (e.g., perennial grasses, ivies, ice plants).
- Do not remove low-growing ground cover.
- Properly dispose of all waste material, including dead vegetation, daily trash, accumulated waste, trimmed and clipped brush, and roof debris.

Federal grants may be available to property owners through National Park Service programs to help pay the costs of major investments in fire prevention—for example, the Wildland Urban Interface Initiative (WUII) which helps to protect areas where homes meet wildlands.

What to Do During and After a Wildfire

If a building catches fire as a result of a wildfire, the procedures that should be followed during and afterward are the same as for other types of fires.

People should also proceed with caution when returning to an area burned by a wildfire. Lingering hot spots can burst into flame without warning. It is important to check for sparks and extinguish them.

Real estate managers should also be aware of potentially devastating consequences of wildfires, including landslides and debris flow (or mudslides). In areas where vegetation is destroyed, surface soil has nothing to hold it in place. Heavy rains can wash the surface soil away, taking structures with it (see the discussion on landslides in *Chapter 19*).

WHEN TO FIGHT A FIRE

Fight the fire only if all of the following are true:

- Everyone has left or is leaving the building
- The fire department is being called
- The fire is small and confined to the immediate areas where it started (wastebasket, cushion, small appliance, etc.)
- You can fight the fire with your back to a safe escape route
- Your extinguisher is rated for the type of fire you are fighting and is in good working order
- You have had training in the use of the extinguisher and are confident you can effectively operate it

If you have the slightest doubt about whether or not to fight the fire—DON'T! Instead, get out and close the door behind you.

If you do fight the fire, remember the word **PASS**:

PULL   Pull the pin. Some extinguishers require releasing a lock latch, pressing a puncture lever, or other motion

AIM   Aim low, pointing the extinguisher nozzle (or its horn or hose) at the base of the fire.

SQUEEZE Squeeze the handle. This releases the extinguishing agent.

SWEEP   Sweep from side to side at the base of the fire until it appears to be out. Watch the fire area in case a fire breaks out again, and repeat use of the extinguisher if necessary.

Most portable extinguishers work according to these directions, but some do not. Read and follow the directions on your extinguisher.

CHAPTER 15:

Winter Storms and Water Damage

Real estate managers who manage properties in Snowbelt communities know that severe winter storms, heavy snowfall, and extreme cold that frequent their area can paralyze a city and immobilize an entire region.

Severe snowstorms or blizzards bring heavy snow, ice, strong winds, and battering freezing rain. They can disrupt communities by impeding road, rail, and air travel, as well as disrupt access for people seeking medical attention, retrieving supplies, and obtaining assistance from emergency services such as fire departments. Powerful winds can knock down trees, utility poles, and power lines. Structures can be severely damaged from wind gusts of 100 mph or more, coupled with the threat that heavy snow and ice can have on structural damage, including roof collapse. Delivery of vital services in such conditions can be delayed for days.

Four physical factors characterize severe winter storms—(1) strong winds, (2) extreme cold, (3) ice storms, and (4) heavy snowstorms.

- Storms with strong winds create blizzard conditions with blinding, wind-driven and drifting snow and dangerous wind chill factors.

- The extreme cold that accompanies a storm, or follows in its aftermath, can become life threatening to humans and animals. Pipes may freeze and burst in buildings that are poorly insulated or unheated. Ice jams may form on rivers and streams and result in flooding.

- Ice storms, characterized by freezing rain or hail, can cause overwhelming accumulations of ice that can bring down trees and utility poles and lines, which can disrupt power and communications for days. Even small accumulations of ice can cause slippery conditions that are hazardous for pedestrians as well as motorists.

- Heavy snowstorms can bring such large accumulations of snow that traffic cannot move. Building structures collapse under the weight of snow, ice, and slush. The cost of snow removal and restoration, as well as loss of business, can cause significant economic losses for property owners.

The physical effects of severe winter storms can be fatal. People exposed to cold weather for prolonged periods of time face the risks of frostbite, hypothermia, and other medical problems. Infants and seniors are especially susceptible to the cold. Strong, sometimes unpredictable storms can create a challenge for unprepared real estate managers.

AREAS AND PROPERTIES AT RISK

Properties located in areas that routinely experience heavy snowstorms are at risk of experiencing similar weather patterns in the future. Because weather systems vary, even areas that normally experience mild winters can fall prey to severe winter storms. In fact, these areas may be even more vulnerable, as neither the properties nor the municipalities may be prepared to meet the needs of residents and commercial tenants or the community. For example, water pipes may not be as insulated in traditionally warm regions of Texas as they would in upstate New York, or other areas that traditionally experience colder climates.

For example, in Alaska, intense storms and wind-driven waves can cause coastal flooding and drive large chunks of sea ice inland, destroying buildings near the shore. In the mountains, the snow builds glaciers, but heavy accumulations of snow can also cause avalanches or collapse building roofs. High winds across the Arctic coast can combine with loose snow to produce blinding blizzards and wind chill temperatures of -90°F. Temperatures of -40°F to -60°F and icy fog may last for days.

Lake effect snow is also a common occurrence, especially near the Great Lakes, which is produced by cooler atmospheric conditions. Cold winds move across long stretches of warmer lake water, providing energy and picking up water vapor, freezing it, and depositing it on the lakeshore. Lake-effect snow can produce narrow but very intense bands of precipitation, which fall at a rate of several inches of snow per hour.

WEATHER ADVISORIES AND WARNINGS

The National Weather Service (NWS) and public broadcast facilities provide warnings and advisories on the progress of severe winter storms and other weather conditions. In order to be prepared for snowstorms, real estate managers need to be aware of the types of weather and the extremes that it can take. The most frequent type of winter weather is categorized in the following list:

- **Flurries**—short periods of light snowfall with little or no accumulation
- **Showers**—brief periods of snow falling at varying intensities with some accumulation possible
- **Squalls**—brief, intense snow showers accompanied by strong, gusty winds and significant accumulation of snow
- **Blowing or wind-driven snow**—snow that reduces visibility and causes significant drifting. The snow may be falling and/or loose snow on the ground that is picked up by the wind
- **Blizzard**—a situation of winds in excess of 35 mph with snow and blowing snow reducing visibility to near zero
- **Freezing rain**—rain that freezes when it hits the ground or other surfaces and creates a coating of ice on roads, cars, and walkways
- **Sleet**—rain that turns to ice pellets before reaching the ground, causing roads to freeze and become slippery

PREVENTIVE MEASURES

The following lists items that could be included when creating the emergency procedures manual as guidelines to minimize loss in the event of a severe winter storm:

WINTER WEATHER ADVISORIES AND WARNINGS

The following lists the various winter weather advisories as used by the National Weather Service:

Winter Weather Advisory—Winter weather conditions are expected to cause significant inconvenience and may be hazardous, especially to motorists.

Winter Storm Watch—Conditions are right for severe winter weather such as heavy snow or ice to develop within 36–48 hours.

Winter Storm Warning—Potentially life-threatening severe winter weather conditions have begun or will begin within 24 hours.

Blizzard Warning—Severe weather conditions are likely to produce deep drifts, life-threatening wind chills, and blinding snowfall with near-zero visibility. Blizzards consist of large amounts of falling or blowing snow with sustained winds of at least 35 mph.

Frost or Freeze Warning—Below-freezing temperatures are expected. Damage to agricultural interests, outdoor fountains, etc. is possible.

Specific advisories may also address freezing rain, sleet, blowing and/or drifting snow, and expected amounts of snowfall (depth in inches).

- Establish procedures for facility shut down and early release of employees; address late opening in the event a storm occurs overnight or throughout a weekend.

- Include winterization instructions; consider winterizing ground-based sprinkler systems (shut off water, blow system dry with compressed air) and HVAC systems (winterize equipment, drain cooling water).

- Drain or install heat tape on all equipment that needs freeze protection.

- Supply emergency heating sources, such as space heaters and use with caution.

- Protect water pipes that may be vulnerable to freezing (insulation; heat tape).

- Periodically inspect roofs and keep gutters and drains clean before the winter season begins.

- Establish procedures to be followed if water pipes freeze.

- Store nonperishable foods for occupants.

- Replenish snow and ice control supplies and equipment—salt, chemical pellets, sand, snow shovels, etc.

- Prepare contracts for winter snow removal. Be sure contracts include the time of day, frequency, and weather conditions when plowing or snow control can occur.

- Keep maintenance personnel on call if a storm threatens.

- Instruct maintenance staff to clear sidewalks of snow and ice. This task should not be started more than one hour prior to the majority of tenants' arrival at or departure from the building. Continue to clear all sidewalks and walkways as needed. For commercial buildings, be sure to clear walkways and parking lots frequently, especially during times of heaviest traffic.

- Insulate the property effectively. Check the efficiency of existing insulation in walls, basements, and attics. Install storm windows or plastic window covers when necessary. Caulk and apply weather stripping around the exterior of doors and windows.

- Make plans to accommodate staff that may have to stay onsite (e.g., water, food, cots, blankets).

DURING A SEVERE WINTER STORM

The following list suggestions what should be taken during a snowstorm to help minimize the harsh effects of winter storms:

- Advise building occupants, if possible, to wear (or have available) layered clothing for extra warmth.

- Keep entrances and walkways clear of snow.

- Be careful when shoveling snow. Overexertion can cause heart attacks—a major cause of death in the winter.

- Inspect the amount of snow on rooftops, and remove if necessary. Heavy, wet snow can cause a roof to collapse. Flat roofs are especially vulnerable to freezing, thawing, and refreezing, which can plug roof drains and add weight.

- When using alternative heating, employ safeguards. If no heat is available, close off unused rooms.

- At night, cover windows and stuff towels or other materials under doors to help eliminate drafts.

- If evacuation is not possible, encourage occupants to consume food and drink fluids; food provides the body with energy to produce its own heat, and fluids prevent dehydration.

- Watch for signs of frostbite—a loss of feeling and a white or pale appearance of areas of the extremities, including fingers and toes. If symptoms are noticed, seek medical help immediately.

- Watch for signs of hypothermia—memory loss, uncontrollable shivering, disorientation, incoherence, drowsiness, and exhaustion. Seek medical help if symptoms are observed.

- Be alert for potential fire hazards, especially if alternative heating devices are used.

AFTER A SEVERE WINTER STORM

After a snowstorm, review mechanical and heating systems and any other equipment that may have been exposed to cold, snow, or ice to determine if there is any weakening or minor damage to repair. The performance of snow removal contractors should be reviewed, and notes should be made for needed adjustments to the contract. Likewise, the performance of maintenance personnel should be reviewed and adjustments made in the procedures followed. Notify your insurance company if any damage has occurred.

When the snow begins to melt, flooding may occur. Make sure all street and building drains are cleared of debris and snow. More information may be found at *www.ready.gov/winter*, a website dedicated to preparation and awareness before, during, and after a winter storm. *Winter Storms: The Deceptive Killers*, published jointly by National Oceanic and Atmosphere Administration, FEMA, and the American Red Cross is also available for download at *www.nws.noaa.gov/om/brochures/winterstorm.pdf*.

WATER LEAKS AND FROZEN PIPES

Water leaks may be the result of ruptured pipes, malfunctioning valves, or broken plumbing seals. The potential for damage will depend on the source and extent of the leak. Plumbing may also fail in extreme cold conditions because of water freezing inside the pipes. Water expands as it freezes and can rupture plumbing pipes and/or connections.

Water leaks are not always easily detected. There may be the presence of water but no clear indication of where it originated. To help determine whether a leak is present, consider using a leak alarm. Leak alarms frequently house small moisture sensors on their underside, triggering a loud signal when those sensors come in contact with water. These alarms can be positioned as a preventative measure any place where a leak is suspected (e.g., basement areas near water pipes and around appliances that use water).

Additionally, there are also firms that specialize in leak detection. It may be appropriate to include such a company as a resource to be cited in the emergency procedures manual. Contact information for the local water department would also be appropriate in the event the water supply has to be turned off and on at the source outside the building.

Turning Off the Water Supply

When a leak is encountered, it may be necessary to turn off the water supply. Depending on the location of the leak, it might also be necessary to disable the power supply. If the problem is in an occupant's space, non-service personnel should be kept away from the area until repairs are made, the water is cleaned up, and water service has been restored. Rarely is there a need for a full or partial evacuation of the building for a disruption of water, though it may be appropriate if the disruption is building wide and for an extended period of time.

Water shutoffs should be located at the water meter and near washer, sink, shower, and toilet hookups. For toilets, water shutoff is usually positioned under the tank. The water supply that leads to a kitchen or bathroom sink is usually controlled by a shutoff located underneath the sink. There are also shutoff valves located at the inlets of water heaters.

Shutting off a valve will only stop water flowing to the areas beyond the shutoff point. In the case of a leak, it is important to locate the valve that will stop the flow to the leaking area. When in doubt, or when it is difficult to locate the appropriate shutoff, the main valve should be closed. Once the correct shutoff is located and closed, water service can be restored to the remaining areas. In large buildings, there may be a shutoff on each floor or building tier, which allows water service to remain uninterrupted on other floors or in other areas.

Care must be taken when attempting to shut off water in a fire sprinkler system. A trained technician may be consulted if it is necessary to shut off a portion of a sprinkler system, and the system water supply should be restored a soon as possible.

Some businesses, such as laundromats and hair salons, are dependent on a continued flow of water. Real estate managers should notify these occupants when the water is to be shut off and when it is expected to be turned on again.

Restoring Water Service

When water service is restored to the building, it may be advisable to turn on faucets and let water flow for a short period to clear out any sediment that may have settled in the pipes while the water was shut off. Also, repair work may have loosened sediment or introduced contaminants.

It is important to take precautions when restoring water service. A difference in water pressure can cause water pipes to blow out when water flow is restarted. A building's water system may need to be cleaned or decontaminated. The water supply should also be checked to see if incoming water needs additional treatment.

CLEANING UP AFTER A WATER LEAK

Sometimes a leak or burst pipe will introduce water where it does not belong. A leak that had been undetected for some time may have introduced water between walls. Even a small leak or breach can release a large amount of water throughout a period of time. It is important that anyone repairing a water leak avoids contact with electrical sources (e.g., outlets or appliances), especially if the person is standing in water. Once the leak has been repaired, it is important to clean up the area where water caused damage.

Standing water can be removed with a wet/dry vacuum, which may be an especially useful method for removing water that is spread out over a large area. Wet/dry vacuums cannot be used effectively when there is a large area of water with measurable depth; a pump may be needed to remove deeper puddles or flooded spaces.

After water has been removed, any puddles or patches remaining can be cleaned up with a mop. Floors should be thoroughly dried—this can be expedited using fans and directing the airflow over the wet surface. A dehumidifier may also be helpful to minimize the threat of mold, mildew, or other damage to the area.

Plaster or drywall should be dried out as soon as possible. Once dried, it should be inspected to determine its condition and the extent of any damage. Extensive damage may necessitate repairs (e.g., patching) or replacement. Wallboard that has been damp for an extended period may harbor mold, which may also grow on other surfaces, including equipment. Where mold is present, it's advisable to consult a mold specialist for categorization and removal.

DEALING WITH FROZEN PIPES

Extreme cold temperatures may cause pipes to freeze, which can deprive residents and commercial tenants' employees of water for drinking, occupational use, and personal hygiene. Frozen pipes can also limit the availability of water to help put out fires or cause water to back up, which may result in causing pipes to burst and thereby flooding of interiors. Plumbing located on or within outside walls is most likely to freeze, especially if the pipes have not been insulated.

Because pipes may not always be insulated as part of building construction, it may be prudent, especially in residential properties, to check potentially vulnerable piping and install or add insulation as appropriate. Sealing around pipes where they enter the building from outside (e.g., through the foundation or walls) may be a good place to start.

Frozen pipes may be suspected if there are one or more reports of low or no water pressure in the building. If the report came from a resident or commercial tenant, check with other building occupants to determine whether the problem is building wide or an isolated incident. If the problem is building wide, it may be a good idea to check with neighboring buildings. If they have water, but your property does not, the problem may be a frozen pipe or meter. If it appears the problem is with your property, the following additional actions are suggested:

- Examine the water meter and check it for leaks.
- Check the frost plate (bottom portion) of the meter. If it's cracked, the meter is probably frozen. Do *not* attempt to thaw the water meter.
- If the water meter is frozen, contact the local water department or other appropriate authority to report the frozen meter and seek instructions.
- In some instances, real estate managers may be instructed to remove the meter. If a maintenance technician on the premises knows how to disconnect the meter from the water line, the meter may be taken to the water department or other authority for replacement.
- If the meter is *not* frozen, proceed to check around the building perimeter, in the basement, or in the crawl space for one or more frozen water pipes.

If water disruption is caused by frozen pipes, it's important to take action to prevent pipe bursting or other damage. The following are steps that may be taken to reduce the possibility of long-term damage:

- Shut off the water supply and open faucets to the frozen pipes.
- Warm frozen pipes with a heat lamp, blow dryer, or portable heater. Boiling water, propane torches, or anything with an open flame should *not* be used.
- If a pipe bursts before preventive action can be taken, turn off the main water supply to the pipe immediately and leave the faucet open until repairs are completed.

Frozen water pipes may also be thawed using special heating tape, but this process should be undertaken with extreme care. Heating tape may be installed as a preventive measure and activated when extremely cold outdoor temperatures are forecast. Automatic tapes include sensors that respond to a preset cold temperature setting and compensate by warming the pipes they are wrapped around. Pipes can also be prevented from freezing by turning on a faucet and letting it drip slowly, keeping water moving within the pipes.

Other Causes of Water Damage

The cause of water damage may not always be the result of a burst or leaking pipe. While plumbing systems and fixtures have a strong potential to cause water damage, tenant and resident-owned furniture or appliances can also contribute—whether it's the result of water leaking from an aquarium, waterbed, overflowed toilet, or a tub or sink left unattended. Occupants, especially in residential properties, need to be made aware of the damage that can be caused by water from their personal furnishings. It may be appropriate to include reminders in resident newsletters and other communications about proper use of plumbing fixtures.

Water may also enter a building as seepage through foundation cracks or chinks in the mortar between bricks or stones of exterior walls. If the source of a leak is not readily found in the water distribution system, seepage may be a likely cause. Regular inspection of the building interior and exterior should reveal where such breaches are beginning to develop so they can be repaired.

As with any emergency incident, it may be advisable to take photographs of the water damage to personal property or to building interior finishes, systems, or equipment before repairs are made or items are replaced. This will assist in cataloging damage for insurance purposes if property policies include coverage for the type of incident.

CHAPTER 16:
Hazardous-Materials Incidents

Chemicals are an ever present and important part of the human environment. They are used in everyday activities such as laundry, bathing, cleaning surfaces and equipment, and treating water supplies. They may even be present in our bodies as part of the daily medication or vitamin supplements we take each day. However, under certain conditions or in large quantities and concentrations, these chemicals can be harmful.

Materials that pose hazards to life and health are present on most, if not all, managed properties. If used, stored, and disposed of properly, the danger can be minimized. However, a hazardous-materials incident can occur anywhere—even at a nearby property, which can have an impact on your property as well.

Real estate managers of properties located near industrial sites, where hazardous materials are used, will benefit from a thorough understanding of the effects of hazardous-materials spills. It's the responsibility of real estate managers to also be aware of the preventive measures that can be implemented to protect people and assets on their properties.

AREAS AND PROPERTIES AT RISK

Because chemicals and other hazardous materials can be transported by boat, train, or truck, it's possible that any property located along a shipping route could potentially be affected by a hazardous-material spill or leak. Properties located near chemical manufacturing plants are also at high risk. Be aware of any industrial activity in the area that uses or disposes of hazardous materials and the types of incidents that might occur.

A hazardous-materials (hazmat) incident can result from a spill or damage to equipment. By knowing what facilities in the area are producing or using hazardous materials, it's easier to prepare for hazmat incidents that may accompany a traffic accident, train derailment, or collision on a waterway. A fire or explosion at a nearby property may release hazardous gases or liquids that pose a danger to occupants of other buildings.

The real estate manager of a property located near an industrial site may want to visit that site to meet with the designated safety officer and discuss the types of hazardous chemicals that could potentially cause problems for the adjacent property, methods of communication in the event of an incident, and safety precautions that could be implemented.

PREVENTIVE MEASURES FOR HAZARDOUS-MATERIALS INCIDENTS

Safe handling and storage of chemicals and other hazardous materials is discussed in regard to industrial properties in *Chapter 11*. Careful handling will generally prevent spills, but immediate cleanup of small spills and proper disposal of the cleaning materials will minimize the consequences of such incidents. The material safety data sheet (MSDS) that accompanies bulk chemicals (or the labels on smaller containers) should provide information on specific hazards and include recommended cleanup procedures. They should also indicate symptoms of exposure and suggested methods of treatment. Real estate managers should also receive copies of the MSDS from tenants who use hazardous materials.

The emergency procedures manual should include steps to be taken in the case of small spills as well as larger incidents, possibly offsite. The local Poison Control Center can provide guidance on how to respond to chemical poisonings. First aid courses for emergency management team members may include treatment for chemical burns. The local chapter of the American Red Cross can also provide helpful information.

WHAT TO DO DURING A HAZARDOUS-MATERIALS INCIDENT

If a hazardous-material spill occurs onsite—or is witnessed near the property—contact the fire department or other appropriate authority to send a hazmat team. These responders are specially trained and have appropriate protective clothing and equipment to handle hazardous materials. People who are not part of the cleanup team should be kept away from the area of the spill. If applicable, it may be necessary or appropriate to evacuate the building. Hazmat responders can provide specific guidance regarding evacuation. If the incident is offsite, but nearby, there are likely to be announcements broadcast on the Emergency Alert System (EAS) through both TV and radio outlets. Alternate methods of notification such as a siren, phone call to building management, or loudspeaker announcement may be used to notify a hazmat spill or evacuation notice.

EXPOSURE TO CHEMICALS

People may be exposed to chemicals in three ways:

1. Inhalation—breathing vapors of a volatile substance or fumes generated when it is exposed to air or water.

2. Ingestion—swallowing the chemical itself or ingesting food, water, or medication contaminated with it.

3. Skin contact—touching the chemical or coming into contact with clothing or other objects that have touched the chemical.

Inhalation and skin contact are most common. Failure to follow label directions and improper handling or mixing of chemicals such as cleaners are common causes of exposure.

Many chemicals are odorless and tasteless. Exposure may occur even though people may not be able to see or smell anything unusual. Some chemicals may be detected because they present a foul odor, or the vapor/fumes they emit may cause watering of the eyes. Fumes may also cause an extremely runny nose or other allergic reaction.

SYMPTOMS OF CHEMICAL POISONING INCLUDE:

- Difficulty breathing
- Irritation of eyes, nose, throat, and/or skin
- Blurring of vision
- Headache
- Dizziness
- Nausea
- Vomiting
- Stomach cramps
- Diarrhea
- Clumsiness or lack of coordination
- Unusual behavior

Chemical poisoning is potentially life threatening. Emergency medical attention should be sought immediately.

Hazmat responders and other authorities will decide if and when evacuation is necessary. Their decision regarding evacuation is generally based on the type and amount of materials released and how long it is expected to affect an area. Weather conditions—especially the direction and speed of wind and local weather forecasts—time of day, and the amount of time to evacuate the area are some other factors that affect the announcements. Specific evacuation routes should also be included in the main announcement. If practical, and if there is time to do so, shut down the HVAC system—close air intakes and vents and turn off fans—to minimize contamination indoors. Depending on the situation, authorities may recommend that people shelter in place rather than evacuate, by closing all windows and air intake vents.

WHAT TO DO AFTER A HAZARDOUS-MATERIALS INCIDENT

Return to the building only when authorities say it is safe to do so. Check exterior and interior surfaces for residue from the spill. Because the residue may be hazardous, it should be carefully cleaned up and disposed of properly. Protective clothing and equipment may be necessary or appropriate. Emergency officials may issue instructions for cleanup and disposal.

Care should be taken in restarting HVAC system components. It may be necessary or appropriate to inspect equipment and ductwork for residue and test for contamination of cooling tower water. It may be advisable to clean out ducts, filters, and other system components before restoring full operation. It may also be appropriate to vent the building before occupants are allowed to return.

Because hazardous materials can contaminate water supplies, including groundwater by leaching through soil, it may be advisable to check with authorities before using water from building faucets for drinking and washing. It may be necessary to boil water for some purposes, especially in a residential property. As an added safeguard, the building's water could be tested for chemical contamination.

Hazardous-materials incidents may result in environmental contamination of air, water, and/or soil, especially if the spill involves a large amount

---

SHELTERING IN PLACE

If instead of ordering an evacuation, authorities recommend sheltering in place, the following precautions should be observed:

- Close all windows and doors.
- Turn off HVAC systems and equipment.
- Move to a level above ground, one with a minimum of windows and doors.
- Preferably, stay in a room with a door that can be closed.
- Take wet towels and jam them into the crack under the door.
- Tape plastic garbage bags (or other suitable plastic sheeting) over windows, doors, and vents. It may be appropriate to cover electrical outlets similarly.
- Close window shades, blinds, or curtains if warning includes the possibility of explosion. Stay away from windows to avoid injury.
- Hold a damp cloth over nose and mouth to prevent breathing hazardous vapors.
- Listen to emergency radio for announcements that the area is safe and/or instructions to evacuate.

Sheltering in place may be recommended in the event of a hazardous-materials incident. It may also be recommended for some types of severe weather or in the event of a terrorist attack.

---

of material or covers a large area. Those who manage industrial sites need to be aware of federal and state regulations that must be followed regarding containment of a spill or release and notification of incidents that occur. An incident on managed property may need to be reported specifically to the U.S. Environmental Protection Agency (EPA) and/or to state and local environmental agencies. It may be appropriate to learn about the reporting requirements, specific material that is spilled, and nature of the hazard(s) it poses.[1]

NATURAL GAS LEAKS

Natural gas is used for cooking, heating, hot water, clothes drying, and residential heating. It may also be used to operate swimming pool and spa heaters. In commercial buildings, natural gas may be used for cooking in restaurants and for heating. It may also be used to operate backup power-generating equipment. Natural gas itself is not combustible; it requires air to burn. The optimum air-gas mixture is 85 to 95 percent air to 5 to 15 percent gas. Because natural gas is odorless, an odorant—typically the smell of rotten-eggs—is added to it.

Natural gas is moved from its point of origin (an underground natural gas field) to urban and rural buildings via pipelines. There are more than one million miles of natural gas pipelines in the U.S., which vary in size from small diameter pipes (approximately 1–1½ inches) entering buildings to very large diameter (24 inches or more) pipes used for transportation for long distances to the local distribution gas mains. The gas is under pressure; in large pipelines, the pressure may be 500 pounds per square inch (psi) or more. Transportation pipelines buried in rural areas—that is, farmlands—are generally marked with a gas company name and an emergency telephone number. Distribution mains in towns and cities are not marked, although they can be precisely located. Most gas utilities participate in a local one-call system that sends locating representatives to mark gas (and other utilities such as electricity and telephone) lines before any excavation is initiated. The party planning to dig must call for this service 48 hours beforehand.

---

1. Additional information on hazardous-materials classification, transportation, and spill reporting requirements can be found on the Hazardous Materials Safety Administration's website at *phmsa.dot.gov/hazmat*. Information on hazardous waste disposal can be found on the Environmental Protection Agency website at *http://www.epa.gov/epawaste/index.htm*. They also publish a Guide for Industrial Waste Management, which can be found at *http://www.epa.gov/epawaste/nonhaz/industrial/guide/index.htm*.

Responding to Natural Gas Leaks

Natural gas leaks create potential fire and explosion hazards. Indoor leaks are recognizable by the smell and hissing sound. A faint odor may be an indication that a pilot light is out, and relighting the pilot may solve the problem. However, a strong, persistent odor requires immediate action including evacuation of the building. Gas utilities recommend the following to prevent injuries:

- Leave the door open after leaving the building to minimize gas buildup in an enclosed space. If possible, ventilate the building by opening doors and windows, beginning where the odor is strongest, but do *not* re-enter the building to do this.
- Use a cell phone or other telephone outside the building to report the leak to the utility company.
- Close the shutoff valve near the gas meter and do *not* turn it on again. The utility company should turn the gas on.

They also recommend *not* operating appliance controls or electrical switches or removing any plugs from electrical outlets, which could create a spark and ignite the gas. One should not light any matches either.

If leaking gas catches fire, the area should be evacuated. The supply of gas must be shut off before the fire can be put out. The utility company and the fire department should be notified immediately.

Outdoor gas leaks from buried pipelines may be indicated by an odor of rotten eggs or a hissing or blowing sound. Visible indications include dead or brown vegetation, dirt blowing into the air, fire at or near exposed piping or coming from the ground, bubbling of surface water, and/or water blowing into the air at a river, creek, or pond. The gas utility should be notified if any of these signs are observed.

Outdoor gas leaks may also result when excavation is done too close to a gas main. A ruptured main can easily be ignited, and the resulting fire can cause a great deal of damage. There may also be an explosion or explosions with such incidents. Gas service to nearby buildings will be disrupted until the main has been repaired. The service disruption may only be hours, but it could be days. Usually utility representatives will relight appliance pilot lights when gas service is restored.

Natural gas leaks and their potential hazards should be addressed in a property's emergency procedures manual. Property management staff should be able to recognize signs of a gas leak and act accordingly. They may be referred to emergency procedures for fire and/or explosion as appropriate. The fire department or other rescue squad may have to be called in if someone is overcome by carbon monoxide. Building occupants also need to be informed about the signs of leaking gas and directed to contact the utility company if they suspect a gas leak.

Preventive Measures for Natural Gas Leaks

Gas-operated appliances and equipment should be inspected periodically to ensure that they are operating properly, have no leaking joints, valves or pipes, and not releasing carbon monoxide. Gas detection meters should be used for routine inspections. Carbon monoxide is created when natural gas is burned without sufficient air. It can be produced when gas appliances are not properly installed, vented, maintained, or used or when vent pipes have gaps, leaks, or plugged with debris. (For more information on carbon monoxide detectors, see *Chapter 14.*)

Gas lines that are downstream of the gas meter (the building side) belong to the gas customer—the building owner. The customer is responsible for maintenance and repair of this portion of the distribution system. Buried gas piping needs to be inspected for leaks and, if the pipe is metallic, for corrosion. It may also be appropriate to test the level of gas pressure.

The local gas utility company may conduct inspections of gas piping, valves, and connections on request. Alternatively, a private contractor may be hired to conduct such inspections as part of a regular preventive maintenance program. Otherwise, a commercial plumbing or heating contractor may be consulted when gas lines need attention.

SECTION 4:

Natural Disasters

CHAPTER 17:
Tornadoes

Spawned from powerful thunderstorm conditions, tornadoes are gray or black rotating funnel-shaped clouds that extend from the bases of thunderclouds to the ground. Their whirling winds can reach speeds of up to 300 mph, uprooting trees and buildings and turning harmless objects into deadly missiles transported with lethal velocity. A tornado's path of damage on the ground can exceed one mile in width and cover a distance of 50 miles or more. Tornadoes typically travel from southwest to northeast.

Within minutes or even seconds, a tornado can devastate a neighborhood, demolish properties, and tear roofs from buildings. When it touches down, a tornado sounds like the roaring of a locomotive. An observer witnessing its approach may see blowing debris from a distance. Other indications of a coming tornado are tree branches being blown in circles and the sky becoming very dark with a green hue. In coastal areas, a tornado may accompany a tropical storm or hurricane. Weather records indicate that most tornadoes occur in the late afternoon and early evening during the months of April, May, and June, but can occur at any time of year. In an average year, 1,200 tornadoes are reported nationwide, resulting in an average of 70 deaths and more than 1,500 injuries.

AREAS AND PROPERTIES AT RISK

Tornadoes are most common east of the Rocky Mountains during the spring and summer months. Although they can occur in any state, Texas has been hit the most. During the spring in the central plains, thunderstorms frequently develop along the "dryline" that separates the warm moist air to the east from hot dry air to the west.

The properties at greatest risk from tornadoes include wide-span or clear-span buildings with roofs supported solely by outside walls (e.g., gymnasiums), pre-manufactured metal buildings, and mobile or manufactured homes. Substantial steel-framed and reinforced-concrete buildings face the least amount of risk.

CATEGORIES OF TORNADOES

Weak: Winds less than 110 mph; duration 1–10 minutes or longer. They represent 88 percent of all tornadoes and are responsible for less than five percent of tornado deaths.

Strong: Winds 110–205 mph; duration 20 minutes or longer. They represent 11 percent of all tornadoes and are responsible for 30 percent of all tornado deaths.

Violent: Winds greater than 205 mph; duration one hour or longer. They represent less than one percent of all tornadoes and are responsible for 70 percent of all tornado deaths.

Source: *Thunderstorms, Tornadoes, Lightning: Nature's Most Violent Storms,* published jointly by the National Oceanographic and Atmospheric Administration, Federal Emergency Management Agency, and the American Red Cross, publication numbers NOAA/PA 99050 and ARC 1122, available online at *http://oceanservice. noaa.gov/education/yos/resource/02ttl.pdf.*

WEATHER ADVISORIES AND WARNINGS

Tornadoes are especially deadly because they often strike with little or no warning. However, Doppler radar at weather stations across the U.S. allow the National Weather Service (NWS) to detect increasing rotation aloft in thunderstorms, which can be indicative of tornadoes. This can allow life-saving warnings to be broadcast before some tornadoes actually form.

Most tornado-prone communities employ sirens to warn residents of approaching tornadoes. Local weather authorities also utilize public broadcast media such as television, radio, and the National Oceanographic and Atmospheric Administration (NOAA) Weather Radio to announce weather watches and warnings.

Real estate managers and emergency teams should become familiar with the significance of the following weather alerts in order to understand the severity of approaching tornadoes and initiate the proper emergency response. One of the first indicators that a tornado might develop is thunderstorm conditions.

- A *severe thunderstorm watch* indicates that such storms are possible in the cited area.
- A *severe thunderstorm warning* indicates that severe thunderstorms are present in the specific area. This is issued when winds gust to more than 58 mph accompanied by hail larger than three-fourths of an inch in diameter.
- A *tornado watch* indicates that tornadoes are possible in the cited areas.

- A *tornado warning* indicates that a tornado has been sighted on the ground or indicated on the weather radar.

People should be alert for approaching storms. If there is a warning and the sky becomes threatening—approaching storm clouds that are dark green or black—everyone should take cover.

EMERGENCY NOTIFICATION SYSTEMS

Weather warnings and watches are communicated in a number of ways. When the NWS issues a watch or warning, local television stations will likely make an immediate announcement through marquee or graphic map to communicate the affected area. Radio broadcasters will similarly make a frequent announcement of watch or warning status, including a list of the affected counties or areas.

THE ENHANCED FUJITA SCALE

EF0: Wind speed 65–85 mph; shallow-rooted trees uprooted, tree branches broken off.

EF1: Wind speed 86–110 mph; moving cars pushed off roads, mobile/manu-factured homes overturned, surface peeled off roofs.

EF2: Wind speed 111–135 mph; large trees snapped or uprooted, roofs torn off of frame houses, light objects become missiles.

EF3: Wind speed 136–165 mph; heavy cars lifted off the ground, trains over-turned, roofs and some walls torn off of well-constructed homes, most trees in forests uprooted.

EF4: Wind speed 166–200 mph; cars thrown about; large objects become mis-siles, well-constructed houses leveled, structures with weak foundations blown some distance off their foundations.

EF5: Wind speed greater than 200 mph; automobile-size missiles move through the air at speeds of more than 100 mph, strong frame houses lifted off founda-tions and disintegrated, trees debarked.

Note: The Enhanced Fujita scale bases wind speed on actual damage.

Source: NOAA (*http://www.spc.noaa.gov/faq/tornado/ef-scale.html*); *Tornadoes*, a publication on hurricane preparedness from the National Hurricane Center of the National Oceanic and Atmospheric Administration, available for download from the Internet at *www.nhc.noaa.gov/HAW2/english/tornadoes.shtml*.

The Emergency Alert System

The Emergency Alert System (EAS) replaced the Emergency Broadcast System in 1997. Like its predecessor, the EAS is designed as the national warning system, capable of reaching 98 percent of Americans if activated nationwide. Standing as a way for the president to address the country in under ten minutes, the EAS is more commonly used to issue weather watches and warnings, AMBER alerts, and emergency information targeted to certain areas.

The FCC requires all compliant broadcasters, cable and satellite providers, and radio stations to allow for broadcast interruptions by the EAS, should an emergency arise.

Wireless Emergency Alerts

Beginning in 2012, FEMA, NOAA, and other government agencies implemented Wireless Emergency Alerts (WEA). WEAs are text or SMS messages with less than 90 characters, which trigger a unique vibration and ringtone alert.

These messages convey localized information regarding severe weather or other emergencies that pose a risk to human life. Unlike other text messages, WEAs are not charged or counted against a monthly allowance by the recipient's wireless carrier. Like the larger EAS, the WEA system can be activated by FEMA acting on orders of the White House.

PREVENTIVE MEASURES

The following preventive measures can help minimize losses from tornadoes:

- Contact your local emergency management office or American Red Cross chapter. Ask about the threat of tornadoes in the area, and learn about community warning signals—whether there is a siren, which NOAA Weather Radio frequency is used, etc.

- Know the county or parish in which the property is situated. Warnings issued by the NWS use these to identify the location or projected path of tornadoes.

- Identify designated shelter areas in advance; these may be public buildings, nursing homes, schools, or shopping centers. Generally these buildings will be constructed of masonry and steel.

- Check local building codes and ordinances regarding wind-resistant building designs and make needed improvements to comply with structural requirements.

- Seek out and secure outdoor objects that might blow away or damage a structure—e.g., trash containers and dumpsters, signs, outdoor furniture, tools, and debris. Instruct residents to keep all patio and balcony items (pots, plants) indoors.

- Inspect roofs and catch basins; remove tools and debris. Repair loose gutters, shingles, and coping. Remove furniture and other items from roof top patios and gardens.

- Prune trees to remove branches that might damage the building.

- Keep a supply of fresh bottled water on hand in case the storm contaminates or disrupts the community's water supply.

- Have a list of emergency supplies kept onsite. Routinely inspect these supplies, and verify quantities and location.

- Evacuate low-lying areas and other areas when directed by emergency personnel.

- Be sure the property carries adequate casualty and liability insurance that includes rent loss coverage.

- Check with commercial tenants in office, retail, and industrial properties to ensure that they maintain proper insurance coverage as required by their leases.

DURING A TORNADO

The emergency procedures manual should include directions to both staff and occupants, instructing them with what to do if a tornado should hit the property. Here are some suggested procedures:

- Listen to local radio or television stations for weather updates.

- Report rotating funnel-shaped clouds to the local police department or weather service.

- Station an emergency team member at a south entrance of the building to watch for the funnel cloud. Identify how those team members will communicate with occupants if the funnel cloud approaches.

- Open windows slightly so pressure will not build and shatter them.

- Stay away from windows, doors, and outside walls. Go to a cellar or basement if possible.

- Advise occupants to seek safe shelter immediately in small interior lower floor rooms without windows; in hallways on the lowest floor; in rooms constructed with reinforced concrete, brick, or block with no windows; or in an interior (windowless) bathroom or other protected areas away from windows.

- If you are in a high-rise building, you may not have time to go to a lower floor or basement. Pick a place in a hallway, interior staircase, or the center of the building.

- In a mobile/manufactured home park, advise residents to evacuate immediately to a nearby shelter or to stay with family or friends offsite.

- Have members of the emergency management team circulate among management staff, building occupants, and others on the property to ensure that everyone has found a safe place to ride out the tornado.

- If people are outdoors and there is no shelter nearby, they should lie flat in the nearest ditch, ravine, or culvert with their hands shielding their heads.

- Do not encourage occupants to out-drive a tornado. Tornadoes move swiftly and may change direction without notice.

AFTER A TORNADO

Once a tornado has passed, the winds will have noticeably died down. Now is the time for the emergency management team to evaluate the damage.

- Check for injuries among the occupants, seeking medical attention where necessary. If first aid is necessary, follow suggestions and considerations presented in *Chapter 13*. Perform a head-count of occupants to identify any missing persons.

- Immediately contact local emergency crews if necessary to assist in the location and removal of injured persons. Maintain dialogue between the local authorities and the building contact person to determine when all injured parties have been removed.

- Contact the insurance company, restoration contractor, and building inspector, and request that they visit the site as quickly as possible.

- In the absence of an insurance adjuster, take pictures and/or videos to document damage.

- Assemble building plans and as-built drawings and have them onsite as soon as possible.

- Inspect the property and appoint cleanup crews.

- Well-built structures may survive a tornado and appear intact. However, use caution when entering the building. Ensure that the walls, ceiling, and roof are in place and that the structure rests firmly on the foundation. If the building has suffered significant damage, have it inspected by a structural engineer and/or local building officials prior to allowing staff and tenant access.

- Wear a hard hat, sturdy boots, and work gloves, if possible.

- Look out for broken glass and downed power lines.

- Watch for live electrical wires and dangerous debris.

- Open clogged drains and catch basins.

- Prepare for possible flooding from the accompanying storm or from damaged water barriers.

- Be alert for potential fire hazards, such as leaking gas lines, pools of water near electrical equipment and appliances, spills of combustible materials, etc. (see *Chapter 16*).

- If the property is damaged, secure it until local officials and/or a structural engineer has inspected the facility and authorized entry.

- Provide security guards, if necessary, to prevent trespass, injury, or theft.

- Apprise the building occupants of the situation and your plans for restoration. Advise them when they can re-enter the premises to collect personal belongings and/or begin the cleanup.

THUNDERSTORMS AND LIGHTNING

Only about one percent of thunderstorms spawn tornadoes. Each year, on average, there are 100,000 thunderstorms across the U.S.—approximately 1,000 of which develop tornadoes.

Severe thunderstorms can produce hail and heavy rains that can lead to flash flooding. Hail can be pea-size or smaller or as large as a softball. It can damage plants and automobiles. Straight-line winds can exceed 100 mph. Thunderstorms are signaled by dark, towering, or threatening clouds, lightning flashes, thunder, and increasing wind. The National Weather Service issues severe thunderstorm watches and warnings.

High winds can be a problem for high-rise buildings. Windows have been blown out of high-rise buildings, causing injuries to pedestrians and damage to vehicles at street level as well as disrupted operations inside the building. If wind damage is a potential problem, the real estate manager can check with the local building department to see if the issue is addressed specifically in the building code. An architect or structural engineer may be able to advise about preventive strategies. Emergency procedures would need to address interior cleanup and window replacement. Also, movable scaffolding used by window washers and building exterior surface cleaners needs to be secured when not in use and should not be used when there are high winds. If such scaffolding should come loose, it may break windows and cause damage to the building exterior. Workers on the scaffolding may be injured or killed, and there are likely to be injuries to pedestrians and damage to vehicles on the sidewalk and street below.

Lightning, which accompanies all thunderstorms, can cause fires. It can also cause injuries and fatalities. Each year, on average, lightning causes 300 injuries and 80 fatalities. A person struck by lightning has received an electrical shock and may be burned, not only at the site of the lightning strike, but also where the electricity left the body. Being struck by lightning can also cause damage to the nervous system, loss of eyesight or hearing, and broken bones. Injured persons should be given appropriate first aid—they may require CPR—and emergency medical help should be called immediately.

Thunderstorms and lightning can cause power outages. If there is no backup power source, electrical equipment should be unplugged—or electricity may be shut off—to prevent damage from power surges when electricity is restored.

Note: More information can be found online at *www.noaa.gov/lightning.html*.

CHAPTER 18:
Hurricanes

Hurricanes are massive weather phenomena composed of tropical cyclones with torrential rains and sustained winds of 74 mph or higher. As one of nature's most destructive forces, they are rather unique in that their winds blow counter clockwise (in the northern hemisphere) around a relatively calm center or "eye." Hurricanes may extend up to 400 miles across and can severely damage areas hundreds of miles inland.

Hurricanes begin as tropical depressions or tropical storms and develop as they gather heat and energy through contact with warm ocean waters. The addition of moisture by evaporation from the sea surface powers them like giant heat engines. Around their core, winds grow with great velocity, generating violent seas; and as they move ashore, they can sweep the ocean coastward, spawning tornadoes and causing huge domes of water (storm surges) to crash into the coastline. As their winds increase, tropical storms are given a new classification as hurricanes. Hurricanes are, in turn, categorized by the National Oceanic and Atmospheric Administration (NOAA) and the National Weather Service (NWS) based on their wind speed. Hurricanes frequently bring widespread torrential rains—often with rainfall amounts in excess of six inches—and can produce deadly and destructive floods.

Violent storms can destroy structures. They can result in broken sewer and water mains, loose and dangling electrical wires, power outages, collapsed roads, and widespread destruction. Foundations can be undermined by water and wind. In addition, there is a greater possibility of fire after a hurricane from gas and electrical damage. Timely warnings due to advanced weather technology and communication have greatly decreased hurricane fatalities in the U.S., but properties continue to sustain major damage and destruction.

AREAS AND PROPERTIES AT RISK

Each year, an average of 10 tropical storms—about six of which become hurricanes—develop over the Atlantic Ocean, Caribbean Sea, or Gulf of

SAFFIR-SIMPSON HURRICANE WIND SCALE

Just as tornadoes are categorized by the Fujita Scale, hurricanes are categorized into five categories as set by the Saffir-Simpson Hurricane Wind Scale.

Category	Winds (mph)
One	74–95
Two	96–110
Three	111–129
Four	130–156
Five	>157

Source: National Hurricane Center, NWS. *http://www.nhc.noaa.gov/aboutsshws.php*

Mexico during the peak hurricane months of May through November. Islands in the mid-Pacific are also subject to hurricanes. Although rarely struck by hurricanes, parts of the southwest U.S. and the Pacific coast suffer heavy rains and floods each year from the remnants of hurricanes spawned off of Mexico. Based on historic tracking, hurricanes strike the mainland with sustained winds of 111–130 mph. The center or eye of a hurricane is relatively calm; the most violent activity takes place immediately around the eye.

Due to limited accessible evacuation routes, barrier islands such as Hawaii and Guam are especially vulnerable to hurricanes, while inland areas such as the Midwest experience associated high winds, floods, and tornadoes.

Coastal areas, especially near the Gulf of Mexico and along the eastern seaboard, are at greatest risk from hurricanes. Inland regions near these areas are also at risk although, generally speaking, the farther away from the coast, the less direct effect a hurricane will have.

The U.S. is becoming increasingly more vulnerable to widespread loss from hurricanes. As shorelines attract large numbers of new homes and condominium towers, cities are being built on coastal sands susceptible to storms. There are more than 63 million permanent residents along the hurricane-prone coastline, with increased seasonal and tourist populations further increasing the number of potential victims.

Technology such as geostationary satellites, Doppler radar, and military reconnaissance aircraft have enabled authorities to notify residents of advancing hurricanes with sufficient time to evacuate. However, the number of roads and their accessibility have not kept up with growing populations, making evacuation increasingly difficult. Seasonal residents and tourists in hurricane-prone areas may have a false sense of security or complacency having never experienced a "major" hurricane.

Structures most at risk from hurricanes are long-span buildings and mobile or manufactured homes. Substantial steel-framed or reinforced concrete buildings are the least risky. On a long-span building, the roof is usually supported solely by outside walls—inside walls are usually false or non-load-bearing. Shopping centers, which are traditionally long-span buildings, are especially vulnerable to roof collapse.

Because of the frailty of mobile homes and manufactured housing, a protective onsite shelter may be included in a mobile home community. In the event of a hurricane, residents should be encouraged to make arrangements to move to such shelters or stay with friends or relatives who live in more stable buildings at the first sign of trouble.

HURRICANE ADVISORIES AND WARNING SIGNS

Heavy rains, increasing winds, and thunderstorms in the vicinity are initial signs of approaching hurricanes. However, it's important to distinguish between a typical storm and a hurricane. A hurricane will be accompanied with major coverage by broadcast media such as television, public radio, hurricane sirens, and the NOAA Weather Radio.

The NWS continuously broadcasts all types of weather advisories and warnings received by NOAA on a special weather radio that alert listeners of approaching weather systems with tone-alert features, and provides descriptions of the approaching weather conditions in relevant areas. Additionally, both FEMA and the NWS have begun issuing severe weather advisories via text message as part of the Emergency Alert System. (For more information about text message weather advisories, see *Chapter 17*.)

Storm surges are a tell-tale sign of an imminently inbound hurricane. Storm surges have abnormally high sea levels that can wash inland for a quarter to half mile, inundating coastal buildings. Residents must evacuate before these surges arrive. Life-threatening torrential rains that are captured in gullies can cause an overflow in nearby streams which results in flooding. Residents of the affected area should evacuate when the order is given by local officials or the NWS.

Weather Advisories and Warnings

Advanced notification of hurricanes come in five forms—(1) tropical storm watches, (2) tropical storm warnings, (3) hurricane watches, (4) hurricane warnings, and (5) short-term watches and warnings. Real estate managers should become acquainted with them in order to understand the current severity of hurricane systems in their areas.

Tropical storm watches are declared when tropical storm conditions are possible in the specified area of the watch, usually within 36 hours. *Tropical storm warnings* are announced when tropical storm conditions are expected within 24 hours in a specified area. *Hurricane watches* are issued when hurricane conditions are possible, usually within 36 hours. During a hurricane watch, prepare to take immediate action in case a hurricane warning is issued.

Hurricane warnings are issued when hurricane conditions are expected in the area within 24 hours. At this point, all storm preparations should

---

HURRICANE ADVISORIES

Advisory: Official information issued by tropical cyclone warning centers describing all tropical cyclone watches and warnings in effect along with details concerning tropical cyclone locations, intensity, and movement and precautions that should be taken. Advisories are issued to describe tropical cyclones prior to issuance of watches and warnings.

Tropical Storm Watch: An announcement for specific coastal areas that tropical storm conditions are possible within 36 hours.

Tropical Storm Warning: A warning that sustained winds within the range of 39–73 mph associated with a tropical cyclone are expected in a specified coastal area within 24 hours or less.

Hurricane Watch: An announcement for specific coastal areas that hurricane conditions are possible within 36 hours.

Hurricane Warning: A warning that sustained winds of 74 mph or higher associated with a hurricane are expected in a specified coastal area in 24 hours or less. (A hurricane warning can remain in effect when dangerously high water alone or combined with exceptionally high waves continue, even though winds may be less than hurricane force.)

Gale Warning: A warning of one-minute sustained surface winds in the range of 39–54 mph inclusive, either predicted or occurring and not directly associated with tropical cyclones.

Source: National Hurricane Center "Hurricane Preparedness—Watches and Warnings." *http:// www.nhc.noaa.gov./prepare/wwa.php*

---

be completed, and evacuation should take place if directed by the local authorities. *Short-term watches and warnings* provide detailed information on hurricane hazard threats such as floods, tornadoes, and high winds. Tornadoes associated with hurricanes can occur for days after landfall, but are usually not accompanied by hail or lightning.

PREVENTIVE MEASURES

Today's satellite imagery enables the NWS to track hurricanes, usually providing ample time for preventive measures to be taken. At the minimum, real estate managers should have one day's notice, as hurricane watches will be upgraded to hurricane warnings when the hurricane is expected to strike an area within 24 hours. The following lists a number of measures that can be implemented during this time to prevent property loss:

- Identify, in advance, locally designated public shelters in the community.

- Closely monitor the television, radio, or NOAA Weather Radio to keep abreast of storms progressing in the area. They will direct you to areas of public shelter. It may also be advisable to check with local broadcaster's Facebook, Twitter, or other social media outlets for immediate announcements and changes on areas of public shelter and storm conditions.

- Learn safe routes heading inland. If possible, provide maps or a list of viable evacuation routes to residents and tenants.

- Review the need for and working condition of emergency supplies and equipment, such as plywood and nails for safeguarding windows, flashlights, and battery-powered radios.

- Clear out clogged rain gutters and downspouts; secure loose gutters and downspouts.

- Seek out and secure outdoor furniture or objects that might blow away or cause property damage, including trash cans and dumpsters, signs, and trash.

- Inspect roofs—repair loose gutters, shingles, and coping; remove tools and loose objects.

- Inspect roof-mounted HVAC equipment for loose debris and improperly fastened panels; make needed repairs.

- Inspect storm sewers and catch basins; clear away debris.

- Close and protect windows and glass doors—board up windows, install storm shutters, and apply masking or electrical tape in an X pattern on both sides of the glass.

- If near a coastline, stream or river, shut off gas and electricity.

- Instruct residents to move all patio and balcony items (pots, plants, etc.) indoors. Remove these items from balconies of residents who are not at home.

- Keep a supply of fresh bottled water on hand in case the storm contaminates the community's water supply or damages distribution lines.

- Evacuate low-lying areas and any other areas when so directed.

- Shut down all three-phase electrical service prior to the hurricane striking.

- Move elevators to the second floor level and lock them off in the event of flooding. Secure elevator doors at lower levels to prevent entry into the shaft.

The National Institute of Building Sciences (NIBS) at the direction of FEMA has developed a standardized methodology, called HAZUS, for assessing losses from hurricane wind damage. The HAZUS methodology has been implemented into a HAZUS program, which is available as a free download through FEMA (*www.fema.gov*).

Compliance with Local Building Codes

Plans to protect a property should be developed well in advance of hurricanes. Permanent storm shutters offer the best protection for windows, although a common alternative is to board up windows with 5/8-inch marine plywood that is precut to fit and ready to install.

Each property should be inspected for compliance with local building codes to ensure that the property will qualify for insurance coverage. Many roofs destroyed by hurricanes have been found to be in violation of local building codes.

Flood insurance is a necessity for hurricane-prone areas. Flood insurance should be purchased well in advance, as there is normally a five-day waiting period before it takes effect. (For more information on floods and flood preparedness, see *Chapter 19*.)

As with other types of emergencies, the emergency management team should know how to shut off utilities, know the locations of gas pilot

HURRICANE PREPARATIONS FOR BUSINESSES:

- In preparation for potential flooding, remove papers from lower drawers of desks and file cabinets; place them in containers or plastic bags on top of the desk or cabinet.
- Use plywood to protect glass showcases; alternatively, turn glass side of case toward an inside wall if possible.
- Store merchandise as high as possible off the floor; merchandise that cannot be stored should be moved away from glass areas and covered with heavy plastic or tarp.
- In warehouses, secure goods off the floor; use sandbags to help keep water from entering.

Source: *Surviving the Storm: A Guide to Hurricane Preparedness* published by the U.S. Department of Homeland Security/FEMA.

lights, and how the heating and air-conditioning systems are controlled. The need for backup systems should be considered, such as battery-operated portable pumps to remove flood water, battery-powered emergency lighting, and alternate power sources such as gasoline-powered generators. Preparations should include measures for securing hazardous materials or plans for removing them from the property.

WHAT TO DO DURING A HURRICANE

The emergency procedures manual should tell both the emergency management team and the building's occupants what to do during a hurricane—should they be unable to evacuate the area. The following lists some suggestions:

- Stay current with the latest updates of the storm's status from television and radio broadcasters or via online news sources.

- Inspect and secure mobile home tie-downs.

- Turn off the gas and electricity.

- Follow evacuation instructions of local officials. Hurricane winds are especially strong at higher elevations, so occupants of high-rise buildings should waste no time in evacuating.

- Stay away from windows and doors, even if they are covered. Take refuge in a small interior room or hallway, where structural support is the strongest.

- Remain indoors—go to designated shelters or basement areas.

- Don't be fooled by the eye of the hurricane if it passes over you.

If it is directly overhead, there will be a lull in the wind lasting several minutes to half an hour or more, and then strong winds and weather will recur.

- Be alert for tornadoes, which can happen during a hurricane or after it passes.

- Avoid using the phone except for serious emergencies. Text messages and online communication (where possible) will likely be the most reliable form of communication during a period of emergency as the cellular network may become overwhelmed.

- Advise occupants of multiple-story buildings that are located away from the water to go to the first or second floors and take refuge in halls or interior rooms, away from windows.

- Wear a hard hat, if possible.

WHAT TO DO AFTER A HURRICANE

After a hurricane, the emergency management team should continue to use the utmost care in ensuring the safety of building occupants and the property. The following lists some suggestions:

- Listen to public broadcast announcements. Wait until an area is declared safe before re-entering an evacuated building.

- Have a first aid kit available for medical emergencies.

- Be extremely careful when moving around the property. Watch for electrical wires (which may be live), shattered glass, splintered wood, and debris, as well as structural damage.

- Inspect the property, and appoint cleanup crews.

- Call the property's insurance company, restoration contractor, and building inspector, and get them to the site as soon as possible.

- Set up a manageable schedule to repair the property. Be aware of symptoms of stress and fatigue.

- Have materials available for making temporary repairs, such as tools, hardware, plywood, sawhorses, and barricades.

- Do not turn on the electricity unless it has been officially declared safe to do so by the utility company.

- Report broken gas, sewer, or water mains to the respective utilities.

- Prepare for possible flooding from the storm or damaged water barriers.

- Be alert for potential fire hazards such as leaking gas lines, pools of water near electrical equipment and appliances, spills of combustible materials, etc. (Refer to *Chapter 14* for an overview of fires that may occur after a disaster.)

- If occupants are permitted by local authorities to evacuate, advise them of safe evacuation routes and roads. Drive only when necessary, as flooding may continue and roads may weaken and collapse.

CHAPTER 19:

Floods, Droughts, and Landslides

DEALING WITH FLOODS

Floods are the second most common natural disaster, after fire disasters. Any real estate manager who has endured catastrophic flooding on a property can attest that flooding is one of the worst natural disasters that can occur. Flooding causes more property damage in the U.S. than any other natural disaster, averaging losses of several billion dollars each year. Most natural floods are due to melting snow, the effects of tsunamis and hurricanes, and prolonged or heavy rainfall. Floods can also result from overflow of inland tidal waters, failure of a dam or levee, a mudflow, or an unusual and rapid accumulation or runoff of surface waters from any source. Flooding inside buildings can also be caused by broken water lines, frozen or bursting pipes, or an unexpected accident.

In the case of natural flooding, real estate managers should be aware of flood forecasts and warnings to determine the possibility of a flood, its expected severity, and when and where it could begin. Severe conditions may require evacuating buildings. Floods can be slow or fast rising, but they generally develop throughout a period of days. Flash floods, however, are like walls of water that develop in minutes—these can be caused by intense rainfall or failure of a dam.

While a flood can cause extensive property damage, it can also cause other potential disasters, including electrical outages, which could impede rescue operations, and result in electrocution of occupants. Drowning is a strong possibility in large regional floods. Depending on the type of property, food, fuel, and water contamination or shortages can also occur.

Areas and Properties at Risk for Floods

Properties with the highest risk of flooding are those located on a flood plain and in areas with histories of flooding. It is wise to check with the local Federal Emergency Management Agency (FEMA) field office to review potential flood risks. FEMA periodically updates public flood zone maps.[1] The Advanced Hydrologic Prediction Service of the National Weather Service (NWS) also provides improved flood forecasting and offers tools to assist in flood emergency planning.[2]

There are several types of floods—each having its own risk factors. River floods occur seasonally when winter or spring rains couples with melting snows, filling river basins with too much water too quickly. They also occur when floating ice accumulates at a natural or man-made obstruction and stops the flow of river water, eventually causing an overflow. Torrential rains from decaying hurricanes or tropical storms can also produce river flooding.

Coastal floods occur when winds generated from tropical storms and hurricanes or intense offshore low-pressure systems drive ocean water inland. Established escape and evacuation routes can be cut off and blocked by high water. Coastal flooding can also be produced by tsunamis, which are ocean waves produced by earthquakes or volcanic activity.

Flash floods are the leading cause of death related to thunderstorms, resulting in more than 140 fatalities each year. Most fatalities from flash floods either occur at night, when the dangers of fast-moving water may be obscured, or involve motorists trapped in their vehicles. Urban flash floods occur where land has been converted from fields or woodlands to paved roads and parking lots, caused by the ground surface losing its ability to absorb rainfall. Urbanization increases water runoff by two to six times more than runoff on natural terrain. During periods of urban flooding, streets can become swift-moving rivers capable of sweeping away vehicular traffic; basements can also become deathtraps as they accumulate water.

Warning Signs and Weather Advisories

Except for flash floods, the average natural flood is preceded by a few potential warning signs. A roaring sound upstream may herald an impending flood. Other common signs include rapidly rising water in a river or stream or water turning muddy. Continuous heavy rains for several days can lead to flooding in low-lying areas—areas that have been flooded in the past often exhibit telltale signs of old waterlines on the sides of buildings. When skies darken and thunderstorms are forecast, look and listen for increasing

---

1. Flood hazard maps can be found online at http://www.fema.gov/mit/tsd.

2. Information from the NWS regarding tools to assist in flood emergency planning can be found online at *www.nws.noaa.gov/om/water/Ahps.shtml.*

winds, flashes of lightning, or sounds of thunder. Severe thunderstorms often lead to flash flooding, but may contribute to river flooding as well.

Local radio, TV stations, and National Oceanic and Atmospheric Administration (NOAA) Weather Radio broadcast watches and warnings regarding flooding in specific areas. A flood watch means a flood is possible in the cited areas, while a flood warning means flooding is already occurring or will occur soon in the area and necessary precautions should be taken at once. Authorities may advise evacuation. The same applies for flash flood watches and warnings. Urban and small stream advisories are issued when flooding of small streams, streets, and low-lying areas such as railroad underpasses and urban storm drains occur. Real estate managers should refer to their emergency procedures guidelines to determine what actions should be taken in each circumstance.

Preventive Measures for Floods and Flash Floods

Certain measures can be implemented to prevent losses that can occur from flooding. The following lists some suggestions:

- Ask your local emergency management office whether your facility is located in a flood plain. Learn the elevation of your facility in relation to streams, rivers, and dams. Research the history of flooding in the area.

- Review the community's emergency plan. Learn the community's evacuation routes and locate the nearest high ground.

- Make sure you can receive updates on current conditions. Consider purchasing a NOAA Weather Radio with a warning alarm tone and battery backup in addition to mobile devices or radios you might use. Check for flood watches and warning updates often.

- Contact the National Flood Insurance Program (NFIP) to find out if the community in which the property is located participates in the program.

- Ask your insurance carrier about flood insurance for your property. This is a separate policy; regular property insurance does not cover flooding.

- Inspect areas in your facility subject to flooding. Identify equipment, records, and other assets that can be moved to a higher location and make plans to move them if a flood is expected.

- Consider the need for backup and recovery systems, such as alternate power sources, portable pumps to remove flood water, and battery-powered emergency lighting.

- Consider the feasibility of relocating vital building equipment (e.g., fire pump motors) if these items cannot be easily moved out of the path of flood water entering the building.

- Consult with a local building contractor or building official as to the best structural materials advised in flood-prone areas. For example, wood has a high water-absorption capacity, and average drywall acts like a sponge, drawing water up above the flood level.

- Know where asbestos-containing materials have been used in the building. Flood-damaged materials that contain asbestos require special handling; services of an asbestos contractor may be needed.

- Use site-planning techniques—sloping lawns, raised patios, improved drainage, flood walls, and levees—to protect a property against floods.

- Keep a supply of sandbags, plastic sheeting, lumber, and plywood for waterproofing at strategic locations and entrances.

- Keep auxiliary pumps on hand.

- Move valuable items to higher ground and advise building occupants to do likewise.

- Disconnect electrical appliances before flooding begins. Do *not* do this while standing in water.

- Identify a safe and elevated location for evacuees to assemble.

- Address dangerous and acceptable conditions for driving from the building. If a car stalls during evacuation, it should be abandoned immediately, and occupants should move to higher ground.

- Participate in community flood-control projects.

The National Institute of Building Sciences (NIBS) with the direction of FEMA has developed a standardized methodology, called HAZUS, for assessing losses from flood damage.[3] HAZUS software is also available for free online (*www.fema.gov*).

What to Do During a Flood

The emergency procedures manual should outline what management should do during a flood or immediately after a flood warning is issued.

---

3. For more information about HAZUS, visit *nibs.org/index.php/hazus*.

FLOOD INSURANCE

U.S. government-backed flood insurance is available to any business owner, homeowner, or renter whose property is located in a community that participates in the National Flood Insurance Program (NFIP). Participating communities must adopt and enforce local flood plain management ordinances that are designed to reduce the risk of flood losses in the future. In such communities, flood insurance can be purchased from a licensed insurance agent or company—for example, the same person who writes the owner's property policies.

Flood insurance is the best means of recovering losses from flood damage. It should be purchased well beforehand because policies do not take effect immediately. The effective date is normally 30 days after purchase.

The following lists what a standard flood insurance policy should cover:
- Structural damage
- HVAC damage
- Cleanup of flood debris
- Damage to floor surfaces (e.g., tile, carpeting)

It is also possible to obtain flood insurance coverage for building contents—furnishings, collectibles, and other personal property.

Note: Information on the National Flood Insurance Program can be found online at *www.fema.gov/nfip* or *www.floodsmart.gov*.

The following lists some possible actions to take:

- Give priority to the protection of power plant and fire pumps, keeping them in service if at all possible. In the event flood waters overwhelm defenses and enter the building, vital fire pump motors or engines should be protected. If they can be moved, they should be relocated. The same should be done for important motors, controls, and emergency power generation equipment.

- If possible, shut down the electricity in the building and distribute emergency flashlights.

- Open basement or lower-level windows to equalize water pressure on the building's foundation and walls.

- Do not use open flames—there may be gas escaping from ruptured mains.

- Watch for and avoid live electrical wires.

- If water enters the building and evacuation becomes impossible, move to an upper floor or rooftop and wait for rescuers.

- While evacuating, avoid attempting to drive through floods or rising water; nearly half of all flash flood fatalities are auto related.

FLOOD PROOFING METHODS

According to FEMA, there are three basic methods for flood proofing a property.

1. Permanent Flood proofing:
   - Where possible, elevate the facility on walls, columns, or compacted fill.
   - Reinforce walls to resist water pressure and seal them to prevent or reduce seepage.
   - Install check valves to keep flood water from entering the building by backing up through sewer lines.
   - Build watertight walls around equipment or work areas within the facility that are particularly susceptible to flood damage.
   - Construct floodwalls or levees outside the building to help keep water away.

2. Contingent Flood proofing:
   - Install watertight barriers, called flood shields, to prevent flood water from entering through windows, doors, ventilation shafts, or other openings.
   - Install permanent watertight doors.
   - Construct movable flood walls.
   - Install permanent pumps to remove flood waters.

3. Emergency Flood proofing:
   - Build walls with sandbags.
   - Construct a double row of walls with boards and posts to create a "crib" and fill the crib with soil.
   - Construct a single wall by stacking small beams or planks.

Permanent flood proofing measures are undertaken before a flood occurs and require no human intervention when flood waters rise. Contingent flood proofing measures are also taken prior to a flood, but some additional action is required when flooding occurs. Emergency flood proofing measures, while generally less expensive than the other types, require substantial advance warning of a flood and do not satisfy minimum requirements for flood proofing as set forth by the NFIP.

Source: *Emergency Management Guide for Business and Industry* published by the Federal Emergency Management Agency (FEMA 141/ October 1993) and available online at *http:// www.fema.gov/pdf/library/bizindst.pdf.*

- It is especially important to develop a specific flood evacuation plan for low-rise residential and commercial buildings because these types of structures are particularly vulnerable to collapse.

What to Do After a Flood

It is important to verify the safety of a building before anyone re-enters it after a flood. If there is standing water next to the outside walls of a property, do not go in. The building may not be safe or structurally sound. Walk around the building before entering it and check for downed or loosened power lines and gas leaks. The real estate manager should either call or appoint someone to call the appropriate utility company if either of these conditions are observed.

Checking for Structural Damage

After a flood, the building should be inspected at the earliest opportunity to assess its condition. The exterior should be inspected before anyone is allowed to enter the building. The following lists what should be inspected before cleanup is started or power is restored.

- Check the foundation for cracks and examine overhangs for missing structural supports. If obvious damage is observed, the real estate manager could ask the city building inspector or fire chief if the building is safe to enter.

- Check ceilings for signs of sagging. If a ceiling is holding water, the wet plaster or drywall will be very heavy and could be dangerous if it falls. Carefully poke or drill a hole in the ceiling at the edge of the sagging area and away from electrical fixtures so that any water trapped there can begin to drain. Walls made of drywall or other water-absorbent materials should also be checked for signs of sagging and treated appropriately.

- Inspect building mechanical systems prior to restoring power to components.

- Determine whether flood damage requires full removal or if cleaning and/or other treatment will suffice. For example, once drywall has been saturated, it generally needs to be replaced.

Restoring the Interior of a Property After a Flood

Provided the exterior of the building has passed inspection and is safe to enter, the following are considerations upon returning to a property after a flood:[4]

- Contact the property's insurance company or agent to file a claim under the flood insurance policy after the property's damage has been assessed.

---

4. Additional information can be found in Floods: The Awesome Power, published jointly by NOAA, FEMA, and the American Red Cross and available for download at *nws.noaa. gov/om/brochures/Floodsbrochure_9_04_low.pdf*.

- Appoint and supervise cleanup crews.
- If the electricity is still on after a flood, it should be turned off immediately. If someone has to step into water to turn it off, call an electrician to do the job.
- Breaker boxes should be turned off using a dry stick while standing on a dry surface.
- Watch for and avoid live electrical wires; do not turn on any electrical appliances until an electrician says it is okay to do so.
- Pump out water gradually to minimize further structural damage (e.g., one-third of the water each day for three days). Draining too quickly could allow the pressure outside the basement to collapse the walls.
- Get fresh air moving throughout the building to reduce moisture and dissipate any leaking gas.
- Properly dehumidify the building and other areas to avoid unhealthy conditions. Use dehumidifiers in conjunction with fans to create laminar air movement and speed up evaporation.
- Affected areas will need to be treated with an antimicrobial solution to kill bacteria and prevent the growth of mold and mildew. Growth of bacteria, mold, and mildew in ductwork is especially dangerous. Water damage or mold/mildew growth may necessitate complete removal of some items. If a building is flooded for 24 hours or more, it may be appropriate to engage a qualified professional to identify and eliminate potential mold and mildew growth.
- Cover holes in the roof, walls, or windows with boards, tarps, or plastic sheets.
- Temporarily repair sagging floors or roof sections by using 4×4 boards as braces in weak areas.
- Check for broken or leaking water pipes. If any are found, turn off the water supply.
- Be prepared for looting; secure the property to guard against potential trespassers.

DEALING WITH LANDSLIDES

Landslides are a global phenomenon. In the U.S. alone, landslides are estimated to cause $2 billion in damage and 25 to 50 deaths each year. Typically associated with periods of heavy rainfall or rapidly melting snow or ice, they tend to worsen the effects of flooding that accompany such events. While landslides often move very rapidly, causing deaths and destroying properties suddenly and unexpectedly, they can also move very slowly and cause damage at a gradual level. The force behind landslide movement is gravity. A number of factors allow gravity to overcome resistance to landslide movement, including steepening of slopes by erosion, alternate freezing or thawing, and saturation by water as well as earthquake shaking and volcanic eruptions.

Areas and Properties at Risk for Landslides

Landslides are common to almost every state in the U.S. and are more likely to occur in areas where vegetation has been destroyed by wild fires or development; on steep slopes or slopes that have been modified for construction of roads and buildings; in channels along a river or stream and where surface runoff is directed; and areas where landslides have previously occurred. Heavy rains after an extended period of drought can also lead to landslides. Even if a property is not in the direct path of a landslide, it can be impacted by landslide damage to electrical, gas, water, and sewer lines and disruption of road and rail transportation.

Preventive Measures for Landslides

Because landslides are so widespread, it is important to learn about the risk of landslides in your area and your property's vulnerabilities. The following lists recommendations to follow as preventative measures:

- Contact local, state, and/or federal authorities to find out if landslides have previously occurred in your area.

- Find out about local emergency and evacuation plans.

- Develop an evacuation plan for the property. This might include alternate driving routes to be recommended to staff and occupants in the event that nearby roads are affected by a landslide. Plan for the possibility that people may not be able to leave the building.

- If your property is in an area prone to landslides, consider having a consultant—civil engineer, structural engineer, or geotechnical engineer—evaluate the property and recommend corrective measures. Local authorities may be able to advise you of the best type of professional to contact.

LANDSLIDES AND MUDSLIDES

Landslides result from disturbances in the natural stability of a slope. They occur when masses of rock, earth, or debris move down a slope. Mudslides or debris flows are a common type of fast-moving landslide. They are rivers of rock, earth, and other debris that develop when the ground becomes saturated. Mudslides often occur without warning in areas where they have never been seen before. They can travel at avalanche speeds, growing in size as they pick up boulders, trees, cars, and other materials in their path. Mudslides are covered under the NFIP; however, landslides are not.

Mudslides usually begin on steep slopes and can be activated by natural disasters. Those that accompany volcanic eruptions are among the most destructive. Wildfires followed by heavy rains can also lead to mudslides.

The California Geological Survey website provides a detailed look at mudslides and how to prepare a property for them at *http://www.consrv.ca.gov/CGS/information/publications/cgs_notes/note_33/index.htm.*

- Landslides are generally not covered by the NFIP or individual insurance providers, however, consult your insurance agent about specific coverage to be sure—debris flow may be covered under the NFIP.

- Avoid gas and water leaks after a landslide by replacing rigid pipe fittings with flexible ones.

- Observe storm water drainage patterns on slopes in your area, especially areas where runoff water converges. Look for signs of soil movement, progressive tilting of trees, and other small changes that may signal the potential for a landslide.

- Consider using heavy plastic sheeting as a retaining barrier to prevent a slide from occurring on a slope.

- Consider landscape elements that can lessen or prevent soil erosion. By preventing erosion, it's likely these plants can help lessen the damage caused by a landslide, should one occur.

- Where feasible, maintain a supply of bags that can be filled with sand or soil to act as barriers around the property.

How to Deal with Landslides and Mudslides During Intense Storms

Emergency information regarding intense rainfall will be broadcast on radio, television, and NOAA Weather Radio. The following lists some indicators that a landslide may be imminent:

- A sudden increase in water level in a stream or creek may indicate a debris flow upstream. A trickle of flowing mud may precede a larger flow.

- A sudden reduction in water level may indicate a debris jam upstream that could eventually cause a more forceful flow when the dam breaks.

- Tilting trees, telephone poles, walls, or fences may indicate shifting of topsoil.

- Unusual sounds, trees cracking, boulders knocking together, general rumbling noises may indicate a landslide or mudflow is approaching.

- If a landslide is imminent, getting out of its path is the best protection. People in buildings may be advised to move above the first floor.

- Consider placing sandbags around the perimeter of the building or the side the landslide is expected to hit.

During a Landslide

The best place to be during a landslide, or if a landslide is imminent, is the inside of a building. Should a landslide occur, consider the following.

- If inside a building, stay inside, take cover under a desk, table, or other piece of sturdy furniture.
- If outdoors, try to get out of the path of the landslide or mudflow and run to the nearest high ground in a direction away from the flow path.
- If rocks and other debris are approaching, run for the nearest shelter, such as a group of trees or a building.
- If escape is not possible, curl into a tight ball and protect your head.

After a Landslide

Even though a landslide has stopped, there may be danger of additional slides or flooding. The site of the landslide should be avoided until the area is declared safe by authorities. Actions that may be taken at a managed property include the following:

- If possible to do so without entering the slide area, check for people who are injured or trapped in debris near the area of the landslide. Direct rescuers to assist them.
- Watch for signs of flooding.

- Report broken utility lines to appropriate authorities.
- Check the building foundation and surrounding land for damage.
- Consult a geotechnical expert for advice on further reducing landslide risks.
- Replant damaged ground to prevent further erosion.
- Remember that flooding may occur after a landslide or mudflow, especially if heavy rain initiated it.

Cleanup of building interiors—removal of water, mud, and debris—may require specialized equipment. A restoration consultant may be able to suggest appropriate vendors who provide this service.[5]

PREPARING YOUR PROPERTY FOR DROUGHT

Drought results when there is a persistent lack of sufficient precipitation to sustain normal function of a geographical area. It can be devastating to farmlands around the world and life threatening to residents of third-world countries that rely solely on their crops and water supply for sustenance. Droughts can also make properties more susceptible to fires and endanger the lives of building occupants.

Droughts not only sap the water out of vegetation to make it dry and brittle, they also deplete valuable life-saving water reservoirs that aid communities in fighting fires. This leaves properties more susceptible to fires, which can arise from intense solar heat and prime dry conditions, arson, or natural and man-made disasters (see the discussion of wildfires in *Chapter 14*).

Where most other types of disasters occur suddenly, often without warning, droughts develop slowly. Communities susceptible to drought conditions can plan ahead by creating water reservoirs and monitoring water usage.

Areas and Properties at Risk for Drought

Though many natural disasters occur specifically in one or two regions of the U.S., droughts can occur nationwide. Areas most susceptible to droughts may be geographically situated away from abundant natural mountain runoffs and where precipitation is rare. However, freak weather conditions can also lead to droughts in areas where precipitation occurs frequently. During a drought, every property type will feel the impact.

---

5. More information on landslides can be found on the U.S. Geological Survey website at *http://landslides.usgs.gov*. Information on landslide emergency preparedness can also be found on the American Red Cross and FEMA websites.

Residential and commercial buildings alike can be vulnerable to its effects.[6]

Preventive Measures for Cases of Drought

Droughts increase the risk of fire due to the dry, flammable condition of brush, crops, and grass. Moreover, if there is a fire, fighting it may be especially difficult due to low water pressure. For these reasons, all of the steps that are taken to prevent human and property loss from fires should be adhered to when there is a drought in the area.

During a Drought

The emergency procedures manual may include a section outlining what should be done during a drought. Recommended precautions include the following:

- Educate residents and commercial tenants on water conservation measures, and encourage them to wash only full loads of laundry or dishes and use the shortest cycle possible.
- Check with the local water department for recommendations on water-saving measures and any incentives they may offer.
- Obey all municipal requests regarding the use and rationing of water.
- Be aware of increased fire hazards. Keep flammable chemicals in cool, dark places.
- Remove flammable items and dead plants that, if ignited, could endanger the property. Keep fire extinguishers and the property's limited water supply easily accessible to prevent fire from spreading once it is detected.
- Familiarize staff and building occupants with precautionary fire safety measures and instruct them to report any fire hazard conditions on the property.

In some areas, it may still be permissible to burn leaves or trash on the property. Especially during a drought, avoid using fire outdoors while close to areas of natural vegetation.

---

6. For information on the drought status of specific areas, the National Weather Service Climate Prediction Center publishes a U.S. Drought Assessment, which is available online at *http://www.cpc.ncep.noaa.gov/products/Drought*.

After a Drought

As with the gradual onset of a drought, the aftermath of a drought is not marked by a sudden change. The emergency procedures manual should outline a gradual return to normal operations:

- Continue to use water conservation measures. Stay in compliance with rationing orders until they are lifted by local authorities.

- Consult the National Integrated Drought Information System, which maintains a drought information center with current conditions (*http://www.drought.gov*).

- Consider implementing permanent measures for reducing the property's water consumption such as installing devices that reduce water usage and recycle water.

- Consider changing the property's landscaping to reduce water requirements. Properties in the Southwest, for example, might consider desert plants rather than grass. In any geographic area, vegetation that is native to the area is likely to be less sensitive to changes in water availability.

CHAPTER 20:

Earthquakes, Tsunamis, and Tidal Waves

The tumultuous effects of major earthquakes can be catastrophic—causing buildings and bridges to collapse, downing telephone and power lines, and causing fires, explosions, or landslides. Oceanic earthquakes may also cause tsunamis—huge waves that travel long distances over the water until they crash into coastlines.

An earthquake can be identified by the rolling, rumbling sound as well as the severe shaking motion. A building and any items in or around it may shake, shatter, rattle, fall, or break. Shaking may begin in different ways—gently, growing violent in one or two seconds, or with a violent jolt like a sonic boom.

DEALING WITH EARTHQUAKES

Unfortunately, it is nearly impossible to predict an earthquake. Scientists can identify regions where earthquakes are likely within a specified range of time, but don't yet have the tools to accurately predict precisely when and where the activity will begin.

Injuries during earthquakes can result from flying glass, overturned bookcases, wall units, and other heavy furniture and even outdoor elements such as fallen power lines, bricks, and concrete. Severe damage can be caused by fires, which can break out due to broken gas lines and electrical short circuits.

Electricity and telephone service may be disrupted as lines and networks become overwhelmed or disrupted. Gas, water, and sewer pipelines may be broken. Fire protection systems are often triggered and sprinklers go on. Strong wind drafts created by the breakage of exterior windows may make the situation even worse. Normal police, fire, medical, and other services may not be accessible, possibly for extended periods of time. Looting may be a possibility as well.

Aftershocks may occur over a period of several days, weeks, or even months, creating more damage. Aftershocks can be nearly as strong as the initial earthquake and pose a significant risk to structures weakened by the initial shock. Many of these aftershocks are sometimes strong enough to be considered dangerous earthquakes in their own right.

Tsunamis may occur in coastal areas as a result of the earth's movement. Still, another concern after earthquakes is the threat of landslides resulting from a new imbalance in ground structure, which can cause both structural and nonstructural damage.

TSUNAMIS AND TIDAL WAVES

Tsunamis are ocean waves that are produced by earthquakes or underwater landslides. They can travel upstream in coastal estuaries and rivers, causing damage inland as well as on the coast. Often referred to incorrectly as a tidal wave, a tsunami is a series of waves traveling at speeds averaging 450–600 mph through the open ocean. While wave heights can exceed 100 feet, waves that are 10–20 feet high can be very destructive.

Tsunamis typically affect California, Oregon, Washington, Canada (British Columbia), and Alaska as well as the Hawaiian Islands and U.S. territories in the Pacific Basin. They also affect countries along the west coast of Central and South America and across the ocean, including Japan, the Philippine Islands, and Indonesia. A strong tsunami can be far more devastating and have more far-reaching impacts than the original earthquake. In fact, the number of people killed from the Tohoku earthquake—the 9.0 magnitude earthquake that rocked Japan in March 2011—were lost during the tsunami and not the quake itself.

Occupants living along the seacoast should consider an earthquake, or sizable ground rumbling, as a warning signal. A noticeable rapid rise or fall in coastal waters is another sign of an approaching tsunami. The following lists what may be issued regarding tsunamis:

- An advisory indicates that an earthquake has occurred in the Pacific Ocean that might generate a tsunami. Subsequent hourly bulletins are issued regarding the situation.
- A watch is issued when a tsunami was, or may have been, generated. It will take at least two hours for the tsunami to arrive onshore; preparation to evacuate may be advised.
- A warning indicates a tsunami that could cause damage was, or may have been, generated; people in the affected area will be advised to evacuate.

Tidal waves sometimes follow an earthquake, but it may also be a great rise of water along an ocean shore due to exceptionally strong winds. A similar phenomenon called a seiche may occur inland on landlocked lakes (e.g., the Great Lakes). A seiche is an oscillation of the lake surface that may be caused by local variations in air pressure—sometimes aided by winds and tidal currents. The oscillation can vary in frequency from a few minutes to several hours and may continue for some time after the atmospheric pressure differences no longer exist.

More information can be found on the National Oceanic and Atmospheric Administration (NOAA) website for tsunamis at *http://www.tsunami.noaa.gov/* and through the International Tsunami Information Center's website at *http://itic.ioc-unesco.org/index.php.*

Areas and Properties at Risk

Earthquakes most frequently occur west of the Rocky Mountains in the Front Range, which runs north-south between Casper, Wyoming and Pueblo, Colorado and rises up to 9,500 feet above the Great Plains. It's important to be aware that other parts of the U.S. are also susceptible. There are 39 states that are potential targets of earthquakes. The area of risk east of the Rockies is the New Madrid seismic zone, which extends more than 120 miles southward from Cairo, Illinois, where the Mississippi and Ohio Rivers converge, into Arkansas and parts of Kentucky and Tennessee.

Real estate managers should determine if their area has a history of earthquakes, the likelihood of another quake occurring, and the amount of damage typically caused by quakes in the vicinity. If real estate managers determine that earthquakes are a potential threat to the property, then an earthquake emergency plan is needed.

It is not surprising that the closer a property is to the center of an earthquake, the greater the likelihood of severe damage. Structures built on solid ground run a smaller risk of serious damage than those built on alluvial or fill soils. Structures most likely to suffer extensive structural damage include the following:

- Properties with asymmetrical towers
- L-shaped structures
- Masonry, brick, concrete block, adobe, and stone buildings with no reinforcing steel
- Reinforced concrete frame buildings with non-ductile or brittle joints (i.e., structures supported by column beam frames and no load-bearing walls)
- One- and two-story commercial and industrial buildings that have concrete, brick, or masonry walls and wood roofs
- Long-span buildings in which only outside walls support the roof (e.g., shopping centers, warehouses, gymnasiums)
- Mobile/manufactured homes
- House-over-garage structures
- Buildings that have not been constructed according to earthquake building codes
- Structures anchored to their foundations improperly or not at all

Buildings that are located adjacent to hills or situated on cliff sides should be constructed with extra structural reinforcement to withstand forceful landslides that can uproot structural foundations, and thrust dislocated soil and debris into building interiors.

Preventive Measures

There are two categories of damage a property may sustain during an earthquake—(1) structural and (2) nonstructural. Structural damage includes damage to foundations, outside and inside load-bearing walls; floor and roof sheathing; slabs, decking beams, and girders; and joists, posts, pillars, or columns.

Nonstructural damage is much more broadly defined. It can consist of damage to ceilings and light fixtures, windows, office equipment and computers, air conditioners, files, electrical and utility equipment, merchandise and inventory, furnishings, and personal property. Damage caused by moving or falling objects—whether during the earthquake or resulting from it—is also considered nonstructural.

Although structural damage is difficult to prevent, it may be possible to reduce future damage by incorporating earthquake-specific building techniques during initial construction and upgrades during major renovation projects. Building codes evolve, and newer codes are more likely to address earthquake damage mitigation. It is a good idea to know when the building you manage was built and what new building codes might apply.

Be sure that the following items are secure by whatever means possible:

- Exterior ornamentation
- HVAC equipment
- Piping
- Suspended ceilings
- Light fixtures, especially suspension type
- Wall hangings and hanging plants
- Computers and other office equipment
- Heavy furniture
- Shelves
- File cabinets (install locks) and other cabinets and cupboards (install sturdy latches on doors)
- Water heaters
- Gas and electrical appliances
- Top-heavy items

Additionally, be sure to inspect for and repair:

- Defective electrical wiring
- Leaky or inflexible gas connections
- Deep cracks in ceilings and foundations
- Store heavy items on lower shelves

- Locate heavy wall hangings, shelving units, and other similar items where they will do the least damage to persons and property if they fall
- Bolt foundations to buildings and mobile/manufactured homes, when necessary
- Ensure that sewer lines and other underground utility connections are structurally secure.

It may be desirable to measure and record earth movement on a property to help in planning preventive measures. This is usually done in consultation with a geotechnical engineer or other appropriate professional.[1]

WHAT TO DO DURING AN EARTHQUAKE

A practiced response to an earthquake is essential. For this reason, the emergency plan should specify what each person should do during the earthquake to avoid personal injury. This applies to occupants as well as members of the management staff. The appropriate response depends on where the person is when the earthquake occurs.

If you are indoors:

- Stay indoors; do not go outside the building.
- Turn off the gas and utilities within immediate reach.
- Locate a sturdy table or desk to protect you. If it is near a window or exterior wall, move it against an interior wall. Crouch under the table or desk, tucking your head to your knees and protecting your head with your arms.
- If the furniture moves, move with it.
- Watch for and avoid falling objects—plaster, light fixtures, heavy items on shelves or in cupboards or closets, mirrors, wall hangings, glass from windows, and swinging doors.

If you are in a hallway:

- Kneel against the nearest interior wall.
- Tuck your head to your knees.
- Cover your head with your arms.

---

1. More specific information on earthquake preparedness can be found on the Federal Emergency Management Agency (FEMA) website at *http://www.ready.gov/earthquakes.* The California Governor's Office of Emergency Services also has a number of publications on earthquake preparedness available for download at *www.oes.ca.gov.* Select Publications Inc. offers *Homeowners' Guide to Earthquake Safety and Environmental Hazards* and *The Commercial Property Owner's Guide to Earthquake Safety,* which may be resources to list in an occupant handbook.

If you are in an elevator:

- Remain calm.
- Be prepared for the elevator's power to shut down and the lights to go off and for the possibility that the elevator may become jammed in the shaft; even if the latter does occur, the shaft should be safe from falling objects.
- Wait for an emergency rescue team when the earthquake is over. Be patient; it may take some time for help to arrive.

If you are outdoors:

- Quickly get as far away as possible from buildings.
- If you cannot move to an open area, position yourself in a building doorway.
- Watch for and avoid falling power lines, chimneys, building and roof ornaments, walls, glass, television antennas, and other airborne objects.

WHAT TO DO AFTER AN EARTHQUAKE

The earthquake itself will probably last only a few seconds, although the time span may seem like minutes or even hours. Likewise, recovery time is usually brief, but it can be chaotic and difficult. The real estate manager may have to cope with limited fire, police, and medical help. Power may be out, and water and sewer facilities may be unavailable for up to 72 hours or even longer.

To get through this post-earthquake period as smoothly as possible, the emergency plan should outline actions that the emergency management team, as well as building occupants, can take. The following lists some suggestions:

- Stay indoors. Do not rush to the exits when the shaking stops. Crowds pushing down stairs or surging through doorways can be as dangerous as the earthquake itself. Moreover, aftershocks may immediately follow.

- Tend to the injured. Do not move seriously injured persons unless it is a matter of life and death.

- Listen to the radio for emergency information. Do not use the phones to obtain this information; keep lines open for emergency services' use.

- Use flashlights only—matches or candles should not be used because of possible gas leaks.

- Avoid fallen and falling glass and equipment.

- Do not flick light switches on or off because this may ignite leaking gas.

- Turn off utilities at main switches, if appropriate.

- Turn off appliances, such as computers, copiers, and washing machines and dryers that were operating when the earthquake occurred.

- Immediately check for evidence of structural damage that could worsen during aftershocks. Such evidence could be in the form of cracks in chimneys (which have a propensity to fall during aftershocks), parking structure instability, and damage to building façade.

- Immediately check for nonstructural damage that could cause secondary problems. These may include broken or leaking gas lines, shorts in electrical equipment or wiring, leaks in diesel fuel lines, and damaged and nonfunctioning elevators.

- Inspect storage areas and make arrangements for the cleanup of dangerous or flammable substances spilled during the quake (e.g., medicines, cleaning solutions, fuels, and chemicals).

- Extinguish secondary fires caused by broken natural gas lines and electrical short circuits; only use fire extinguishers designed for these types of fires.

- Secure the building against looting.

- Do not turn on utilities until given the go-ahead by the appropriate utility companies. Then, restore electrical power one floor at a time and one piece of equipment at a time to avoid a power surge.

- Check sewer main lines before attempting to use toilet facilities. If sewers are inoperable, use plastic bags to line wastepaper baskets for temporary toilet facilities; close bags after each use and dispose after several uses.

- Open cabinet, cupboard, and storage area doors slowly and cautiously to avoid being injured by items that might tumble out.

- Make people at the property as comfortable as possible for as long as necessary by providing games, books, and magazines from the property's emergency provisions. Provide food and drink, which go a long way toward calming nerves and avoiding panic.

EARTHQUAKE DAMAGE TO ELEVATORS

- Elevator cars may stop between floors.
- Hoistway doors may bind so they cannot be opened.
- Hoistway door locks may break, allowing doors to sag or leaving the hoistway open.
- Counterweight rails and guide shoes may be loosened.
- The suspension system may fail due to loosened beams and/or deflector sheaves or broken ropes.
- Machine room equipment may also be damaged.

For additional information on potential damage to elevators as the result of an emergency, see *Chapter 12*.

- Pay particular attention to anyone who may be injured and to senior residents, those with special needs, and children.

- Be advised of the threat of land or mudslides. (See *Chapter 19* for specific preparations for landslides and mudslides.)

It may be necessary or appropriate to have a structural engineer inspect the building. If the property owner is responsible for water, sewer, and other underground utilities between the building and the connections to the main lines—often the case even though the utility may have performed the installation—it may be necessary to have appropriate professionals check out the integrity of such utility lines and connections. A plumber can detect breaks in sewer lines using a video camera.

The National Institute of Building Sciences (NIBS) at the direction of FEMA has developed a standardized methodology, called HAZUS, for assessing losses from earthquakes and other natural hazards. HAZUS uses geographic information system software to calculate, map, and display earthquake hazards and damage.[2]

---

2. Information about HAZUS is available online at *http://nibs.org/index.php/hazus*. Additional information can be found at the U.S. Geological Survey National Earthquake Information Center website at *http://neic.usgs.gov* and in Earthquakes by Kaye M. Shedlock and Louis C. Pakiser, published online by the U.S. Geological Survey at *http://pubs.usgs.gov/gip/earthq1*.

CHAPTER 21:

Volcanic Eruptions

Volcanic eruptions are capable of hurling hot rocks for distances of 20 miles or more—airborne ash can travel hundreds of miles. Dangerous floods and mudflows can occur in valleys leading away from volcanoes. Molten rock and mudflows can block roadways, uproot trees, and destroy buildings and bridges.

AREAS AND PROPERTIES AT RISK

Volcanic eruptions are most likely to occur in the Pacific Rim, including the states of Alaska, Washington, Oregon, California, and Hawaii. The greatest likelihood of damage to populated areas is around the active volcanoes in Alaska and Hawaii—although active volcanoes in the Cascade Mountain Range in California, Oregon, and Washington have also created problems. While the danger area around a volcano covers an approximate 20-mile radius, there may be some danger up to 100 miles or more from a volcano, which means states such as Idaho, Nevada, Montana, and Wyoming are also at risk.

EMERGENCY PLANNING

People who live near a known volcano, whether it is active or dormant, should be ready to evacuate at a moment's notice. Emergency preparations for volcanic eruptions should anticipate other hazards that can accompany them, including earthquakes, tsunamis, flash floods, landslides and mud-flows, airborne ash, and acid rain.

Real estate managers in areas near volcanoes should find out how the local community warns residents about impending volcanic eruptions. Emergency plans should include procedures to be implemented before, during, and after an eruption. It may be appropriate to inquire about the likelihood of ashfall (e.g., past incidents in the general area) to determine what emergency procedures may be needed. The various hazards that can accompany volcanic eruptions should also be addressed—especially if they are not among the commonly expected emergencies for the locale. Specific preparations might include the following items:

- Compile information to facilitate evacuation of the building and departure from the area. Include area evacuation routes in occupant emergency procedures.

- Ensure that everyone on the property knows and understands how warnings of a volcanic eruption will be announced and what to do when evacuating the building and area.

- Stockpile disposable dust masks and goggles for property personnel (also for occupants if possible and practical to do so). Encourage occupants to also have these available for themselves.

- Purchase or prepare appropriate covers to protect sensitive equipment. For some items, covers of plastic sheeting may be adequate. Equipment with slots or vents may need closely fitted covers to keep out volcanic ash.

What to Do During a Volcanic Eruption

During a volcanic eruption, people should avoid areas that are downwind of the volcano. If there is time to take precautions, close building windows, doors, and vents; turn off machinery and equipment; and protect it from dust. This is especially important for rooftop installations (e.g., HVAC equipment). People who are outdoors should seek shelter. If caught in a rockfall, they should roll into a ball to protect their heads. Avoid low-lying areas where poisonous gases can collect. If caught near a stream, be aware of mudflows. Mudflows occur when rain falls through clouds containing volcanic ash or when rivers are dammed during an eruption. If a mudflow can be heard approaching, it's important to move upslope. Mudflows are most dangerous in areas that are close to stream channels.

What to Do After a Volcanic Eruption

After a volcanic eruption, seek updates from radio broadcasts, televised news, or online sources on the current state of the emergency, including how widespread ashfall has become. Volcanic ash should be avoided as it poses serious health risks—particularly to those with respiratory ailments. Wear protective goggles and a dust mask, and keep skin covered to avoid burns or irritation. Because volcanic ash is very heavy and can cause buildings to collapse, it should be cleared off of roofs as soon as possible.[1]

---

1. More specific information can be found online at *http://www.noaawatch.gov/themes/volcanoes.php* and *http://volcanoes.usgs.gov.* The U.S. Geological Survey (USGS) site includes information on specific volcanoes in the U.S. The Federal Emergency Management Agency (FEMA) website includes background information and a link to a fact sheet on volcanoes at *http://www.ready.gov/volcanoes.* States with active volcanoes include emergency information on their official websites.

SECTION 5:

Crime and Terrorism

CHAPTER 22:

How to Deal with Crime on a Property

Real estate managers are justifiably concerned when it comes to crime on the properties they manage. Crime not only endangers a property's staff, tenants, and damages physical premises; it also threatens a property's value, reputation, and income.

A high crime rate will cause a property to suffer from a poor reputation, lower morale among employees and occupants, and have a detrimental effect on prospective residents, commercial tenants, customers, and employees.

Criminal activity comes in many forms, among them includes:

- Burglary
- Robbery
- Vandalism
- Assault
- Rape
- Murder
- Child or spousal abuse
- Fights
- Drug activity
- Gang violence
- Gunfights
- Hostage situations
- Riots

CRIME PREVENTION MEASURES

Real estate managers can implement any number of preventive measures to combat crime. To help thwart some crimes, it's important to be aware of the two types of perpetrators—(1) outsiders and (2) insiders. The following lists the suggested measures to be taken in each case:

1. Outsider Perpetrators

- Ask to assist unfamiliar persons on the property, which may help decrease the risk of theft.

- Ask to see identification for service or maintenance persons.
- Escort delivery persons or messengers to their destinations.
- Ask to see identification for food vendors and repair persons.

2. Insider Perpetrators

- Check references and background information before hiring employees
- Educate employees and change negative attitudes if there is a strong sense of low morale.
- Instruct security personnel to screen all employees according to an appropriate list of criteria, and have them utilize uniforms with the company's and person's names.
- Provide uniforms for maintenance personnel that exhibit the property identification and person's name; require them to carry and show property-specific identification.
- Institute a sign-in/sign-out program for clients of property management or commercial tenants if the building has a lobby security guard.
- Establish and enforce screening procedures for potential/future residents.
- Require visitors in high-rise buildings either to sign in and out at a main desk or wear visitor badges while on the property.

The following lists some other crime preventative measures:

- Inspect the property and make appropriate repairs/replacements for flickering, broken, and burned-out lights, which can create dimly lit corridors, stairwells, staircases, restrooms, and other secluded areas. Verify that all doors are properly locked, and there are no broken windows.

- Inspect the outside areas of the property to ensure safety of residents and commercial tenants' employees. Be sure that the landscaping (e.g., bushes, trees, shrubs) is not overgrown, which could be used as potential hiding places.

- At properties that have security patrols, consider providing a guard to escort occupants and visitors to their cars after sunset. Instruct security guards to regularly patrol the property.

- Safeguard records of safe and vault combinations and computer passwords in the office; lock and secure critical and confidential files; and shred confidential documents before discarding.

- Use individual keys instead of master keys and keep track of all copies; be able to account for all keys; maintain a list of commercial tenants who are given keys to restrooms that are kept locked or use electronic locks that require a numeric code or a magnetic swipe card to gain access.

- If a property uses sign-in/sign-out sheets, maintain security by keeping them out of public view.

- Distribute a list of emergency telephone numbers, such as building security, managers, police, fire department to each occupant—residential or commercial tenants.

- Instruct employees *not* to let callers know when persons of authority are out of town or are not on the property.

- Develop programs with public-victim services agencies and mental health centers for any victims of crime on the property.

IMPLEMENTING A SECURITY SYSTEM

Seek advice from security professionals regarding appropriate use of safes and vaults, access controls (door locks and other hardware, electronic locks, and key pads or swipe cards), intrusion alarms, and closed-circuit television cameras, and the benefits of employing security patrols using onsite personnel or a contracted security service. Remember, however, that security measures, once implemented, are difficult to alter without raising questions about security being reduced by such a change.

Meet with other real estate managers to devise a communication network arrangement with the police department that will notify others of specific criminal activity if or when it happens. The network may include sophisticated voicemail systems that automatically contact all users of the system. The arrangement may also include an ongoing program in which real estate managers meet with police officials to receive periodic updates on crime statistics, trends, and prevention techniques.

It is also a good idea to use an occupant newsletter or occasional flyers to remind residents and commercial tenants' employees to take precautions for their personal safety and to report criminal activity to the proper authorities. Subjects that might be addressed include who to contact if they are the victim of a crime, proper use of dead-bolt locks, safeguarding cash and credit cards, and the need to be aware that pickpockets are more active in areas of heavy retail traffic—especially during lunch hours and holiday shopping seasons.

CRIME MAPPING: HOW TO INVESTIGATE COMMUNITY CRIME REPORTS

Many police departments prepare daily criminal activity reports which include reported information on specific city streets, the time when incidents have taken place, and a brief description of the incidents. The listed incidents are unverified, meaning that they have not yet been checked by the police to confirm the occurrence or nature.

Police use these reports to analyze crime trends, assign patrols, gauge the crime rate in given areas, and gain a better insight for responding to crime. Such reports may be helpful to managers; however, they are not always inclusive of all types of criminal activity and generally require follow-up investigations. Real estate managers can use police reports to obtain information on specific types of crimes—for example, if a car thief is working in the property's vicinity. Criminal activity reports can also be used to help stop rumors that tend to exaggerate the frequency and seriousness of crimes.

BEING AWARE OF GANG ACTIVITY

Gang activity, including violence, occurs when the community at large allows it. In order to help preserve the safety of people on managed properties—including visitors as well as residents and commercial tenants' employees—real estate managers should actively combat gang-related activity on their premises.

The following lists what real estate managers can do to become more aware of a gang presence on their property and how to detect gang insignia:

- **Identify Gangs.** Gang members often identify themselves by use of certain hand signals, haircuts, jewelry, and styles of dress that include specific colors.

- **Be Firm.** Make it clear that anyone who violates property rules will be prosecuted. Gangs repeatedly target properties that have a reputation for being "soft" on offenders such as vandals. Real estate managers should work with local police to establish firm criminal and procedural discipline for gang members who violate property or community conduct policies.

- **Remove graffiti immediately.** It is often used as symbols to mark a particular gang's territory, which is painted in a process called "tagging." Graffiti should be painted over or removed immediately (and continuously) to discourage violators from returning and

224

to discourage clashes between gangs who paint over each other's symbols. Before removing graffiti, be sure to photograph it as evidence—police may be able to identify which gang was responsible.

- **Reflect the Community.** Employ security officers who reflect the demographics of the area surrounding the property to encourage a sense of community. An effective security officer is one who is highly trained and well equipped, self confident, with a professional demeanor, and good communication skills to send a credible message to gang members.

- **Create an Active Record.** Police may be able to provide descriptions of locally active gang members. Such a file will allow management staff to know whom to watch out for.

- **Identify Loitering.** Immediately address groups of people loitering in a particular area for an extended period of time—especially if they display obnoxious behavior. The longer people are allowed to loiter, the more trouble they could potentially cause.

- **Be Consistent When Prosecuting Criminal Offenders.** Local police cannot assist a property unless someone is willing to prosecute. A complaint must be signed by a resident or a commercial tenant's representative, management, or security staff to effectively combat problems.

VIOLENCE IN THE WORKPLACE

Workplace attacks are primarily instigated by irate customers, disgruntled employees (both current and former), and estranged lovers or spouse reflect a stressed-out, downsized business environment, and a changing society, according to Joseph Kinney, executive director of the National Safe Workplace Institute. "People are increasingly deciding that violence is a way to respond to problems."

According to Alan Bell, manager of Intercon Security Limited's corporate resource group, real estate managers have no control over commercial tenants' hiring practices, business procedures, or whether or not they have security programs in place. Furthermore, commercial tenants tend to keep problems within their own organizations to themselves. Therefore, real estate managers are encouraged to give heed to early warning signs, particularly when employees are involved. Ignoring potential problems can lead to costly litigation for the companies and properties involved.

The following lists what can real estate managers can do to protect their properties against workplace violence:

- **Design a safe workplace by considering issues of safe access.** Be sure that offices with sensitive information are not accessible near elevators. Consider the use of pass cards or magnetic locks to prevent trespassers. Install a panic button at the reception desk, which can signal an alarm to building security or the police. By not posting names on office doors, it makes it difficult for hostile intruders to locate their targets.

- **Employ stringent hiring procedures.** Pre-employment screening is essential in reducing workplace violence. Criminal and employment background checks reveal patterns that can signal potential problems. For example, substance abuse and incidents of workplace violence go hand in hand.

- **Train managers to detect warning signs.** Certain behavioral changes that cause suspicion and merit investigation include sudden drastic changes in employees' personalities, overreaction to changes in corporate policies, persecution complexes, boastful remarks concerning the use of weapons, or previous incidents of violence, such as spouse abuse, threatening co-workers or supervisors, repeated violations of organizational policies and procedures, increased emotional swings, and symptoms of alcohol or drug abuse.

- **Train employees to report threats.** Employees should always report threats to their personnel departments or supervisors and trust that their concerns are being taken seriously.

- **Establish policies and procedures.** Threats of violence, intimidation, harassment, or violent acts should not be tolerated. Employees should be aware of a company's zero-tolerance policy and that threats or incidents of violence will result in immediate termination. There should be specific procedures for addressing incidents of violence that occur in a tenant's space, including actions to be taken by employees who encounter threats or experience varying kinds of workplace violence.

- **Take precautions when downsizing.** Job losses may trigger incidents of workplace violence. Therefore, layoffs and individual dismissals should be sensitively treated. Termination checklists provided by the real estate manager are especially important in buildings that employ access control systems. All work-related keys, identification cards, and pass cards that provide access into the building, the commercial tenant's space, and parking garage should be retrieved. Real estate managers should also be informed by tenants' human resources personnel about the terminations. Unreturned building access cards can be flagged in the system by the real estate manager, triggering an alarm when the card is used without permission. Violent reaction to job loss is not necessarily immediate. Sometimes a delayed reaction may occur months later if the individual has difficulty finding new employment.

CRIMES AGAINST SENIOR RESIDENTS

Nearly every state has enacted legislation addressing abuse, exploitation, or other victimization of senior residents. Seniors are frequent targets of consumer fraud schemes, as well as robbery and physical abuse. They are also more likely to be injured in a criminal incident and to need medical care.

An almost standard feature in adult protection statutes is mandatory reporting of abuse or neglect as defined by law. States vary in stipulating who must report and whether any penalty exists for not revealing known or suspected abuse. The following lists the signs for maintaining a strong sense of awareness for crime against senior residents:

- Signs of physical abuse include frequent injuries without plausible explanations, overmedication, and multiple bruises in various stages of healing.

- Neglect is akin to physical abuse. It includes deprivation of food and medical care, as well as living in a filthy environment. Lack of needed glasses, hearing aids, and/or dentures may signal neglect, as may poor personal hygiene.

- Emotional or psychological abuse is not as easily recognized. It may take the form of denying the senior resident any role in decision-making or berating the person as a burden. Signs include sudden dramatic changes in the senior's behavior.

- Exploitation may involve illegal use of the senior resident's funds, misuse of the guardianship function, or use of the senior resident's funds in a legal manner that is not in the person's best interest (e.g., through guardianship or power of attorney). Signs may include foreclosure on a home or eviction for nonpayment of rent, unusual activity on the person's bank account, and lack of food, clothing, or personal supplies.

Senior residents, whose mental and reasoning abilities may be waning or impaired, can also be susceptible to consumer fraud, including fraudulent charitable solicitations. Real estate managers of residential properties should foster sensitivity among their staff and encourage security personnel to pay particular attention to the welfare of senior residents.

STRIKES, DEMONSTRATIONS, OR PROTESTS ON A PROPERTY

Real estate managers of commercial properties (office buildings, retail properties, and industrial facilities) may face the possibility of a strike from a tenant's disgruntled employees. Strikes could be created by employees who are laid off, fired, or are discontent with their work environment, benefits, or wages. The latter may be part of a labor union strategy to obtain management concessions or the result of contract negotiations breaking down.

Real estate managers should be vigilant for threats that may be made by individuals or groups of protestors. Physical attacks may even be made upon the person or property of workers involved in the strike. Therefore, it is important that before, during, and after the strike, real estate managers should take a firm position that any type of threats, violence, or intimidation will not be tolerated and that offenders will be dealt with severely. As flare-ups between workers or against the company may likely occur within the first day or two, security forces should be adjusted.

Demonstrations by people supporting a cause or protesting an action related to a company or organization can lead to similar types of threats and actions. These are often short-lived events. In cities, a permit is usually required and law enforcement is present to maintain the peace. However, demonstrations have gotten out of hand, resulting in injuries to bystanders, as well as demonstrators, and damage to properties. These types of public displays should be subject to the same "rules" as strikes by workers. If the participants in the demonstration have no valid reason to be on the property—if they do not work on the premises—call the police to have them removed.

DRUGS AND CRIME ON A PROPERTY

Crack houses and other illegal drug operations threaten the sanctity and safety of communities by luring potentially violent customers into the area and presenting potential chemical hazards. While illegal drug manufacturing laboratories may be set up in commercial buildings, drug trafficking is more often seen in residential areas. When drug activity is present or suspected, the real estate manager should work closely with the police.

Potential Signs of Drug Activity

The following indicators might not always be present, but the presence of any of the indicators could mean that criminal or drug activity is taking place. However, taken individually or in an aggregate, the following list suggests things to be vigilant for:

- Increased traffic to the property by vehicles and pedestrians who stop for only a brief period of time
- Visitors who appear to be acquaintances rather than friends
- Visitors who sit in the car for a while after leaving the residence or who leave one person in the car while the other visits
- "Lookouts," frequently younger people, who tend to hang around the property during heavy-traffic hours
- People exchanging small packets for cash; people using drugs while sitting in their cars; syringes on the lawn and other paraphernalia lying about
- Motorcycle and bicycle riders making frequent late-night trips to and from a property where other indicators of drug activity are being observed
- A dramatic drop-off of suspected activity within minutes before police arrive; this may indicate that the criminal is using a radio scanner to monitor police broadcasts
- Unusually strong fortification of a residence or individual rooms with blacked-out windows, window boards, or extra dead-bolt locks
- Large dollar amounts spent on alarm systems and requests for or willingness to pay high dollar amounts for installation of window bars and other fortifications.
- A willingness to pay rent months in advance, particularly in cash— if applicants offer six months' rent in advance, resist the urge to accept, and require them to go through the application process
- A general tendency to pay in cash, combined with a lack of visible means of support

Methamphetamine and Other Drug Laboratories

Real estate managers who discover or have reason to believe that there is a methamphetamine laboratory on their property should immediately leave the property, wash their face and hands, and call the police. If there is reason to believe exposure has been extensive, they should contact their doctor without delay, as some of the chemicals involved are highly toxic.

The following are some warning signs that indicate the presence of a methamphetamine laboratory:[1]

- Strong smell of ammonia
- Maroon-colored residue on aluminum material in the house—the acid used in the ephedrine process of methamphetamine production leaves this residue, but does not have the ammonia smell
- The presence of flasks and beakers—used for secondary purposes
- The odor of either chloroform or other solvents
- Large amounts of baking soda, tin foil, or electrical wiring—used in various drug production or growing operations
- The presence of unusually sophisticated weight scales, using grams and smaller units of weight
- Drums and other chemical containers with their labels painted over
- Individuals leaving the premises just long enough to smoke a cigarette, particularly if other suspicious signs are present
- The presence of ether on the premises, which is highly explosive and used in methamphetamine production
- Large quantities of empty medication boxes, especially those medicines which contain pseudoephedrine (or similar compounds), which may be found in a number of decongestants and can be used to stimulate methamphetamine

Identifying Possible Marijuana Growing Operations

The following lists some warning signs that indicate marijuana is being grown at the property:

- General signs of excessive fortifications or overly paranoid behavior such as blacked out or obstructed windows

---

1. Some of these indicators may signal active laboratories that produce other illegal drugs.

- A sudden jump in utility bills—growing operations require strong lighting and excessive electricity

- Persistent, powerful lighting left on all night in the attic or basement

- Evidence of tampering with wiring and hooking directly into power lines for growing operations—this will overload the power rating for the residence and can burn the wiring, potentially resulting in fires

- Rewired circuitry due to some operations that use 1000-watt bulbs that require 220-volt circuits—this exceeds the power rating for the residence and can burn out the wiring, possibly resulting in an electrical fire

- Basements and attics filled with plants, lights, and highly reflective material which help speed the growing process

- A surprisingly high humidity level in the residence—growing operations require great quantities of moisture.

Real estate managers may find it appropriate to include language in their leases, indicating that drug activities (trafficking, manufacturing, or growing) are prohibited in leased premises and that violators will be prosecuted. Legal counsel can best advise on specific language that will stand up to adjudication in a court of law. Be sure to also check with local, state, and federal laws regarding possession and growing of marijuana. Some states are voting for the possession, growing, and selling of marijuana for medicinal purposes.

WHAT TO DO DURING A CRIME

Real estate managers should be able to refer to the property's emergency procedures manual for guidance in responding to criminal activity as it occurs on the premises. The following are some suggested guidelines:

Reporting Crime Activity to the Police

- When talking to the police, stay calm, and state the problem. Give police all the relevant information, including the property's address and nearest cross streets. Clearly state your name, address, and telephone number.

- Answer all the operator's questions, and stay on the phone until the operator says that it is all right to hang up.

Waiting for the Police

- Real estate managers and staff should not subject themselves to any physical endangerment at the scene of the crime.
- Never argue or debate with an assailant, thief, or robber—they could be carrying a weapon.
- Never fight back forcibly, unless forced to in a life-threatening situation.
- If possible, look carefully and get a full description of the perpetrator(s) of the crime, including height, weight, age, sex, hair color, hairstyle, and distinguishing features such as scars, birthmarks, eye color, complexion, and clothing.
- If the perpetrator attempts to escape, pay attention to which direction they were headed. Try and capture vehicle information such as make, model, color, and license plate number.

WHAT TO DO AFTER A CRIME

The emergency procedures manual should also provide guidance for responding after a crime has occurred. The following are suggested actions to take:

- Upon arrival at the scene of a crime, be sure not to disturb anything, as it may disrupt a police investigation.
- Keep everyone confined to the building until authorities give the all-clear signal to leave. Also, do not allow access to anyone, tenant or visitor.
- Do not invite a copycat crime by revealing too many details of the crime to the media.
- Never report large losses or overly detailed descriptions of stolen items to the media. Doing so could inspire a future theft.

CHAPTER 23:

Bombs, Bomb Threats, and Explosions

An explosive device or explosion on a property can be devastating to both human life and the property itself. Acts of terrorism and major bomb threats reinforce the need for real estate managers to educate their staff about how to properly respond if there is a bomb emergency on the premises. Real estate managers should have a bomb threat plan in place to share with staff members, who should also be assigned to different activities—for example, someone (usually security guard) who should prevent uninvited people from entering the building, or someone who should be required to wait for the police after the call is made, or even someone who visits the tenant or resident who received a potential threat over the phone. These are just a few items that should be outlined in your plan.

AREAS AND PROPERTIES AT RISK

Though all properties can be vulnerable to bombs and bomb threats, major metropolitan areas are more vulnerable because they offer all the ingredients bombers seek—numerous targets, many people whose attention they want to get, and crowds of people, among whom they can conceal themselves. Large cities may also be a target because of their opportunity to impact cultural significance or reputation through an attack on a landmark or other famous building. Given the well-developed infrastructure that may exist in a large city, there are also opportunities to make relatively small attacks that cripple a system. Metropolitan areas will also likely have a high media presence, drawing national and international attention immediately following an act of terrorism.

SECURITY MEASURES TO THWART BOMB THREATS

Real estate managers may conduct a security review of a property to pinpoint vulnerable areas within the building. A physical assessment of the facility includes checking the access control systems, employee identification system, alarms, surveillance cameras, and physical barriers. Not all buildings have or need the full array of these security measures.

Building mechanical systems (e.g., plumbing, electrical wiring, communications cabling, HVAC equipment) as well as emergency generators should be checked to ensure they are not easily accessible to the public. Real estate managers can choose from numerous security measures and options, depending on property type, security needs, and location of the property. The following lists some measures to consider:

- **If the building utilizes security patrols, review the patrolled areas and schedule.** Are stairwells and corridors regularly patrolled? Should the frequency of patrols be increased? Should the hours of patrol be extended to cover hours earlier in the morning and/or later in the evening?

- **Review the communications systems within the building.** Do management staff and security patrols have and use portable communication devices? Is there a backup system available, should the primary building-wide system become inoperable?

- **Check the lighting systems for elevators and stairwells.** Are battery-operated lights available to serve as backup to current emergency lighting systems?

- **Check the condition of building exit signs.** Are there additional phosphorescent signs posted to facilitate evacuation if lighted exit signs do not work?

- **Review methods by which deliveries are made to the property.** Do any procedural controls need to be added?

- **Be aware of suspicious or unattended items.** Has someone left a strange package or unidentifiable object in a strange location?

The information derived from the security review can help determine if new or additional preventive measures should be implemented. The emergency procedures manual should include procedures for responding to a bomb threat or the discovery of a bomb. The local police department or bomb squad should be consulted for specific guidelines. Recommendations vary regarding evacuation of a building that receives a bomb threat. There is and should be concern that immediate evacuation may expose people to greater danger. Evacuation routes are usually through public corridors, stairwells, and lobbies—the places most likely to contain an explosive device because they are accessible by the public. A general panic during an evacuation could cause injuries to people and damage to the property.

RESPONDING TO A BOMB THREAT

When a real estate manager or tenant receives a bomb threat or notice that a bomb has been found on the premises, there should be emergency procedures already in place. Response procedures will differ slightly, depending on whether the threat arrives by telephone or mail. The following lists guidelines for responding to a bomb threat received by phone:

- Never transfer the call. Try to keep the caller on the phone as long as possible to obtain information about the bomb and its whereabouts.
- Never assume the threat is a hoax.
- Never shrug off the threat as a bomb scare that can be ignored.
- Never argue with or ridicule the caller.
- Have a prearranged signal with others in the office so that someone can listen in without the caller's knowledge.
- If at all possible, record the conversation.
- Have a prepared checklist readily accessible to help identify the caller.

A bomb threat checklist is available at no charge from the Department of the Treasury, and Bureau of Alcohol, Tobacco, and Firearms.

The following are guidelines for responding to a bomb or a bomb threat received by mail.

- Save all received material—envelope, packaging material, and contents. Do not touch the package if there appears to be an object enclosed.
- Take care in handling the envelope or package so that fingerprints will be preserved.

The U.S. Postal Inspection Service recommends observing the following precautions if a suspicious parcel is received:

- Do not open the package.
- Isolate the suspicious parcel and evacuate the immediate area.
- Do not immerse the bomb in water or put it in a confined space (desk drawer or cabinet).
- If possible, open windows in the immediate area to assist in venting potentially explosive gases.
- Contact the Postal Inspection Service and the local police.

The person who receives the threat should immediately report it to supervisory personnel. If the supervisor is not the site manager, the site manager should be notified immediately. At this point, the property

BOMB THREAT CHECKLIST

1. When is the bomb going to explode?
2. Where is the bomb right now?
3. What does the bomb look like?
4. What kind of bomb is it?
5. What will cause the bomb to explode?
6. Did you place the bomb?
7. Why?
8. What is your address?
9. What is your name?

EXACT WORDING OF BOMB THREAT

_____
_____
_____

Sex of caller: _____
Age: _____   Length of call: _____
Telephone number at which call is received: _____
Time call received: _____
Date call received: _____ / _____ / _____

CALLER'S VOICE

____ Calm		____ Nasal	
____ Soft		____ Angry	
____ Stutter		____ Loud	
____ Excited		____ Lisp	
____ Laughter		____ Slow	
____ Rasp		____ Crying	
____ Rapid		____ Deep	
____ Normal		____ Distinct	
____ Slurred		____ Whispered	
____ Ragged		____ Clearing throat	
____ Deep breathing		____ Cracking voice	
____ Disguised		____ Accent	

____ Familiar (If voice is familiar, who did it sound like?)

BACKGROUND SOUNDS

____ Street noises	____ Factory machinery
____ Voices	____ Crockery
____ Animal noises	____ Clear
____ PA System	____ Static
____ Music	____ House noises
____ Long distance	____ Local
____ Motor	____ Office machinery
____ Booth	____ Other (please specify)

BOMB THREAT LANGUAGE

_____ Well spoken	____ Incoherent
_____ Irrational	____ Message read by threat maker
_____ Foul	____ Taped

REMARKS: _____

Your Name: _____

Your Position: _____

Your telephone number: _____

Date checklist completed: ___ / ___ / ___

management staff should exercise discretion regarding who is informed about the threat in order to avoid panic. Panic from a threat can be as dangerous as an actual bomb. The caller often knows this; creating a disruption of the property's normal operations may be the objective the caller is trying to achieve.

First and foremost, the police department should be called. The police can provide advice about the threat level, since they are aware of the current activity in the area. If the recipient is a site manager, he or she should contact the real estate manager, who decides what action should be taken based on the property's emergency procedures. Once this call has been made, the real estate manager could:

- Contact the fire department.
- Inform the property's occupants to coordinate the evacuation of the property on a voluntary basis.
- With assistance of professionals, search the property for the bomb.

The emergency procedures plan should provide options based on the information available. When a bomb threat is made by telephone, the response is based on whether the caller has made threats against the property in the past and the amount and nature of detailed information the caller provides. If the building is evacuated, management staff should perform a visual search as they exit the building. Any suspicious objects or packages should be reported to real estate managers, their supervisors, or the police or bomb squad if they are on the scene.

CHARACTERISTICS OF BOMBS SENT THROUGH THE MAIL

Any of the following indicators, alone or in combination, should raise suspicions about a parcel:

- Excessive postage
- Fictitious or nonexistent return address
- Postmark different from the return address city
- Restricted endorsements—"personal" or "private"
- Distorted handwriting or homemade labels or cut-and-paste lettering for addressee information
- Unprofessional wrapping with different types of tape, may include special labeling such as "Fragile—Handle with Care" or "Rush—Do Not Delay"
- Irregular shape, soft spots, or bulges
- Protruding wires, aluminum foil, oil stains, or peculiar odor

More information can be obtained from the U.S. Postal Inspection Service at *www.usps.com/postalinspectors/bombs.htm.*

Searching for a Bomb

Every bomb threat should be assumed to be real until it is proved otherwise. It is important to act quickly to prevent an explosion. The immediate actions may include searching the property for the bomb. This should be done by local authorities (e.g., police or bomb squad), but it may be necessary, only when under police direction, to begin a search before they arrive. The emergency procedures manual should list detailed procedures for performing such a search, including (1) how to conduct the search and (2) who makes up the search team. It is recommended that the following steps be followed in the order shown:

- Search the suite and the common areas on the floor where the bomb threat was received.
- Next, search outdoor areas most accessible to intruders.
- Begin at the lowest level and search entrances, shrubbery, trash containers, dumpsters, piles of leaves or refuse, patios and terraces, recreation areas, window ledges, air-conditioning units and equipment, building ornaments, signs, parking lots, parked vehicles, and manholes. Move upward along the exterior of the building, searching fire escapes and roof areas. Extend the search 25 to 50 feet in all directions or to a natural boundary line (e.g., curb, wall, hedge, parking lot, and property line).
- Continue with an interior search. Start with the most accessible areas, such as areas open to the public, reception areas, restrooms, areas containing service equipment, and stairwells.
- Move up through the building systematically, floor by floor. Search each room thoroughly, and listen for unusual sounds.
- Divide each room into equal parts, depending on how many items there are in the room and how large an area there is to search. Assign a team member to each part. After the team members have searched their areas, rotate areas and search again.
- Search in sweeps—from floor to waist height, from waist to chin height, from chin to ceiling, and finally the ceiling area (e.g., light fixtures, false ceiling, and smoke alarms).
- Keep in mind that the use of walkie-talkies or other radio devices while searching for a bomb could activate a device.

A thorough search can take up to several hours, depending on the size and layout of the building and the number of people on the search team.

INDICATIONS OF TAMPERING

If a bomb threat is received, consider that a bomber will generally only have had access to public areas of the building. While it is logical to search for an object, it is also appropriate to search those public areas of a building looking for signs of an intruder. The following are some indicators to look for:

- Suspicious persons loitering in the area
- Pictures or other hanging objects that are not hanging straight
- Disturbed soil in potted plants or potted plants that are moved
- Broken cabinet
- Furniture or objects recently and obviously moved out of place
- Torn coverings on upholstered furnishings
- Ceiling tiles that appear disturbed
- Doors or door locks that have been tampered with
- Any object that looks out of place in its surroundings
- Freshly painted or plastered areas

The following lists suggested team members to include as a part of this search team:

- Local authorities and trained searchers
- The onsite management staff
- People who will be able to identify new, foreign, or unfamiliar objects
- Persons having access to locked doors
- Trained security guards
- Trained maintenance crew members

The emergency procedures manual should list names and current telephone numbers of search team members and designate a clear chain of command. The leader makes the critical decision whether to evacuate, calls the police or fire departments, coordinates the search teams, supervises the command center, and communicates with the media, the public, building occupants, and public agencies (unless another spokesperson has been appointed).

What to Do When a Bomb is Found

If a bomb is found (or what is thought to be a bomb), staff should consider the following precautions:

- Do not touch or disturb the bomb or suspicious article unless police or other official instructs you to do so.

- Evacuate occupants immediately to a distance where they will be safe from flying glass and debris, usually at least 300 feet. Do not allow anyone to return to the building until re-entry is officially authorized.

- Call police explosive specialists to take charge of the situation. Property management personnel should never try to defuse a bomb.

- Do not submerge the bomb or suspicious item in water; do not cover it, hoping to diminish its blast. Doing this could hasten explosion and create additional debris.

- Assemble the building's first aid team.

- Initiate damage control procedures at the advice of the police. Open all windows and doors to vent a blast. Shut off all utilities (e.g., gas and fuel oil) that might contribute to fire or explosion.

- Remove any flammable materials.

- Construct a protective barrier around the bomb—but not on top of it—using material that will not fragment (e.g., a double row of sandbags, mattress, or overturned furniture). The material(s) should be placed between the bomb and the nearest vulnerable wall, with the barrier *not touching either*.

Recovering from a Bomb Threat

The real estate manager's main responsibility after a bomb threat is to ensure the safety of the building occupants. If an evacuation was ordered, the real estate manager should permit all occupants to return to the building and assure them the situation is under control. However, not all bomb threats result in building evacuation.

Finally, no unnecessary mention or public announcement should be made of the bomb or bomb threat. Word of one bomb threat may spawn copycats.

PREVENTIVE MEASURES FOR EXPLOSIONS

While an explosion may be the result of a bomb being detonated, there are other causes to consider in regard to managed properties. A boiler used to provide steam heat can explode if excess steam pressure builds up. A gas leak ignited by a spark can explode. Chemicals that are themselves not potentially explosive may cause an explosion if exposed to certain other chemicals in an accidental spill. A fire may detonate potentially explosive materials, or an explosion outside a building can cause damage to the

WHAT TO DO IF TRAPPED IN DEBRIS

- If possible, use a flashlight to signal your location to rescuers.
- Avoid unnecessary movement so that you don't kick up dust.
- Cover your nose and mouth with anything you have on hand. (Dense-weave cotton material can act as a good filter. Try to breathe through the material.)
- Tap on a pipe or wall so that rescuers can hear your location.
- If possible, use a whistle to signal rescuers.
- Shout only as a last resort. Shouting can cause a person to inhale dangerous amounts of dust.

Source: Federal Emergency Management Agency (FEMA) website *www.ready.gov.*

interior as well as the exterior of the building, and that damage can lead to injuries.

Regular inspection and preventive maintenance can ensure that boilers and other pressure vessels are in good condition and operating at proper settings. Compliance with the Occupational Safety and Health Administration (OSHA) workplace safety rules and proper handling of chemicals within tenants' premises can reduce the potential for an explosion to occur accidentally. Information on potential ignitability and reactivity, if known, should be included on the material safety data sheet (MSDS) for an industrial chemical. (Information on preventing gas leaks can be found in *Chapter 16,* and fire prevention measures are discussed in *Chapter 14.*)

IF AN EXPLOSION OCCURS

If there is an explosion, people should exit the building as quickly as possible, using stairways rather than elevators. Stairwells and stairs should be checked for stability before using them for evacuation. There may be smoke or fire, in which case, evacuation procedures for a fire should be followed. The emergency management team should account for building occupants as quickly as possible.

The fire department and rescue squad should be called immediately. If people are trapped in debris, they may also be injured. Rescuers may have to proceed with caution to avoid destabilizing debris. Even if there is no fire, there is likely to be fine dust in the air. If the explosion is chemical related, there may be toxic gases as well. Rescuers should wear appropriate respiratory protection—at a minimum, dust masks.

If people are trapped and communication is possible, let them know that help is on the way. Devise a signal they can use to help rescuers pinpoint their location.

CHAPTER 24:

Nuclear Accidents, Attacks, and Radiation Exposure

Designed to provide an efficient means of generating electricity, nuclear power plants have been operating in the U.S. for decades. There are 104 commercial nuclear power reactors licensed to operate at in 31 states.

There are two basic types of reactors used in nuclear power production: (1) boiling water reactors, which generate steam to power a turbine that produces electricity, and (2) pressurized water reactors, which circulate water through the reactor under pressure to heat it. The heated water moves to a steam generator where it heats another secondary water supply to make steam that spins the turbine.

While nuclear accidents are very rare, the 1979 incident at Three Mile Island in Pennsylvania and the 1986 incident in Chernobyl, Ukraine, and the 2011 nuclear incident at Fukushima Dai-Ichi in Japan have proven that the threat of nuclear accidents exists. Real estate managers of properties located near nuclear power plants will benefit from an increased understanding of the effects of nuclear accidents and a general awareness of preventive measures they can implement to protect people on their properties.

Each power plant is equipped with extensive safety systems to prevent or cope with an accident. Unlike the familiar images of a nuclear attack or explosion—an atomic bomb exploding and creating a fireball and a mushroom cloud—nuclear accidents do not cause explosions. Instead, they release radioactive gases into the atmosphere. The effects of such accidents represent only a small fraction of the concentrated capacity of a nuclear explosion. However, all nuclear accidents should be taken seriously because exposure to radiation could be fatal. The specific hazard depends on the type of accident, amount of radiation released, and weather conditions at the time of and after the accident.

In addition to accidents at nuclear power plants, a radiological incident could occur anywhere that radioactive materials are used, stored, or transported, including hospitals, research laboratories, industrial plants, and major highways, railways, and shipyards.

GOVERNMENT REGULATION OF THE NUCLEAR INDUSTRY

The Nuclear Regulatory Commission (NRC), successor to the Atomic Energy Commission (AEC), was created in 1975 to regulate the various commercial and institutional uses of nuclear energy, including power plants. In addition to its responsibility to protect the public health and safety, the NRC has three principal functions:

1. Establish standards and regulations.
2. Issue licenses for nuclear facilities and users of nuclear materials.
3. Inspect facilities and users of nuclear materials to assure compliance with regulatory requirements.

The NRC is also responsible for ensuring that the risks of accidental nuclear emissions are maintained at acceptably low levels. The NRC regulatory program also establishes limits for exposure of the general public to radiation.

In 1979, President James Carter appointed the Federal Emergency Management Agency (FEMA) to take the lead in offsite planning and response to radiological emergencies, assisted by the NRC in carrying out this role while also carrying out its statutory responsibilities for public health and safety. Currently, federal oversight of emergency planning for licensed nuclear power plants is shared by the NRC and FEMA.

After the events at Three Mile Island, the NRC issued regulations stating that before a plant could be licensed to operate, the NRC must have "reasonable assurance that adequate protective measures can and will be taken in the event of a radiological emergency." In addition, emergency plans must be prepared for evacuation or other actions to protect the residents in the vicinity of nuclear plants. These plans usually cover an area about 10 miles in all directions around each nuclear plant. The utility has its own emergency plan to notify government officials and provide them with information and recommendations in the event of a potential or actual radiological emergency. State and local governments also have detailed plans for sheltering and evacuation of residents, if necessary. In the event of a nuclear accident, the NRC is responsible for closely following how utility companies respond to the accidents and to investigate its causes. These emergency plans are tested through emergency exercises that simulate a serious reactor accident. The exercises may sometimes include small-scale evacuation drills for schools, nursing homes, and other institutions.

In addition, the federal government has established a system of "no-fault" insurance for nuclear power plants to provide liability coverage in the event of a major reactor accident. Initiated under the Price-Anderson Act, the program combines commercial insurance and self-insurance by the nuclear industry. Large nuclear plants are required to have the maximum amount of liability insurance commercially available. The Price-Anderson Act also provides liability insurance coverage for actual damages incurred by anyone affected by a major reactor accident.

It is important for real estate managers to become familiar with the regulatory provisions for nuclear power plants, especially if the property is located near a nuclear facility. This knowledge will aid real estate managers to determine where to turn for guidance in developing emergency procedures and help to provide assurance of the many regulatory safeguards currently in place to protect the public.[1]

NUCLEAR ACCIDENTS

Areas and Properties at Risk for Nuclear Accidents

There are two zones for nuclear emergency preparation, and a property's location within either of these zones will affect how it should prepare for and respond to a nuclear accident. The first zone is the area within a 10-mile radius of a nuclear power plant. In this area, direct exposure to radiation from an accident is possible and potentially harmful. The second zone is the area within a 10-to-50 mile radius. In this zone, indirect exposure to radiation is possible if radioactive particles enter the food chain through contamination of water, crops, or grazing lands. Although the areas and properties closest to a nuclear power plant are at greatest risk, the entire U.S. population could suffer the effects of indirect exposure.

Risks of Tenant Exposure from Non-Power Use

Exposure to radioactive materials may occur without a nuclear emergency. In addition to power generation, radioactive materials are used in medical diagnosis and treatment and in some manufacturing processes. Consequently, it is possible that such materials may be present at managed properties such as medical office buildings and industrial sites. If that is the case, it may be appropriate to consider addressing this issue in the lease. In particular, the tenant may be required to comply with NRC regulatory

---

1. Additional information can be found in NRC—Independent Regulator of Nuclear Safety published by the U.S. Nuclear Regulatory Commission and available for download at *http://www.nrc.gov.*

245

requirements regarding use, storage, disposal, and transportation of radio-active materials—and to have appropriate liability insurance coverage.

The real estate manager may wish to consult with the owner's insurance agent or other risk management advisor regarding emergency plans for the property and potential liabilities that may arise out of a nuclear accident.

PREVENTIVE MEASURES FOR NUCLEAR ACCIDENTS

An emergency plan for nuclear accidents is built around three methods to minimize radiation exposure:

1. **Shielding**—placing heavy, dense materials between oneself and the radiation source
2. **Distance**—placing as much distance between oneself and the source of radiation—in a serious nuclear accident, local officials will likely call for evacuation
3. **Time**—limiting the amount of time spent near a radiation source—radioactivity weakens fairly quickly

Real estate managers should develop guidelines and procedures for evacuating occupants to shelters, depending on the amount of radioactive material released and also based on public announcements.

Inclusion of potassium iodide (KI) tablets in the property's emergency supplies or first aid kit may be advisable. Authorities may recommend taking KI in the event of a nuclear accident. A medical professional may be able to advise real estate managers regarding the need for and use of potassium iodide (KI). It may be desirable to encourage occupants (residents and commercial tenants' employees) to acquire their own supplies of KI.

Every community near a nuclear power plant is legally required to have an emergency plan in place for all residents within 10 miles of a nuclear power plant. Real estate managers of properties within such communities should find out what plans the local government has in place and what is recommended for the private sector. Radioactive gases released into the atmosphere may require the same precautions as a fallout from a nuclear attack.

During a Nuclear Accident

Actions to be taken are somewhat similar to those for a nuclear attack:

- Listen to the radio or television for official information regarding the incident. This may include instructions to evacuate the area or to shelter in place.

POTASSIUM IODIDE (KI)

Radioactive iodine (^{131}I also called radioiodine) released in a nuclear accident can cause thyroid cancer if inhaled or ingested. Children are especially vulnerable. Potassium iodide (KI) has been found to be a safe and effective means of protecting against thyroid cancer when exposure cannot be prevented by evacuation, sheltering, or control of food and milk supplies.

As a general rule of thumb, the Food and Drug Administration (FDA) recommends that adults age 18 and older receive 130 mg of KI and children ages 3–18 receive 65 mg. The dose of KI should be taken daily until there is no longer risk of significant exposure to radio iodines.

Federal policy regarding KI was revised in 2002 such that the decision to use KI to protect the general public has been left to the discretion of individual states and, in some cases, local governments. As of October 2003, the following 18 states have received KI tablets through FEMA: Massachusetts, Connecticut, Maryland, Vermont, Delaware, Florida, Alabama, Arizona, New York, New Jersey, North Carolina, South Carolina, Pennsylvania, California, Ohio, Virginia, Mississippi, and New Hampshire.

More specific information can be found in the FDA publication Guidance: Potassium Iodide as a Thyroid Blocking Agent in Radiation Emergencies, which can be downloaded at *http://www.fda.gov.*

- All persons should shield themselves from potential radioactive gas or run-off water by creating a barrier between themselves and the contaminants, such as staying indoors in a basement.
- If officials order an evacuation, all persons should immediately evacuate to a designated shelter. Radioactive gases can travel rapidly, especially if there is wind. Seeking shelter should take priority over anything else.
- If there is no designated shelter, seek cover in building mechanical areas or stairwells.

After a Nuclear Accident

Radioactive contamination could affect areas as far as 50 miles away from the accident site. Government authorities will indicate when it is safe to return to the affected area.

- Continue to listen to radio and television for updated emergency information.
- Do not drink from community water supplies, which could be contaminated. Local authorities will advise when water is safe for drinking and hygienic uses (e.g., bathing, dishwashing, or laundry).

- Be prepared for looting during any evacuation or chaos that might ensue.
- Buildings and soil at properties may be contaminated with radio-activity from a nuclear accident. Have the condition of the building evaluated professionally. It may be necessary to demolish the building. Radioactive soil and construction materials should be removed from the site and disposed of properly by trained professionals.

Depending on the type of radioactive material released and the extent of the area involved in a nuclear incident, it may be a very long time before anyone can get close to a contaminated property.[2]

NUCLEAR ATTACK

Explosion of a nuclear bomb produces an intense pulse or wave of light, air pressure, heat, and radiation. While it is not immediately likely that a country, group, or individual would attack an area in the U.S. with nuclear weapons, the availability of nuclear weaponry at military compounds around the world demands attention. It would benefit real estate managers to become aware of ways to safeguard the property they manage in the event that such a tragedy should occur.

The damage and other consequences of a nuclear attack differ from those resulting from an accident at a commercial nuclear power plant. Nuclear weapons are created specifically to cause the maximum damage possible. They are capable of killing or injuring very large numbers of people and destroying or damaging properties and infrastructure over very wide target areas.

The fireball from a nuclear explosion forms an upward rising mushroom cloud, vaporizing everything in its path, including soil and water. As the vaporized radioactive material cools, it condenses into dust-like particles and falls back to earth. This "fallout" can travel long distances on wind currents, spreading to areas that are miles away from the explosion and contaminating anything it touches, including food and water supplies.

The immediate effects of a nuclear attack are unmistakable. They include a flash of intense light followed by a blast of heat and radiation. The secondary effects are from radioactive fallout. The extent of immediate and

2. Additional information on nuclear accidents can be found on the FEMA website at *http://www.ready.gov/nuclear-power-plants*. The Centers for Disease Control and Prevention (CDC) website includes information on preparing for a radiation emergency at *http://www.bt.cdc.gov/radiation/index.asp*.

HEALTH EFFECTS OF AN ATOMIC BLAST

Injury or death may result from the blast itself or from debris thrown by the blast. Human skin may receive moderate to severe burns. Those who look directly at the fireball could experience temporary blindness or even retinal burns. While severe burns may appear in minutes, other effects may take days or weeks to appear. These effects range from mild (e.g., reddening of the skin) to severe (e.g., cancer or death), depending on the type of radiation, the radiation dose (amount absorbed by the body), the route of exposure (e.g., external by absorption through the skin or internal by inhalation or ingestion), and the duration of exposure.

secondary effects will depend on the following several factors:

- Size and type of nuclear device exploded
- Use of the area affected by the blast
- Height of the explosion above the surface of the earth
- Distance of people and objects from the explosion
- Weather conditions during and after the explosion—stronger winds will intensify the damage and disseminate fallout over a larger area; rain may also concentrate the radiation in an area
- Thickness of protective material between the person and the fallout (e.g., bagged sand or gravel, concrete, bricks, wood, or earth)
- Amount of time spent in a shelter after the initial explosion

People near the explosion most likely would be killed or seriously injured by the initial blast, heat, or radiation. People several miles away from the explosion would be endangered by the initial blast, heat, and subsequent fires. Others may survive but would be exposed to dangerous radioactive fallout.

Areas and Properties at Risk for Nuclear Attack

Areas of the U.S. that are at greatest risk of a nuclear attack are those with significant military, political, and economic importance. Properties located near military bases may be particularly vulnerable, especially during wartime. The risk of exposure to radiation from fallout extends well beyond the boundaries of cities and military bases.

Preventive Measures for Nuclear Attack

Local government agencies may have constructed shelters or designated

249

certain structures (buildings, subway tunnels) as fallout shelters. However, these may not accommodate everyone in the area who needs shelter.

The only precaution a real estate manager can take to prevent loss due to a nuclear attack is to provide an emergency shelter for those on the property at the time of an attack. The shelter could be a special building or underground bunker, where possibility for destruction from the impact of the nuclear blast is minimized. Water and nonperishable food may be stored in the shelter to sustain its inhabitants for a period of days or weeks. Ideally, the real estate manager should determine ahead of time—as part of the emergency planning process—where the safest areas(s) of the building might be. This is, however, not always practical and requires a significant amount of planning for an unlikely emergency.

Because building occupants (property staff or commercial tenants' employees) cannot be forced to shelter in place at their workplace, it is important to involve them in the planning process to maximize their cooperation in the event of a disaster. Planning to shelter in place at the workplace might include some of the following items:

- Determine whether all personnel will shelter in place or if some will leave the building before shelter procedures are implemented
- Develop an accountability system, which may include sign-in sheets to document who is entering and leaving the designated shelter area.
- Assign specific duties to individuals and making backup assignments
- Plan and conduct drills, assessing the drills for needed improvements
- Encourage individual tenants to make plans and preparations for their employees to shelter in place[3]

If an underground shelter is not available, the real estate manager could advise people on the property to seek safety at an alternative location in a building that has both walls and a roof thick enough to absorb radioactivity emitted by fallout.

Inclusion of KI tablets in the property's emergency supplies or first aid kit may be advisable. Authorities may recommend taking KI in the event of a nuclear attack.

---

3. The National Institute for Chemical Studies has published *Shelter in Place at Your Office: A General Guide for Preparing a Shelter in Place Plan in the Workplace* online at *www. nicsinfo.org.*

The same preventive measures may apply in the event of a terrorist attack that releases biological or chemical agents or explodes a dirty bomb (see *Chapter 25*).

During a Nuclear Attack

In the event of a nuclear attack, federal, state, and local governmental agencies would activate a national emergency response plan. The following lists suggested steps for people to take at a managed property:

- Immediately evacuate to a designated shelter. Radioactive fallout travels rapidly, so seeking shelter should take priority over anything else.
- If there is no designated shelter, seek cover in mechanical areas or stairwells in the building.
- Shield your body from the explosion using solid material such as sandbags.
- Protect your eyes; do not look at the light from the blast.

The World Health Organization (WHO) has published suggested actions for individuals to take under different circumstances, depending on where they are when a nuclear attack occurs.[4]

After a Nuclear Attack

After the intense heat, rumbling noise, and obvious fallout have noticeably ceased, a person in a shelter may think that it is safe to leave the shelter area. However, this is not the case. Radioactive dust and other particles can remain airborne for extended periods of time, and the earth may still be subject to fallout. Once these particles hit the ground, they decay fairly rapidly; but it is recommended that people remain inside the shelter for as long as physically possible to avoid radiation exposure. The following lists some actions to consider:

- Stay indoors for at least the first 24 hours after the initial explosion. This is the most dangerous period, when radioactive particles fall to the earth's surface.

- While in the shelter, continue to listen to the radio and television for announcements about affected areas and when it is safe to leave the shelter. It may not be necessary to remain in the shelter more

4. Additional information can be found on the CDC website at *http://www.bt.cdc.gov/radiation/nuclearfaq.asp*

than one or two weeks. People may be able to leave the shelter for short periods of time after a few days.

- Do not drink from community water supplies, which could be contaminated. Local authorities will advise when water is safe for drinking and hygienic uses (bathing, dishwashing, or laundry).

- Be prepared for looting during any evacuation or chaos that might ensue.

- Buildings and soil at properties may be contaminated with radio-activity from the nuclear blast. Have the condition of the building evaluated professionally. It may be necessary to demolish the building. Radioactive soil and construction materials should be removed from the site and disposed of properly.[5]

---

5. More specific information on radiological emergencies, including nuclear blast, can be found on the CDC website at *http.//www.bt.cdc.gov/radiation/index.asp.*

SUGGESTED ACTIONS TO TAKE DURING A NUCLEAR ATTACK

Emergency procedures for building occupants may include the following actions suggested. These are primarily actions for people to take individually.

People near the blast should:

- Prevent damage to your eyesight by turning away from the blast and closing and covering your eyes.
- Lay face down with your hands under your body.
- Remain flat until the heat and two shock waves have passed.

People who are outside when a blast occurs should:

- Use a handkerchief or other cloth to cover your nose and mouth.
- Go to a ventilated area and brush, shake, or wipe dust from your clothing; keep your mouth and nose covered while doing this.
- Remove clothing (it may be contaminated); if possible, take a shower, wash your hair, and put on fresh clothing before entering the shelter.
- Move to shelter (preferably a basement or other underground area located away from the direction of the wind).

People in a shelter or basement should:

- Listen to local radio or television stations for information about the areas affected by the blast and instructions to follow. Authorities may direct people to shelter in place or evacuate to a safer location.
- Keep your mouth and nose covered with a face mask or cloth until the fallout cloud has passed.
- Clean and cover any open wounds on your body.
- Turn off the ventilation system and seal doors and windows until the fallout cloud passes. After it has passed, unseal doors and windows to allow for air circulation.
- Stay inside until authorities say it is safe to come out.
- Use stored drinking water and food; do not drink water from open water supplies or eat local fresh food until told it is safe to do so.
- If you go out, cover your nose and mouth with a damp towel.

CHAPTER 25:
Terrorist Acts

Terrorism is the unlawful use of force or violence against persons or property for purposes of intimidation or coercion. The goal of terrorism is to create fear of the unknown and the unknowable. A terrorist can strike at anytime, anywhere. The Federal Bureau of Investigation (FBI) differentiates two types of terrorism—(1) domestic and (2) international—referring not to where an incident takes place, but to the origins of those responsible for it.

1. **Domestic terrorism** involves groups or individuals who direct terrorist activities at elements of the U.S. government or population without foreign direction. Most incidents in the U.S. have involved small extremist groups who use terrorism to achieve a specific objective. The 1995 bombing of the Murrah Federal Building in Oklahoma City is one example.

2. **International terrorism** involves groups or individuals whose terrorist activities are foreign-based and/or directed by countries or groups outside the U.S. or whose activities transcend national boundaries. The 9/11 terrorist attacks are examples.

All manner of man-made disasters could be acts of terrorism. Explosions are usually more spectacular than acts of arson, but the latter can also be a component of a terror campaign. Sabotage of infrastructure components is also a possibility—an explosive device detonated at a nuclear power plant could result in the release of radioactive material while also causing a power outage. An obstacle on railroad tracks could derail a train and possibly disrupt freight shipments and passenger train travel for a period of time. Even a bomb threat, whether real or a hoax, is a terrorist act.

A terrorist act may rely on chemical or biological warfare materials to cause harm. Terrorist devices can employ high-powered explosives combined with radioactive material—a "dirty bomb." While there is likely to be property damage from the conventional explosives used in a dirty bomb, biological and chemical weapons are used strictly to kill and injure people.

In the event of a terrorist attack, the aftermath is likely to be chaotic, the following is likely to be expected:

- Large numbers of casualties and extensive damage to buildings and city infrastructure; employers should have up-to-date information on employees' emergency contacts (e.g., spouse, parent, or other family member)
- Increased law enforcement at all levels of government, which may include more visible police and other law enforcement personnel and restrictions on people's movements
- Large numbers of people may be evacuated from the affected area
- Hospitals and mental health facilities in affected communities are likely to be overwhelmed
- Buildings (i.e., workplaces, schools) may be closed—or they may be commandeered for use by government emergency personnel; there may be restrictions on travel inside and outside the U.S.
- Media coverage will be extensive; strong public fear is likely
- Clean-up may take a long time; months or even years

Regarding media coverage, unedited video footage and repeated images of a terrorist attack and people's reactions to it can be very upsetting. People may want to gather in groups and take turns listening to the news so they can be informed without being psychologically and emotionally overwhelmed. Real estate managers whose buildings include live media displays in lobbies or common areas need to be sensitive to the need for information.

AREAS AND PROPERTIES AT RISK

Because the nature of an act of terrorism is difficult to anticipate and more difficult to thwart on the part of a real estate manager, all areas of the U.S. and all types of managed properties can be considered at risk. Because possible targets include infrastructure components, it is likely that those properties near nuclear power plants, chemical manufacturing plants, transportation centers (railway stations, and airports), and utilities are at greater risk for damage than those located away from such facilities. Major high-rise buildings (especially named buildings) could be specific targets, and any adjacent properties would likely experience some devastation because of their proximity. High-profile tenants, landmarks, monuments, and major international sporting events might also be targets.

PREVENTIVE MEASURES

A real estate manager cannot completely prepare for every type of potential terrorist attack, but some general precautions recommended for other types of disasters would apply for a terror attack as well. Written emergency procedures that address bombs and bomb threats, power outages, elevator emergencies, fire, hazardous-materials incidents, nuclear accidents, and medical emergencies will cover many types of terrorist acts and their consequences. The following lists additional precautions to consider:

- Check the effectiveness of security measures implemented at the property. Consider having a security professional conduct a risk assessment to identify potential vulnerabilities, especially in regard to a terrorist attack. Implement additional measures if appropriate.

- If you do not currently have security personnel on your property, consider making arrangements and adjustments as you see fit to increase the general security on the property. For example, if the Department of Homeland Security (DHS) issues threat information via the National Terrorism Advisory System (NTAS) try to contract for security guards to patrol the property. If this is not a possibility, locate someone willing to patrol and the property as an added security measure.

- Ask commercial tenants to provide a list of names and telephone extensions for all of their employees. This should include phones in unoccupied offices or workstations and other locations in their leased premises. In the event of a terrorist attack, or if there is an intruder in the building, this information can help emergency response personnel locate the site of a reported incident (e.g., by linking the caller who reports an incident to a specific phone in a particular location).

- Designate one employee (or one from each work shift if applicable) to be the safety coordinator and make decisions relating to employee and customer safety, perhaps including the safety of the property itself. This person should know how to contact the building owner or manager at all times.

- If you have a voicemail system, designate one extension for emergency use to record messages for employees and building occupants. Make sure the phone number is provided to all who may need it.

- If you have programmable call forwarding, use that feature to reprogram phones to ring elsewhere.

THE NATIONAL TERRORISM ADVISORY SYSTEM

The Department of Homeland Security (DHS) initially established a color-coded threat alert system known as the Homeland Security Advisory System (HSAS) to advise citizens and businesses when they need to take action to protect themselves from possible terrorist acts.

Phased out in 2011, it was replaced by the National Terrorism Advisory System (NTAS), which corrects many perceived flaws in the HSAS by eliminating what might have been considered arbitrary or unclear threat levels.

NTAS issues two levels of threat alerts:

1. **Imminent Threat Alert**—warns of credible, specific, and impending terrorist threats against the U.S.

2. **Elevated Threat**—warns of a credible terrorist threat against the U.S.

NTAS alerts are released to audiences relevant to the type of terrorist threat for which they are issued. For example, they may be released solely to law enforcement or affected areas of the private sector in one instance, and the public at large in another.

Each alert includes a sunset provision, stating that an individual threat alert is issued for a specific time period before it automatically expires. The alert may be extended if new information becomes available or the threat evolves.

Threat alerts are communicated through state and local partners, the media, and directly to the public via e-mail, social media, and online.

For more information, visit the DHS website for NTAS alerts at *http://www.dhs.gov/files/publications/ntas-public-guide.shtm.*

- Use battery backup systems and surge protectors to protect sensitive equipment such as computers in the case of a power outage (see *Chapter 12* for specific information on power outages). Ensure critical data has been backed up or stored online or offsite (see *Chapter 4*) to allow continued operations in the event the property is compromised.

- Secure locks or latches on cabinet doors and drawers to prevent them from opening and dumping their contents in the event of an explosion.

- Install automatic fire sprinklers if the building has none.

- Consult your insurance agent about types and levels of insurance coverage in place and what might be advisable adjustments. Business continuity insurance should be considered. Valuable equipment and personal property may be covered under special riders. It may be possible to obtain specific insurance coverage for terrorist acts.

Real estate managers can prepare the people who live and work in the buildings they manage—and the buildings themselves—by finding out what types of incidents local police and fire departments and area hospitals are preparing against. Government preparations are likely to be broader in scope than those needed for an individual property or location, and information the authorities share may be for "public consumption"—information they are required to provide—rather than specifics. On the other hand, there may be an opportunity to work with local authorities to the benefit of your property by volunteering to participate in their planning processes. To seek specific information regarding preventive measures, the Lawrence Berkeley National Laboratory has published *Advice for Safeguarding Buildings Against Chemical or Biological Attack* online at *http://secure-buildings.lbl.gov*. There is also a publication from the National Institute for Occupational Safety and Health titled, *Guidance for Protecting Building Environments from Airborne Chemical, Biological, or Radiological Attacks*, which can be found online at *www.cdc.gov/niosh/bldvent/2002-139.html*.

FEMA offers a series of risk management publications that can be downloaded at *www.fema.gov/fima/rmsp.shtm*; several are related specifically to

FEDERAL TERROR PREVENTION MEASURES

In the aftermath of the September 11th terrorist attacks, the federal government enacted a series of laws and executive orders aimed to disrupt and prevent future terror attacks. Two such measures, the U.S.A. PATRIOT Act and Executive Order 13224 have some impact on real estate managers.

The U.S.A. PATRIOT Act—the acronym stands for "Providing Appropriate Tools Required to Intercept and Obstruct Terrorism"—addressed security issues from 9/11.

As a result of the act becoming law, residential properties intensified their screening of rental applicants, in particular, the verification of each prospect's identity and citizenship or immigration status. Commercial properties increased security measures and paid more attention to the activities of their tenants, visitors, and guests.

Further enforcing the spirit of the law, Executive Order 13224—issued by President Bush on September 23, 2001—took precautions a step further by requiring those leasing commercial space to check the names of officers of prospective tenant companies against the *Specially Designated Nationals and Blocked Persons list,* which identifies individuals suspected of terrorism or related activities.

For more in-depth information on the PATRIOT Act, visit the U.S. Department of Justice website at *http://www.justice.gov/archive/ll/highlights.htm*.

terrorism. Additional information on terrorism preparedness and mitigation can also be found on the FEMA website at *www.fema.gov/hazards/terrorism/*. The American Red Cross includes terrorism-related information on their website at *www.redcross.org/pubs/dspubs/terrormat.html*. Many of the documents can be directly downloaded.

SPECIFIC TERROR THREATS

The following sections discuss the different types of terrorist attacks, including descriptions of some likely chemical and biological agents;

QUALIFYING RESIDENTIAL RENTAL APPLICANTS AS A PREVENTIVE MEASURE

Because it is possible that terrorists may be planning to attack apartment buildings, many in the multifamily industry are taking greater care in qualifying rental applicants to avoid problems on their properties. The following includes some options to consider:

- Verify the identity of all rental applicants. Require all adult applicants (over age 18) to complete a written rental application form and provide original documents to verify identity (social security card, driving license, or other government photo-ID), show evidence of employment (pay stub or W-2 form) or school enrollment (student ID or current class schedule), and proof of U.S. citizenship or the applicant's right to live in the U.S. (birth certificate; visa or green card for non-citizens).

- Obtain consumer reports to verify identity and authenticity of social security numbers and other information provided by applicants regarding their financial/credit status. If there is no credit record, a search can be made based on the applicant's social security number—this is done by a service separate from the credit reports. Such a search can verify social security numbers, identify addresses and employers associated with the applicant over time, provide additional names the applicant may have used, and help identify application fraud. It is also possible—and desirable—to obtain a rental history and information on any landlord-tenant disputes.

- Review the information to be sure that the information on identification documents and credit reports is consistent across all the documents and in agreement with that provided on the application form (i.e., social security numbers, names, addresses, birth dates, etc., are the same in all instances).

It is also a good idea to ask for and verify personal references. To comply with fair housing laws, applicant screening procedures should be the same for all applicants. Also, confidential information provided in the application process should be protected to prevent inadvertent or improper disclosure, which could lead to identity theft.

however, both categories include many more agents than are mentioned here. In the event of a biological or chemical attack, authorities are likely to instruct people to either seek shelter where they are and seal the premises or evacuate immediately.

The Centers for Disease Control and Prevention (CDC) provides information on large numbers of potential biological and chemical agents on its website at *http://www.cdc.gov* under "Emergency Preparedness and Response."

Fact sheets on radiation and radioactive materials, including dirty bombs, can be found on the Nuclear Regulatory Commission (NRC) website at *http://www.nrc.gov/reading-rm/doc-collections/fact-sheets*. Real estate managers can find real estate industry specific information and resources on homeland security and emergency preparedness on the Real Estate Information Sharing and Analysis Center website at *http://www. reisac.org.*

REAL ESTATE INFORMATION SHARING AND ANALYSIS CENTER (ISAC)

The real estate industry has taken a proactive approach to preventing terrorism and responding to terrorist acts when they occur. Specifically, the Real Estate Roundtable organized the Real Estate Information Sharing and Analysis Center (ISAC), which serves three roles:

1. Disseminate information from the federal government, including terror alerts and advisories to real estate industry participants.

2. Facilitate real estate industry reporting to government authorities regarding credible terrorist threats to real estate assets.

3. Bring together private- and public-sector experts to share useful information on specific issues, including risk assessment, building security, and emergency response planning.

Founding members of the Real Estate ISAC include the National Association of REALTORS® (NAR), the Institute of Real Estate Management (IREM®) which is an affiliate of NAR, the Building Owners and Managers Association (BOMA) International, the International Council of Shopping Centers (ICSC), the National Association of Industrial and Office Properties (NAIOP), and the National Association of Real Estate Investment Trusts (NAREIT).

Other industries—including the chemical, electric power, financial services, food, information technology, oil and gas, telecommunications, and water industries—also operate ISACs in partnership with the federal government as part of efforts to protect America's critical infrastructure from terrorist attacks.

Information on the organization, current alerts, and incident reporting as well as links to member websites and resources can be found online at *http://www.reisac.org.*

Biological Attack

A biological attack is the deliberate release of bacteria, viruses, or other biological agents that can cause illness and, in some cases, death. Some agents (e.g., the smallpox virus) are potentially contagious—and can be spread by contact with people who are infected. Others (e.g., anthrax) are not contagious. Unlike an explosion, a biological attack may not be immediately obvious. As with the 2001 anthrax mailings, local healthcare workers may report increased numbers of sick people seeking emergency medical attention or a pattern of unusual illness. The general population will most likely learn of the danger from media reports.

Smallpox. Smallpox is a serious, contagious, and sometimes fatal disease caused by the variola virus. Except for laboratory stockpiles, the variola virus has been eliminated. Smallpox is spread by prolonged face-to-face contact with an infected person, direct contact with contaminated body fluids, bedding, or clothing. The most common form of smallpox—*variola major*—is also the most severe. Symptoms include extensive rash and high fever, and there is a fatality rate of about 30 percent. The less common form—*variola minor*—is much less severe, with a fatality rate of one percent or less. Symptoms develop after an incubation period of one to two and a half weeks. Initial symptoms include fever, malaise, headache, and body aches, sometimes coupled with vomiting. After two to four days, a rash emerges; about four days later, the rash turns into open sores. Smallpox is most contagious during the first 7–10 days after the onset of rash, but contagion continues until the last smallpox scab falls off. Treatment is symptomatic. The disease does not respond to antibiotics.

Anthrax. Anthrax is caused by *Bacillus anthracis,* a spore-forming bacterium. Anthrax can be contracted from eating undercooked meat from infected animals, handling infected animal products, or inhaling spores from infected animal products such as wool. Anthrax can also be weaponized. Because anthrax could potentially be sent through the mail, the postal service and onsite mailrooms in commercial buildings are likely to be points of contact. Symptoms of anthrax infection depend on the method of exposure. Skin contact may produce a small sore that develops into a blister and then into a skin ulcer with a black center. None of these are painful.

Ingestion of anthrax can cause loss of appetite, nausea, bloody diarrhea, and fever followed by stomach pain. Inhalation produces cold or flu-like symptoms, including sore throat, mild fever, and muscle aches. Symptoms can appear within seven days of contact; however, symptoms following inhalation may take up to six weeks to develop. Anthrax can be treated with antibiotics, with treatment usually lasting for a period of at least 60 days. Success depends on the method of exposure and how soon treatment is started. Antibiotics can also be used to prevent infection in persons exposed to anthrax, but who have not yet become ill. Anthrax can be prevented by a vaccine, but that has not been available to the general public.

Real estate managers of buildings that include an onsite mail center can find information on emergency planning for such facilities in the U.S. Postal Service publication 166, *Mail Center Security Guidelines.*

In addition to smallpox and anthrax, there are numerous other biological agents that could be used in a terrorist attack. These include bacterial infections like plague and tularemia, hemorrhagic fevers caused by viruses, and botulism caused by a bacterial toxin.

During a Biological Attack

Public health officials may not be able to provide information immediately in the event of a biological attack. It will take time to determine the nature and cause of the illness, how to treat it, and who is in danger. Official news on the radio, television, and online will detail specifics, which are likely to include:

- What geographic area or population group authorities consider in danger
- Signs and symptoms of the disease caused by the agent
- Whether medications or vaccines are being distributed and where to obtain them
- Who should receive medications and/or vaccines; segments of the population—infants, children, or senior citizens—may be especially vulnerable and need to seek treatment or may be cautioned against using specific medications or vaccines
- Where those who become sick should go to obtain emergency medical care

People who are potentially exposed to a biological agent should follow instructions of doctors and public health officials. They should expect to receive medical evaluation and treatment. However, some medical facilities may not accept victims out of fear that they will contaminate the hospital population. If the disease is contagious, those exposed may be advised to stay away from other people or deliberately quarantined.

Chemical Attack

A chemical attack is a deliberate release of a toxic substance (solid, liquid, or gas) that can poison people and contaminate the environment. There are many chemicals that could be used for this purpose, among them are nerve agents such as sarin (liquid), hydrogen cyanide (flammable colorless gas or liquid), chlorine (gas that is heavier than air), and sulfur mustards (heavy, yellow to brown, strong-smelling liquids). Ricin toxin from castor beans is considered both a chemical and a biological agent. Chemical agents can be inhaled, ingested, or absorbed through the skin and eyes, and their effects can appear fairly quickly. Many people may suddenly exhibit common symptoms, such as redness and watering of the eyes, difficulty breathing, choking, twitching, loss of coordination or other indications of a nervous disorder such as drooling, excessive sweating, and confusion. Large numbers of sick or dead animals, birds, fish, or insects may also be an indicator.

Sarin. Sarin is a man-made chemical warfare agent that acts on the nervous system. In its pure form, sarin is a clear, colorless, odorless, tasteless liquid that can evaporate into a gas. People can be exposed to sarin in the air by skin or eye contact or inhalation. Because sarin readily mixes with water, it can be used to poison water and food. Symptoms of exposure to low or moderate doses of sarin by inhalation, ingestion, or skin contact may develop within seconds or throughout a period of hours. These include runny nose, blurred vision, cough, tightness of the chest, rapid breathing, diarrhea, drowsiness, confusion, or headache. Large doses of sarin can cause convulsions, paralysis, loss of consciousness, and respiratory failure leading to death. There are antidotes to sarin but they must be used quickly to be effective. Treatment consists of removing sarin from the body as soon as possible and providing supportive medical care at a hospital.

Ricin. Ricin is a deadly poison. It is extracted from the "mash" of castor oil when it is extracted from castor beans. It can be injected into the body, dispersed in a mist or powder, or used to contaminate food or water. Accidental exposure is highly unlikely; it would take an intentional act to make ricin and use it as a poison. Symptoms of ricin poisoning depend on the route of exposure and the amount received. Inhaling ricin would likely cause difficulty breathing, cough, nausea, and fever with heavy sweating within eight hours after exposure. Ingestion in food or water would likely lead to vomiting and diarrhea accompanied by severe dehydration in less than six hours. Exposure of skin or eyes to ricin mist or powder can cause redness and pain. In severe cases, death could take place in 36–72 hours. There is no antidote for ricin. Victims should receive supportive medical care by treating the symptoms they exhibit.

During a Chemical Attack

People who see signs of a chemical attack should try to find clean air as quickly as possible. The following lists what to do during a chemical attack:

- If possible, try to define the affected area or identify where the chemical is coming from.
- Leave the area immediately.
- People inside a building where the chemical agent is present should get out of the building (without passing through the contaminated area, if possible).
- Those who are unable to exit the building should move as far away from the contamination as possible and shelter in place.
- People who are outside during an attack should quickly decide on the fastest way to find clean air (leave the area or enter the closest building and shelter in place).

Those who think they have been exposed to the chemical, or are exhibiting symptoms, should immediately remove their clothing and wash themselves with any source of water at hand, preferably with soap, but being careful not to scrub the chemical into the skin. Then they should seek medical attention. Exposure to chemical agents can be fatal. There is no assistance an untrained person can offer that would likely be of any value to the victims of chemical agents.

Dirty Bomb Attack

A dirty bomb combines a conventional explosive with a radiation source. In application, the conventional explosive in a dirty bomb would be more lethal than the radioactive material. This is because the difficulty and danger in obtaining more refined, high-level radioactive materials make it more likely that low-level sources, such as materials used in medical diagnosis and treatment, would be used in a dirty bomb. Such sources are unlikely to yield enough radiation to kill people or cause serious illness. However, it is also possible that a powerful source of radioactivity could be hidden in a public place (e.g., a waste receptacle in a subway or train station) so that people passing close to the source might receive a significant dose of radiation.

In the U.S., radioactive materials are carefully regulated. Users are licensed and are required to secure the materials from unauthorized access and theft. Lost or stolen material must be reported immediately, and local authorities make a determined effort to recover it.

The extent of local contamination from a dirty bomb would depend on the amount and type of radioactive material, the size of the explosive, and weather conditions. Because radiation cannot be seen, felt, tasted, or smelled, those at the scene of an explosion will not know whether radiation was released.

After a Dirty Bomb Explosion

The following actions are recommended for people at or near the scene who have not been severely injured by the blast.

At the blast site:

- Follow instructions from emergency personnel; stay in the area until you are released.
- Stay calm; decontamination does not have to start immediately.
- Cover your nose and mouth with a handkerchief.

Near the blast site:

- Stay calm.
- Cover your nose and mouth with a handkerchief.
- Leave the area—preferably on foot. To avoid contaminating vehicles, do not take public transportation. If driving a car or truck, do not use the heater or air conditioner.
- As soon as possible, remove clothing. Shower twice and wash your hair thoroughly.
- Listen to local radio or television stations for information about the emergency and the response to it. If radioactive material was released, people will be advised where to report for monitoring, blood testing, etc., to determine whether they were exposed. News broadcasts will also advise how to discard contaminated clothing and clean your vehicle.

As with a nuclear accident, it is important for people to limit the amount of radiation they are exposed to by using shielding, distance, and time (see *Chapter 24*). Those who become ill from radiation exposure in the range of 75–200 rem (the unit used to derive equivalent dose) may have nausea, vomiting, fatigue, and loss of appetite. Recovery may take a few weeks. Higher doses of radiation (>300 rem) can cause bleeding and changes in blood cells, and exposure in excess of 600 rem causes hair loss and suppresses the ability to fight infections—this is usually fatal.

For perspective, the natural environment includes a certain amount of low-level radioactivity that does not harm humans. Radiation exposure from a chest x-ray is equivalent to 1/100 rem. Because potassium iodide (KI) only protects the thyroid gland from exposure to radioactive iodine, and it is unlikely that a dirty bomb would contain radioactive iodine, KI would probably not be beneficial.

SECTION 6:

Business Continuity Strategies

Written by David Mistick, CPM® and Debbie Mistick, CPM®

CHAPTER 26:

Introduction to Business Continuity Planning and Risk Analysis

In 2003, a University of Minnesota study of disasters reported that 80 percent of businesses that experience an extended disaster go out of business within five years. When the first edition of *Before Disaster Strikes* was published, business continuity planning was not the industry it has become today. Since that time, the importance of technology to real estate managers has moved beyond record keeping and word processing; it has become a gateway for connecting to colleagues, employees, tenants, vendors, and others.

The contemporary notion of business continuity planning began to develop in late 1970s, when professionals first identified the need to protect their data and mainframe computers. The next decade saw the rise of the disaster recovery profession—a subset of the industry built specifically around information technology and computer systems. However, it wasn't until the 1990s that the term "business continuity" was coined, when it became clear that entire business enterprises—not just their data centers—needed the planning and protective services developed by disaster recovery experts.

Rooted in the complex world of computing systems, disaster recovery concepts and methods were historically not easily understood by many in the business world. A further level of complication arose in that continuity concepts were often shrouded in secrecy to protect sensitive data, leaving many with a feeling that the entire process of business continuity planning was just as secretive—difficult to understand.

Planning for business continuity means making sure that critical business functions, such as project management, system backups, change control, engineering services, and support will be available to necessary customers, suppliers, vendors, regulators, and others. Business continuity planning is not a series of actions to be implemented at the time of a disaster, but refers instead to those activities performed daily to maintain service, consistency, and recoverability. The term *business continuity* describes a mentality or methodology of conducting day-to-day business, whereas *business continuity planning* is an activity determining what that methodology should be, and must be followed by everyone in an organization on a daily basis to ensure normal operations.

WHAT IS BUSINESS CONTINUITY MANAGEMENT?

Business continuity is an understanding of what might go wrong and having a plan in place to overcome it. It's what real estate managers have long done for their properties, if not for their businesses. It goes beyond what has been done to prepare for fires and floods, winter storms, and power outages—business continuity management includes recovery and resumption of normal business operations with the ability to efficiently and effectively handle an insurance claim and reduce rent loss and business interruption costs.

Business continuity is about knowing that after a disaster strikes, the real estate manager has a responsibility to preserve and protect the property from further damage, and that they will have the knowledge of how to do it. It forms a complete package of preparing, responding, and recovering from an event that can disrupt regular operation—recognizing that it's sometimes the smallest, simplest interruption that can be the most disruptive. Business continuity helps make sure your business will survive a disruption and recover in the most effective and efficient manner possible.

ELEMENTS OF BUSINESS CONTINUITY PLANNING

Traditionally, business continuity planning includes five core developmental processes: (1) risk assessment, (2) business impact analysis, (3) strategy development, (4) testing and exercising, and (5) maintenance and evaluation.

Performing a Risk Assessment

Risk assessment is the process whereby the potential for a disruption is assessed, whether that disruption occurs from loss of facilities, computer systems, loss of data, communications, or loss of key personnel.

Business Impact Analysis

Business impact analysis helps to identify which parts of a business can be affected by any of the risks identified by a risk assessment. While performing a business impact analysis, consider how those disruptions can affect revenue, market share, reputation, and productivity. In this phase, interdependencies between departments and external resources begin to become identifiable, allowing for the establishment of priorities for those business functions that are most critical to regular operations.

Strategy Development

Strategy development helps to identify strategies for reducing risks, mitigating impacts, and responding to disruption with an organized, teachable methodology. In this stage, consider and choose a strategy or methodology for recovering data and other systems for a return to normal operations.

Testing Systems

In the typical terms of business continuity planning, people and systems are tested. Both exercising and testing systems are critical to ensure the best chance of continuity. Testing systems can take a variety of forms from evacuation drills and tabletop exercises to checklist tests and simulations. Testing will provide feedback as to the efficacy of the plan. Any post-test evaluations will highlight gaps or shortcomings present in the existing plan.

Maintenance and Evaluation

Just as people need to be trained routinely, all parts of a continuity plan need to be regularly reviewed. Changes in personnel, upgrades in equipment, and changes in location all merit immediate attention in your plan. Prepare a schedule for routine maintenance or revision to the plan as well, just as routine maintenance might be done on a boiler system or emergency generator. The emergency procedures manual is a compilation of routine, tested action. Your business continuity plan should be established on the same grounds.

RISK ASSESSMENT

To ensure the continued operation of your business, begin with understanding the risks. Only by understanding the risks posed to a property or business can you create a comprehensive strategy for business continuity.

Real estate managers have long identified risks to their properties, whether in areas prone to earthquakes or hurricanes, or if their tenants' operations use hazardous materials, etc. Business continuity takes the notion of risk further than loss of physical asset, and asks that the risks inherent to a business be examined as well. At the broadest level, begin with a consideration of previous disruptions or other disastrous events that have impacted your properties and business over time. This provides an obvious baseline—what is most likely to be experienced is based on historical data.

Next, consider threat sources, including natural, manmade, and technical disruptions. *Section 4* of this book discusses a wide variety of natural and manmade disasters, but business continuity also looks deeply at the potential for technical failures—disruptions to data, communications, and utilities. Consider the following questions:

- Is your fee-based management company supported primarily by a single owner that might change?
- Are your residential tenants employed by a single large firm in the area that could move those jobs to another location or lose them altogether?
- Are your own systems and data protected with network backups and redundancies?
- In the event of a regional disaster, will your staff be able and/or willing to report to work?

Once risks are identified, consider how these events might impact critical operations or processes at our properties or businesses. Also, consider the impact on every part of your operation, from janitorial and maintenance functions to payroll and human resources, and from security to reporting requirements. How extensive could a disruption be? How long might the disruption might last? For example, take loss of power as a disruption that could impact almost every aspect of what you do every day.

BUSINESS IMPACT ANALYSIS

To fully appreciate the risks on your business, you must also identify the potential financial and intangible impacts of each risk exposure. What will the financial consequences be on a daily, weekly, monthly, or annual basis? This information is generated by each of the critical functions or departments that could be impaired.

By looking at risk exposures, the impacts on business processes, and financial ramifications, you can get a perspective on the requisite hierarchy for mitigation response and recovery. A well-conceived analysis will highlight the most significant financial and intangible exposures, and lead to establishing maximum tolerable downtimes for the various facets of the business.

When calculating the costs to the business, you may use either a quantitative or qualitative analysis. In financial, quantitative terms, consider loss of rental income, sale, leasing, and ancillary income. Also calculate the costs of fixed expenses that will continue—even if the business or property cannot operate as usual. Additionally, consider extra expenses that may be incurred during the disruption, outside of normal operating costs. All of these expenses will impact corporate valuation.

Similarly, there are intangible, qualitative impacts. A business disaster may affect your brand or goodwill in the marketplace. This may produce loss of investor confidence, market share, or competitive edge. It may impair relationships with tenants, vendors, and suppliers. You may also lose employees who are essential to routine operations. Understanding the potential loss of value helps create a hierarchy for recovering or restoring property or business functions in a well-established order.

RISK MANAGEMENT STRATEGIES

Identifying risk is the first step in developing strategies to address them. Generally there are four primary approaches to risk management: (1) elimination, (2) reduction, (3) transfer, and (4) acceptance.

Elimination

What can you do as the real estate manager to eliminate possible risks? Are there cost effective steps to be taken? Replacing a worn electrical service entry line is an example.

Reduction

Can you make reasonable investments to reduce risk to an acceptable level? In a flood zone, for example, storing valuables above the first floor could be a solution.

Transfer

"Transfer" is the terminology used for insuring against a risk. The cost of your insurance policy, in effect, transfers risk to the insurance carrier.

Acceptance

There may be risks that can't be mitigated, or for which the cost of mitigation outweighs the benefits. Imagine your building is located near a railway leading to a chemical plant. You may decide there are few cost effective alternatives to eliminate or reduce the exposure to a possible chemical spill. The risk is recognized, monitored, and accepted.

CHAPTER 27:

The Crisis Management Team and Crisis Communications

Similar to the emergency management team (addressed in *Chapter 2*) the crisis management team is the group that will make strategic decisions about how to continue operations in the event of a disaster. The emergency management team's primary responsibility is the physical safety of building occupants and securing the property. The crisis management team, on the other hand, may not always be composed of the most senior members of a department, but individuals with thorough knowledge, good communication skills, and are respected for their cooperative drive. This team will address issues such as whether or not workers will need to be relocated or reassigned. The crisis management team will decide if the company will need an on-going media plan and the specific message to communicate. This team provides the overall, broad management control over response and recovery efforts.

The following lists potential members of the crisis management team:

- Chief Financial Officer (CFO)
- Chief Information Officer (CIO)
- Risk manager
- Facility manager
- Human resources
- Health and safety officials
- Customer service
- Legal
- Public relations and communications
- Primary departments' critical process collaborators

The crisis management team has a different set of objectives than the emergency response team, and their success or failure can easily spell the success or failure of the company.

CASE STUDY: CHICAGO TYLENOL MURDERS

In 1982, Tylenol capsules laced with potassium cyanide were responsible for the deaths of seven people in the Chicago area. Johnson & Johnson—the parent company of Tylenol manufacturer McNeil Consumer Healthcare—made quick and swift decisions to handle the crisis. Johnson & Johnson issued a recall of all Tylenol products from store shelves—an estimated 31 million bottles with a retail value of more than $100 million. In addition, they pulled all advertising and issued warnings to hospitals. When it was determined only capsules were involved, they offered to exchange capsules for other products in stores.

Currently considered to be a paradigm case in crisis public relations and business continuity, Johnson & Johnson was, at the time, praised by the Washington Post, who said they had "...effectively demonstrated how a major business ought to handle a disaster." Immediately following what was deemed the Chicago Tylenol Murders, Tylenol lost nearly 75 percent of its market share—plummeting from 35 percent to 8 percent. After Johnson & Johnson's proactive response, the market share recovered in less than one year.

However, the actions taken by Johnson & Johnson weren't isolated to Tylenol alone. Following the murders, pharmaceutical companies began to transition away from traditional capsules to tablets shaped like capsules. By altering the physical form of the medication, manufacturers were able to make it more difficult to tamper or alter a product. They also introduced the now ever-present, tamper-proof seal beneath the cap of over-the-counter medications.

CASE STUDY: 2010 DEEPWATER HORIZON OIL SPILL

The 2010 Deepwater Horizon oil spill, also known as the British Petroleum (BP) oil disaster, is the largest accidental marine oil spill in the history of the petroleum industry. The spill stemmed from a sea-floor oil gusher that was created by the April 20, 2010 explosion of Deepwater Horizon, which drilled on the BP-operated Macondo Prospect. The explosion killed 11 men working on the platform and injured 17 others. By the time the floor gusher was capped in July, it had spilled approximately 4.9 billion barrels of oil into the Gulf of Mexico.

To understand the magnitude of failure in handling this disaster, it's important to begin by examining BP's Initial Exploration Plan, dated March 10, 2009—"it is unlikely that an accidental spill would occur" and "no adverse activities are anticipated to fisheries or fish habitat." On April 29, 2010, Louisiana Governor, Bobby Jindal, declared a state of emergency after weather forecasts predicted the oil slick would reach the Louisiana coast.

Citing example after example, the Associated Press summarized: "While a disaster as devastating as a major oil spill will create some problems that can't be solved in advance, or even foreseen, BP's plans do not anticipate even the most obvious issues, and use mountains of words to dismiss problems that have proven overwhelming."

Supporting what might have been seen as harsh allegations in the media, BP CEO, Tony Hayward, told the BBC that the company's contingency plans were inadequate and that the leadership "were making it up day to day." Consequences of the failed planning and recovery efforts had global reach. Family businesses and the generations who supported them, wildlife, and the gulf shore beaches all suffered devastating consequences. BP also suffered consequences that nearly bankrupted them.

As a result, in January 2011, the White House oil spill commission blamed BP and its partners for making a series of cost-cutting decisions and the lack of a system to ensure safety. In September 2011, further investigation revealed that the main cause was a defective cement job, which also put most of the fault for the oil spill with BP.

CRISIS COMMUNICATIONS PLAN

One of the primary goals of crisis management is to protect your brand through assured support via clear messaging to staff, stakeholders, and the public. In any organization, large or small, there should be one single spokesperson for the organization. This may be someone in public relations or communications in a large company or simply a trained staff member in a small organization.

Responding to the Media

There are general guidelines that should be followed when dealing with the media. (*Chapter 5* provides a more in-depth discussion on dealing with public relations.) However in terms of a crisis, consider the following suggestions:

- All media requests or inquires should be directed to the designated spokesperson. This overarching policy should be well known to *all* employees. All requests referred, without exception.

- Before responding to a request for information, the spokesperson should know who the person or reporter is and who they represent. The spokesperson should also know the subject of the interview and the deadline for response.

- Answer all questions with candor and honesty.

The following lists key talking points that should always be covered in any statement to (or interview with) the media:

- Describe the nature of the disruption, accident, or disaster.

- Express empathy and concern for employees, tenants, residents, and visitors.

- Describe what the company is doing to mitigate the impact on all parties involved.

- Clearly state the implication or impact for the property and all business units.

Creating Press Releases

During a disaster and the recovery phase, press releases are a mechanism for providing newsworthy updates to media outlets and to the general public, employers, customers, and suppliers. A press release should provide assurance about the steps being taken to facilitate recovery and return to normal business operations. Effective and timely distribution of press releases will minimize loss of clients, customers, and tenants—and can even help minimize distractions for staff. (A sample format for press releases can be found in *Chapter 5*.)

COMMUNICATION WITH STAFF, TENANTS, AND CLIENTS

Automated Mass Notification

There are a variety of options available for providing immediate notification of a disaster or disruption, as well as updates on the response process. Mass notification solutions typically allow the company to identify multiple groups for notification—for example, onsite staff and at a corporate office, tenants or residents, and contractors or vendors. The user may also be able to develop event-specific messages to be sent to different groups if a fire, flood, tornado, etc. occurs. You may also choose to create messages as needed. System options for distribution will typically include text message, mobile phone, home phone, work or other phones, and e-mail.

Look for a notification system that provides a perpetual record of deliveries, with information that can include the date sent, to whom it was sent, how the message was delivered, confirmation or time of delivery, and the body or text of the message. It may also be advantageous to include the ability for a recipient to respond to the notice. Maintaining these records is important for determining the effectiveness of your communication system, and may be a factor in liability management.

Toll-Free Phone Numbers with Pre-Recorded Messages

Companies should consider utilizing multiple toll-free numbers to provide timely messaging for clients, staff, tenants, and families. During a disaster, existing primary business phone numbers are often overwhelmed, or may be severed by the event. It is advisable to look for toll-free solutions that travel different trunk lines that can provide specific, timely information. Use one phone line to provide information for staff, give directions, and update them with developments, such as where and when to report for work. Use a separate line for tenants and customers to ensure easy access for callers and easy updates for the company with information such as access, hours, office relocation information, and new contact information.

Online Options

Organizations must have multiple options for both e-mail and online notification in the event the primary source goes down. Clients and tenants will find it wholly unacceptable that they cannot access you via e-mail. Obviously, e-mail provides the opportunity to distribute information to groups, as previously described. Social media and other online options also offer solutions. Information may be posted on the company website in a section identified for emergency messages. The company's Facebook page, Twitter account, LinkedIn profile, or Google+ page can also be used. Alternatively, the company may choose to provide online, internal message boards as a method of communication for employees or suppliers. Twitter is a particularly effective tool for real time communication—explored by both nonprofits and government agencies, such as FEMA and the Department of Homeland Security, in the event of an emergency.

Mobile Phones

In the event of regional disasters, wireless network systems may be out of service or overwhelmed by the volume of traffic, making their utility somewhat marginal at the onset of the event. However, text messaging and online connectivity may remain an effective option as it utilizes different bands for transmission.

Satellite Phones

In the aftermath of a major disaster, satellite phones provide a superior calling solution. Although this may have been an extremely expensive alternative in prior times, it is now a more affordable method of communication. In the past, satellite phones required a significant upfront investment for the antenna, car adapters, and batteries, along with the calling plan. Today, satellite phones may be rented and data plans purchased much like other wireless phone plans; however, they can usually be turned on and off as needed.

IMPLEMENTATION OF A CRISIS PLAN

Ultimately, the effectiveness of business continuity and emergency response plans relies upon communications at their core. A company's ability to respond in a coherent, coordinated manner is dependent on its redundant methods of messaging. The implementation of a comprehensive, successful crisis communication plan will help gain control in response and recovery situations, while also protecting people, property, and profits.

CHAPTER 28:

Business Continuity Processes for Real Estate Management Companies

At the onset of business continuity planning, it is imperative that critical business processes are identified through a questionnaire, series of group meetings, or interviews. This survey should ask key department members to consider which vital internal and external resources must be available for successful continuation of their process or department operations through any disaster. This exercise looks at creating a hierarchy of resources, but also leads the group through an examination of the links between departments—upstream and down. During the process of creating this survey, ask "What functions in this organization rely upon your department's ability to perform, and what departments do you rely on to perform?"

Essential resources are broken down into their component parts such as labor, material, and equipment. This survey inquires about timelines, resources, and accessibility at the most basic levels. Survey responders must consider how they operate under normal conditions, and then reflect upon how they could be affected by reallocation, redirection, or procurement of contingent components. The ultimate goal of this exercise is to develop an understanding of the critical process linkages within the business and the required resources to keep each at the requisite level of performance.

This "what if" exercise will usually generate more than a single solution. All of the options identified should be itemized, along with the potential costs of implementation. With this information in hand, the planning team may consider a cost-benefit analysis of each recovery solution and then choose the most appropriate. These recovery strategies then get codified for the company's guidance. The amount of time spent producing emergency procedures for onsite staff and tenants should also be applied for developing recovery procedures for the crisis management team. The following sections in this chapter discuss some commonly used strategies for business continuity.

SELECTING YOUR DISASTER CONTRACTOR

As with many disaster relief or preparedness services, you should not wait until you need a restoration contractor to establish contact. This is an important consideration in your everyday work and is critical when you suffer a significant loss. Your contractor needs to know your property, the building's equipment, access requirements, and staging opportunities before a disaster strikes or a disruption begins.

Conduct an annual review of the pricing of emergency services with your contractor or insurance carrier to head off any disagreement about service costs. Get the specifics on the table and document the discussions and resolution. Do not wait until after the emergency to discuss acceptable pricing with the insurance company—dealing with this negotiation after the fact will cost you time, cash, interest, and legal and accounting fees. It's important to always be proactive and also engage your insurance broker in this endeavor. Let your broker make this an annual process at renewal time. Review procurement issues, purchase orders, contracts, payment terms, and unit costs for time and material billings, as well as the presentation and documentation of time and material invoices.

Your contractor should have experience working on your type of property. They should provide information about their safety program, employee training, and certifications. The following lists some items that you should ask the contractor:

- What is their labor pool?
- What percentage of the work crew are permanent employees?
- Will temporary labor be employed?
- Does the contractor perform background checks and drug screening?

These are important considerations as the crews may be working in vacated premises with access to corporate and personal assets and residential tenants.

Review the contractor's insurance coverage and focus on the limits of that coverage. Very often the restoration contractor may have very low limits that would be reasonable for working on a single-family home, but are not acceptable for multifamily, commercial, or industrial real estate. In the aftermath of a disaster, do not increase your risk exposure by having under-insured contractors on your property. It's important to plan ahead to resolve these qualification issues. You do not want to be sifting through the smoldering ash or standing in a foot of water while trying to perform your due diligence.

A qualified disaster contractor brings more to the table than immediate emergency service. They have knowledge and resources for many restoration techniques that are not widely known in our industry. For example, a contractor will help create temporary power, communication, and IT systems, along with trash removal. Other important elements, such as performing a power study for your building in order to size your temporary power generator, or having a switch installed to run the generator are other ways that a contractor can help. When it comes to protecting your electronic equipment from water and smoke, it's important to know how effective immediate drying and cleaning may be to save computers, phones, and elevator controls, etc.

When dealing with a major construction on a property, it's essential to begin with the proper plans, specifications, and pricing. This basic approach should be applied to any potential business-ending event by always identifying the core elements for response and recovery.

CHOOSING ALTERNATE SITES AND BRANCH LOCATIONS FOR OPERATIONS

Moving some or all of your operations to an alternate site is a simple strategy, but it must be considered well in advance. For a single occupant building, corporate real estate property, or single division or department, relocation to an alternate site may be part of your business continuity solution.

The continued growth of digital data storage—at the heart of many industries—has led executives to consider this as the most vital corporate function. This posture gave rise to three main site concepts: (1) hot sites, (2) warm sites, and (3) cold sites. These sites are generally described in terms of the number of seats available—i.e., the actual number of chairs—and the related equipment employees can use.

A cold site is the most inexpensive as it includes no data or equipment outside of what is required for staff use. It is simply a generic space to which staff can relocate when necessary. It would require an immediate investment and installation of necessary power, hardware, software, phone, and internet connections.

A hot site is a duplicate of the original site with full computer and network systems with data backups. Real time synchronization may be used to completely mirror the data environment of the original site. Following a disruption at the original site, the hot site is activated so that the organization can relocate with minimal losses to normal operations. Ideally, a hot site will be up and running almost instantaneously, although consideration must be given to the time required to fully relocate personnel. Though it may be a near duplicate of the original location, a hot site may not have the same capacity, so it's important to identify the essential number of people to occupy the site.

A warm site is a compromise between hot and cold. These sites will have computer systems and connectivity already established. They will generally have backup information on hand, but that information will likely need to be downloaded or restored at activation instead of being mirrored in real time. Depending on the procedures and routines in place for data backup, this may result in loss of the most current data.

Today the surge in home-based offices—network sophistication and cloud computing—provide many options to manage workflow during chaotic times, although communications and network accessibility still require sufficient advance planning to be effective. One thing is certain— the successful ability to utilize any of these options is based on a thorough planning process.

WORKING WITH YOUR STAFF

Often overlooked in business continuity planning is the importance of dealing with people. Many planning groups mistakenly assume their staff will be available to implement response and recovery strategies. While this may typically be true if a disaster is limited to your site, it is an invalid assumption when considering a large-scale regional disaster.

If your staff and their families are significantly impacted by a disaster, the staff's primary concern will be with the health and safety of their families. Your staff are not likely to appear onsite when their families are without food, water, shelter, or needing medical attention. They will be torn in many directions from the onset of the disaster, and working overtime in finding remedies, making repairs, or settling their own insurance claims. Additionally, even if you staff hasn't been directly impacted at home, they may have limited access to your property. Public transportation may not be running, roads may be closed or impassable, or the area may be blocked by public safety officials.

If work can be performed remotely, do you have a plan and infrastructure for communications and network accessibility to support your staff?

Even if staff can make it into work, it will readily become apparent to everyone that long and stressful work conditions can result in burnout, illness, ineffectiveness, or unsafe conditions. Recognize in advance the possibility that additional labor and resources may be required.

Far-sighted municipalities and companies in high-risk areas develop plans to provide assistance to families of critical personnel, so that those critical personnel can tend to essential government services or business functions and be confident that the needs of their families are being met.

Ultimately, a plan that cannot be implemented by the people essential to the plan is no plan at all. Employees will recognize and appreciate your company's commitment to them by providing support in the event of a disaster.

CHAPTER 29:
Business Records Management

Data is the lifeblood of most organizations. Critical elements of business operations include contact information, e-mails, customer records, accounting, personnel records, and basic inventory. Core business processes are typically recorded both on paper and as electronic data. Loss of data can create a temporary inconvenience or a sweeping financial catastrophe. Generally, data preservation and storage solutions are created to protect against human error and equipment failure.

ELECTRONIC BACKUPS OF RECORDS

There are two primary types of backup in use by business managers: (1) file backup approach and (2) disk imaging. File backups address the issue of human error, which may be initiated by the user or as a network operation. Backing up files should be a daily activity at minimum. The system selected for this operation may provide a secure environment, both on or offsite, and should maintain data within the time parameters that are deemed appropriate. The backup system should provide retrieval and recovery that reduces potential financial or operational crisis, which is often referred to as a recovery time objective. An initial backup may require a significant period of time to create. Subsequent backups scan files to identify which need to be updated because they are newly created, modified, or deleted.

For the smaller business owner, data backing up files can be as simple as transferring data to an external hard drive or to online storage. This solution is especially suitable for office files, such as documents, database records, or spreadsheets. Since these files change regularly, it is best to have a solution that tracks chronological versions of these files.

If your business uses a local network, a decision needs to be made between backing up each computer individually or backing up the entire network. Generally, it is advisable to back up all of the computers in the network, along with your file server. You can manage this process utilizing a single backup system for the entire network.

Backups that protect organizations against equipment failures requires a system that protects the broad spectrum of business processes. The goal is to be able to recover an entire system of files and applications. Typically, this option requires a considerable amount of storage space in order to maintain complete copies of the information systems, often in partitioned disks. The benefit of such a system is instant recovery anywhere on the network, which is often accomplished by running mirrored servers that write data to both the primary drive and the backup drive simultaneously. This provides excellent protection against hardware failure.

For smaller businesses, it may be more cost effective to back up data on the primary disk to a secondary disk—utilizing the same software that would support the mirrored solution. The only disadvantage is that if the primary disk fails, your backup will only contain data as of the date and time of the last backup. Data saved to the primary disk in the intervening while will be lost, and may only be recoverable at a substantial cost of both time and money—if at all possible. Disk image backup is the only practical way to maintain software backup viability. Trying to reinstall software after hardware failure is an endeavor fraught with possible problems. It's important to remember to routinely upgrade software or install patches over time. Attempting to reinstall software from multiple downloads can be a costly investment of both time and money.

Dealing with Equipment Failure

There must be a specified work-around procedure in the event that a particular application or the entire network in inaccessible. A straightforward outline for continuing to operate without automation must be presented to staff during the planning process. Lack of planning for equipment failure could potentially create a decrease in customer service and satisfaction, as well as a negative impact on income and cash flow.

Dealing with Paper Records

Many companies still retain large volumes of paper files. These may be stored on or offsite in file boxes for long-term storage, which may consist of regular or fireproof filing cabinets, or rolling file-management systems. Although property management software applications have minimized the type and volume of paper stored, the field is not yet entirely paperless.

Often, retained paper records include older tenant or financial records, original contracts, and building plans and specifications. In the planning process, identify any material that should be converted to a digital format. The remaining paper records that are of critical interest—or required by a regulatory agency—should be clearly identified and their location noted in the plan so they can be promptly salvaged if required. It's also important to identify access limitations and authorizations and list those parameters in the plan.

An important consideration for your insurance program is to insure coverage for the cost of recovering documents and data. Insurance will include recovering electronic data from damaged media as well as the cost of air drying or freeze drying and recovering vital paper documents.

UNDERSTANDING COMPLIANCE REQUIREMENTS

Whatever your backup strategy and policy consists of, it must be consistently applied. Often, regulatory requirements for companies detail how long data must be stored, how it is encrypted, and how access is controlled. There are a variety of compliance standards applicable to specific industries. For example, public corporations are bound by the Sarbanes-Oxley legislation, health related companies are bound by the Health Insurance Portability and Accountability Act (HIPPA), and real estate trusts are bound by the Securities and Exchange Commission. Owners and real estate managers should consult accounting and legal professionals to clearly understand regulatory requirements for their specific industry.

Maintaining Asset and Building Information

Almost every site manager or real estate management company has basic information about their building's construction, design, and systems at hand. Sometimes there will also be records of equipment, contents, and furnishings. Often these records do not exist in a consolidated format that can be updated at regular intervals.

In the planning process, it is important to assemble a comprehensive record of these items to assist in proper inspection and maintenance, mitigate against certain disruptions, and provide a source of data to guide development of response and recovery procedures.

You will generally have the following elements as primary information:

- Blueprints of the building
- As-built drawings (including changes made for improvements or tenant build-outs)

- Construction completion date or year
- Information of contractors, architects, and engineers
- Occupancy permit
- Photo or video documenting conditions prior to any building loss.

Equipment and content information should be organized along the following guidelines, which can be customized according to the specific item involved:

- Manufacturing information: make, model number, serial number, name of the manufacturer and contact information, and initial cost information
- Servicing information: service vendor and their contact information, routine maintenance performed, and the most recent date of maintenance
- Warranty information
- Replacement cost
- Roof type, size, and location
- Elevator lift mechanism type and weight capacity

Even though the previously mentioned records may already exist as part of maintenance or engineering files, there are several benefits to collecting this information as part of your disaster preparation planning. It is also much easier to effectively and efficiently update your plan if this information is included. Lack of organization will promote chaotic decision making, resulting in lost time and money.

Other benefits to maintaining a strong organization of business records may be less obvious. The most important benefit applies directly to basic valuation. A well-prepared and maintained asset inventory will help in establishing values when buying insurance coverage. Having specific business records readily available following a disaster will jumpstart repairs or replacement by expediting the procurement process. If business records and other important information is lost in a disaster—or you are prohibited access by public safety officials or cause and origin investigators—you could experience costly delays in accessing the information required for recovery.

The data relative to equipment, specifications, costs, and contractors are all valuable for limiting downtime and the cost of the disruption. Having a good compilation will assist in the prompt submittal of an insurance claim. Frequently, the preparation of repair estimates by your insurance company can be time consuming. Preparation of an accurate repair or replacement value is also dependent upon investigation of the physical equipment or property remaining, coupled with information you may provide about assets that are lost or destroyed in the event of a disaster. Being able to produce a thorough description and value of the asset, along with photographs, helps to assure that the adjuster is estimating "with like kind and quality." Your best effort in organizing your assets is one of the single best efforts you can make to a prompt and accurate valuation and claims settlement. The return on investment for the time required to compile the information is immense.

CHAPTER 30:

Examining Insurance Coverage and Managing Claims

Many business owners and real estate managers believe that once insured, there is no reason to worry. In reality, insurance is only one element of a well-conceived business continuity plan. Begin by working through the risk assessment as a good starting point for insurance program development.

POTENTIAL INSURANCE PITFALLS

Examine your insurance coverage to guard against potential insurance pitfalls. Inadequate coverage can be the result of bad information—for example, a poor property appraisal—or it can reflect the lack of updated information as the property, equipment, and contents are modified.

Co-Insurance Penalties

Co-insurance penalties arise when the carrier or adjuster determines the value of the property, equipment, or contents was not accurately identified when coverage was purchased. This inadequate coverage—a result of under-valuing the replacement cost of the asset—will result in payment that only covers partial cost of repairs or replacement; hence, the co-insurance penalty.

Business Interruption and Loss of Rents

The legal definition of business interruption insurance compensates a business for certain specified categories of costs in the event of catastrophic events. Three categories that may be covered are:

1. Profits that would have been realized if the disaster had not occurred
2. Operating expenses that must be paid despite inability to operate
3. Expenses incurred because business operations had to be moved while damaged original premises were restored for use

Business interruption coverage is generally purchased as part of a business owner's policy. Although business interruption coverage will replace lost income sources and cover some expenses, it does not address the entirety of the costs of the interruption or downtime. For example, if your building suffered a significant fire and was forced to be evacuated for six months, business interruption would cover your loss of rents, but it would not cover other costs, such as marketing and leasing expenses, for securing new tenants when the property is finally available for occupancy.

The business interruption policy may also exclude additional costs incurred in moving, securing new space, or outfitting the space with required utility or communications resources. For these types of expenses, you may need to acquire coverage for additional expenses as a rider.

Another area of confusion about business interruption coverage revolves around business losses and expenses caused by an event that did not occur at your property. For example, an earthquake and tsunami might create an interruption in the supply chain to automobile manufacturers resulting in a drop in production and automobile sales. The costs of this interruption may not be covered unless business owners maintain contingent business interruption insurance and identify this specific risk. According to U.S. Legal, Inc., contingent business interruption coverage is an insurance policy that provides benefits, if earnings are reduced, because of damages to another business on which one's business is dependent. Contingent business interruption (CBI) insurance can also extend to lost profits and extra expenses resulting from an interruption of business at the premises of a customer or supplier. Companies purchase this type of insurance as an extension to their standard property insurance.

Insurance Deductibles or Retention

In today's competitive business environment, companies may choose to have higher retentions/deductibles in order to reduce annual premiums. This means that the business owner or real estate manager is retaining more of the cost of repairing or replacing assets in the event of a loss. The first dollars on a claim come from the owner in escalating numbers. Essentially, the owner looks at the cost/benefit of the coverage value and retention in light of the potential risk and agrees to pay more from their own pocket before the first claim dollars flow from the insurance carrier. These retention values may reach into millions of dollars per occurrence for the largest corporations.

This decision to accept higher retention levels provides even greater incentive for companies to invest in effective business continuity plans. The ability to manage a business through a disaster in the most cost-effective and efficient manner is key to minimizing the extent of losses in terms of duration and costs. The return on investment can be very significant.

VENDOR CONTINGENCY PLANS

Every real estate manager works with a cadre of service and maintenance companies that provide essential services, such as equipment maintenance, janitorial services, landscaping, payroll, etc. These companies can usually be relied on to respond to a single disruptive event on your property. They are utilized on an ongoing contractual or project-specific basis. Should you experience a disaster on an individual property, you can assume these companies will be able to service you promptly. In preparing a solid solution set for potential disruptions, you need to consider the ability of your key vendors and contractors to respond in the event of a significant regional disaster. The following lists important questions to be asked when preparing your plan:

- What happens when several hundred square miles are impacted?
- Will your vendors and contractors be victimized by the event?
- Will their building equipment and inventories be lost?
- How will they manage the influx of service requests that may increase exponentially?
- How will they prioritize their service schedule?

Your group of vendors and contractors should be involved in the discussion and testing of your plan. They should be engaged in a collaborative fashion. You should provide them with an overview of your planning efforts, and clearly identify the importance of their participation in creating an effective strategy. This is where you realize, as the adage goes that "a chain is only as strong as its weakest link." Your business continuity is largely reliant on the business continuity of your vendors and contractors. It's difficult to realize—after overcoming inertia and spending time and money on your plan—that a key vendor or supplier has no plan or that the plan is solely an answering service for service calls.

Companies that are required to have a business continuity plan by a regulatory agency or corporate clients have confronted these issues for some time. For many, though, vendors and suppliers have no idea of the importance of their role. You can assume that vendors with locations statewide or nationally have a depth of resources. They may be able to reroute or handle an overload of calls. They may also have a plan to bring in labor from other locations to provide emergency services or meet deadlines. Companies that are local, or with single-site operations, may need further direction from you. You must communicate the need for them to be pro-active in finding a solution if they are to be your chosen supplier or long-term vendor. Independent operators may consider their options to be slim, and would not want to turn to other companies in the same business for assistance. However, it is essential for your success. Oftentimes, vendors may have "friendly" competitors, which can be a difficult point to navigate because they do not want to jeopardize their business. Failing to participate in developing a contingency solution, however, may harm their business relations with you. These are important points to communicate.

MUTUAL AID AGREEMENTS

The loss of a specific piece of equipment can be devastating to a company's operations, whether it's a specialized printer or a piece of manufacturing equipment that is critical for continued operation. When a business requires a specialized piece of equipment that cannot be replaced or repaired within an acceptable lead-time, a mutual aid agreement could solve the problem.

A mutual aid agreement involves working with an outside organization, with comparable equipment, that is willing and able to perform the neces-sary operations. These agreements must be worked in advance. Often, the vendor who sells or services the equipment is a good source for finding a company with similar equipment. Issues to be considered when imple-menting a mutual agreement are primarily the proximity to your location and hours the equipment might be available.

Similar to a mutual aid agreement, a real estate management company might want to negotiate an arrangement with a nearby property to pro-vide temporary shelter after an evacuation, or temporary office space. Sometimes you may need additional space for staging equipment, mate-rials, or parking in the response or recovery phase. These are all issues to be considered in advance.

FILING AN INSURANCE CLAIM

Navigating your way through a significant property claim can be a daunt-ing and often challenging process. For the new or inexperienced real estate manager, it may be perceived as a never-ending series of crises long after the initial event has ended. For the seasoned real estate manager, it is a methodical process of communication and documentation to obtain every reasonable benefit from the property policy that was purchased. This is another area where advance planning can have a major impact on the ultimate cost and scope of business interruption, loss of tenants, and repairs.

In order to initiate the claims process, you will need basic information including the name of the insurance carrier and how to file notice of the initial claim. For instance, determine whether you need to call a toll-free number to a national claims service or to a local broker. When submitting the claim, you will be asked for the insured's name, policy number (if possible), the date and time of the loss, a description of any injuries, and a general description of the extent of damage.

The insurance company may ask if you need a referral for a disaster restoration contractor to provide emergency mitigation services, or if you have existing resources. The claims staff will remind you of a contractual responsibility to take whatever actions are necessary to protect the property from further damage. Examples of actions to prevent further damage include patching a hole in the roof, removing wet materials, or securing the site. For more detailed information on protecting a property from further damage after a disaster, see *Chapter 4*.

REVIEWING THE INSURANCE POLICY

Always begin by reviewing the policy to understand the terms and conditions of coverage. Review the policy to learn what perils are covered, and if there are endorsements that provide additional coverage for code and ordinance requirements. Also be aware of the retention or deductible. The insurance policy should also cover costs of bringing the property up to current building codes. Other endorsements may include the following:

- Business interruption, contingent business interruption, or extra expense
- Vital documents recovery
- Environmental coverage (mold, lead, or asbestos)
- Electronic equipment coverage

Having a grasp of this information in preparing your disaster plan will help you to effectively marshal necessary resources with insight about your coverage and cost of recovery. Often, uninformed real estate managers make decisions that result in expenditures that may not be covered (e.g., mold remediation or the extra expense for relocating and setting new computer systems). Understanding coverage and limits will allow you to develop response and recovery strategies that are most efficient and effective.

THE PROPERTY ADJUSTER'S ROLE IN THE CLAIM

Once the claim is filed, the insurance carrier will assign an adjuster to manage your case. The property adjuster will interpret the coverage, provide direction per the policy, and review and negotiate the settlement.

For significant property claims, the adjuster may retain a stable of experts and consultants on the carrier's behalf, which may include engineers, contractors, cost consultants, environmental experts, or forensic accountants. You need to clearly understand that these consultants are employed by the insurance company to represent their interests. Although it is important to obtain their input and reports, you should not rely upon them with blind faith to represent your best interests. If there are technical or financial points of contention, you must secure your own professional services. In certain instances, the owner may engage a public adjuster who represents the owner in the overall settlement process, managing a team of subject experts for a percentage of the final settlement value.

DOCUMENTATION OF INSURANCE RECORDS

From the beginning of the loss, it is critical to document all aspects of the event and your responses to it. The real estate manager, or their designee, must prepare an initial incident report that captures the periods immediately before and after the loss. It's important to describe the scene and activities in as much detail as possible. Take photographs or video to provide visual records. List injuries, deaths, interactions with first responders, and actions taken by your staff.

Create a log to track expenses including purchase orders, credit card charges, cash transactions, and contracts. Also, log the contractors you have requested to respond and identify the scope of their work. Additional topics that should be documented or noted in a daily log include the following:

- Records of safety meetings onsite
- List of contractors onsite each day and the work completed
- Meetings with local government representatives including police, fire, building code officials, etc.
- Proposed work plan for each day

- Tenant needs and wants; document your communication with them
- Interactions with the media

Continue this written and photographic record from inception through the completion of the emergency or mitigation services. Your ability to recover expenditures from the insurance carrier will be directly impacted by the record keeping and backup documentation provided for the initial response to the loss. The adjuster, or the adjuster's consultants, will want to have a well-supported submittal in order to authorize payment.

In an effort to keep everyone's knowledge and expectations in line, you should issue meeting minutes after all significant meetings with a focus on mitigation and recovery. Stipulate your understanding of the decisions made or agreements reached during the meeting. You should also request any recipient of the minutes to notify you within 48 hours of distribution whether or not they agree with your statement of decisions. A strong attention to detail on an ongoing basis is essential for preventing an adjuster's denial of work, months after they have been completed or incurred. Additionally, you should ask the adjuster to support all requests from you for information in written form.

INVOICING FROM CONTRACTORS

Ideally, when real estate managers employ a contractor to work on a property, they always define the scope of a bid or proposal, providing drawings and specifications. When engaging contractors to perform emergency services of a disaster mitigation, they proceed to work immediately after the loss; however, the scope in such a transaction is defined as the event evolves. Initial response activities are generated from initial damage assessments.

Your emergency planning should include qualifying potential response contractors. In this process you should be provided pricing for labor and materials that would likely be utilized by the contractor. This is especially important in the selection of your disaster recover or restoration contractor, who may not work for you on a regular basis as does other maintenance contractors.

ONGOING TESTING AND MAINTENANCE

Understand that an untested plan is not a plan at all. Testing and exercising your plan validates your assumptions and procedures. It will also provide feedback regarding potential shortcomings by allowing you to assess the timelines and effectiveness of your responders, both internally and externally. Testing on a regular basis also creates an unconscious competence among the group. This is the effect you ultimately seek—people who are rehearsed, who know potential risks, responses, and options so that they are not paralyzed by looking for information.

Items to be tested include all manual and automated procedures, backup and recovery configurations, call trees, contact lists, inventory, and more. It might seem tedious, but as harmless as a wrong phone number may seem, when running a test or exercise, an out-of-date number of a critical supplier can derail the entire recovery process.

Although there are a variety of testing options available, the tabletop exercise may have the most value as a routine property management process. Tabletop exercises allow you to test against a variety of events occurring to your property without a major interruption of your business.

The process involves bringing coordinators or liaisons from your various departments together in a conference room setting to collaborate through an exercise. In advance, the facilitator should consider a potential disaster to discuss and also provide an overview of the testing scenario and review the process and objectives. An official scribe should also be identified to record the process.

The facilitator should describe the day of the week, time of day, and disastrous event that could potentially befall the property. The meeting participants should share their responses to the event, and each subsequent escalation of the event as presented by the facilitator. This meeting should be conducted in a non-judgmental fashion in order to engage the participants without fear of recrimination for mistakes. Inevitably, this process will highlight the good, the bad, and the ugly. Upon completion of the exercise, the group should prepare a post-incident summary, which will be used as a guide to make modifications as necessary to improve the overall effectiveness of the plan.

Additional testing methods can include a simple checklist test, such as verifying the names and phone numbers listed on a call tree. A "desk check" could take place, which tests the individual responsible for each component of the plan and reviews it for accuracy and completeness. Evacuation drills are an obvious test of evacuation procedures, and routine checks of smoke alarms and sprinkler systems are also tests that should be recorded in your plan.

APPENDIX:

Additional Resources

Natural Disasters—Weather Related:

- National Weather Service (NWS)
  http://www.weather.gov
- National Ocean and Atmospheric Administration
  http://www.noaa.gov
- U.S. Geological Survey (USGS)
  http://www.usgs.gov
- National Flood Insurance Program (NFIP)
  http://www.fema.gov/national-flood-insurance-program
- National Fire Protection Program (NFPA)
  http://www.nfpa.org

Emergency Response Agencies:

- Federal Emergency Management Agency (FEMA)
  http://www.fema.gov
  http://www.ready.gov
- U.S. Fire Administration (USFA)
  http://www.usfa.fema.gov
- American Red Cross
  http://www.redcross.org
- Centers for Disease Control and Prevention (CDC)
  http://www.cdc.gov

Other Federal Agencies and Policy Resources

- U.S. Department of Homeland Security (DHS)
  http://www.dhs.gov
- U.S. Environmental Protection Agency (EPA)
  http://www.epa.gov
- Occupational Safety and Health Administration (OSHA)
  http://www.osha.gov
- U.S. Department of Housing and Urban Development (HUD)
  http://www.hud.gov
- U.S. Citizenship and Immigration Services (USCIS)
  http://www.uscis.gov
- American National Standards Institute (ANSI)
  http://www.ansi.org
- U.S. General Services Administration (GSA)
  http://www.gsa.gov

EMERGENCY PLANNING FORMS:

To access the forms that were made to accompany this book, please visit the following address:

www.irem.org/disasterforms